THE BIG BOOK OF
ORGANIC BABY FOOD

THE BIG BOOK OF
ORGANIC BABY FOOD

Baby Purees, Finger Foods, and Toddler Meals For Every Stage

Stephanie Middleberg MS, RD, CDN

PHOTOGRAPHY BY SHANNON DOUGLAS

SONOMA
PRESS

To my lively son, Julian;

my best friend, Andrew,

without whom none of this would be possible;

and my biggest supporters,

Mom and Dad.

Thank you all for keeping me inspired

and cleaning up the kitchen.

Contents

Introduction xii

SMOOTHIES AND FINGER FOODS 136

8

TODDLER MEALS 176

12 MONTHS AND UP

FAMILY DINNER 214

Introduction

Five months into being a new mom, right when my son Julian was taking his first bites of food, I began to think about his future. No, not what college he would go to or whether he would be an astronaut, but would he become some who loves good, healthy, real food? Or would he come to see food as simply fuel to keep his motor going? Thinking about him made me reflect on myself.

Growing up, I was a picky eater, which was very convenient, as my mom didn't exactly *enjoy* being in the kitchen. Yet she always made sure we had a side of veggies and sat down together for meals (thanks, Mom!). Whether the food on our table was organic was never a consideration, let alone a topic of conversation.

I started caring about what was on my plate—and what was *in* what was on my plate—only when I stumbled into the nutrition field in my mid-twenties. It was then, while I was learning all there was to know about nutrition and health, that I met my husband, Andrew. It should've been obvious, but I needed him to shine a light on the huge disconnect between my career and my life. Even though I spent my days prescribing home cooking to all my clients and

their young children, my own kitchen contained roughly the following: a stack of paper plates, a bunch of condiment packets, and what was left of the Ikea knife set I had bought in college.

Andrew, on the other hand, loved to cook. He turned to me one day and asked, "Shouldn't you learn how to do this? You know, for your clients and all?"

Ouch. His question struck a chord. I could barely hard-boil an egg. That started me down the path of practicing what I preached. Today, my entire nutrition philosophy is grounded in building and maintaining a healthy relationship with food. This starts with eating real, ideally organic, food, but also includes developing a certain level of comfort in the kitchen, regardless of skill level.

In an age when it's difficult to pronounce the ingredients in a granola bar, let alone know what chemicals and pesticides might be in it, people are looking to determine what's best to eat. This issue is even more pronounced when it comes to babies and their first bites. Every day, clients, friends, family, and total strangers ask me for wholesome recipe ideas, which foods are the best for babies, and what to feed—and not feed—their precious little ones. This issue is compounded by the concerns that often accompany the transition to real food: *Am I feeding her enough? Is he getting all the nutrients he needs? Is the texture right for this age? Can I afford to feed my baby only organic?*

As a new mom myself (hi, Julian!), I completely empathize. I also feel the added weight of my day job as a dietitian urging me to be an exemplary chef for my little guy. But if there's one thing I know without a doubt, it's that babies are no different, really, than we are. Yes, their digestive systems aren't entirely developed and their lack of teeth will make the blender your best friend, but tiny humans and grown humans should abide by the same food philosophy: Eat real food. Real food comes from the ground, a plant, or an animal. If anything was added to or taken away from it between harvesting or packaging and when you cook it, it isn't real food. Giving your baby (eventually, your toddler) the

Julian, 8 months

most wholesome and delicious foods is what this book is about.

The Big Book of Organic Baby Food is an easily digestible (though, alas, not edible), comprehensive resource for new parents to ensure their little ones are eating healthy and having fun in the process. The over 200 recipes will save you time and keep your little one excited and satiated! I start you with the basic, single-food purees and take you all the way through fully composed meals the whole family will enjoy for years. We'll also go through my recommendations for pantry staples and great ways to add flavor and spice to develop those little palates.

I remember how I felt when confronted with the high chair for the first time, and I want to make it as easy as possible for new parents to enjoy cooking for their little ones, today and every day after.

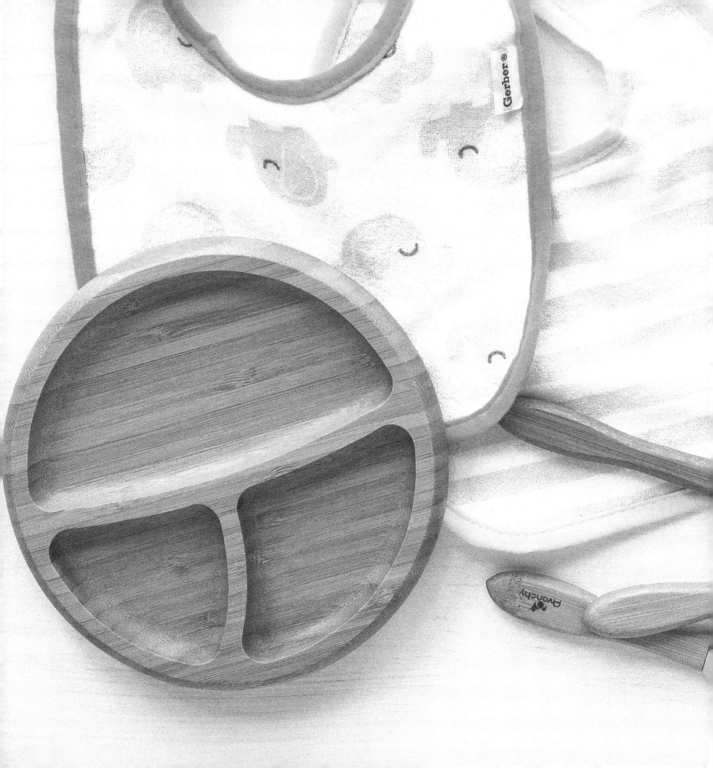

PART 1

ONLY
THE BEST

1
CHOOSING AN ORGANIC START

Congratulations on taking this first step in your baby food–making journey! Just when you've finally settled into a comfortable routine, it's time to change everything. I know it can be nerve-racking, and you're probably feeling both excitement and trepidation. It doesn't help matters when people tell you that your baby's first few bites of food will set the tone for her entire culinary life. Talk about pressure! But pat yourself on the back; you've already taken a step in the right direction—to create healthy, delicious meals with the purest foods available. And don't worry; that "flavor window" doesn't completely shut, so there is always an opportunity to help your baby develop an appreciation for all types of food. Get ready to have a lot of fun!

There is something both empowering and gratifying about making your own organic baby food, especially when your baby opens up that adorable little mouth and leans in for more. No matter what, know you are nurturing your little one with the most wholesome ingredients available.

From the Heart

Every new parent wants the absolute best for their little ones. We spend hours combing through reviews for all sorts of products and gadgets, always searching for the perfect item to enrich our child's life. It is with that same care and passion that we choose to pull out a blender and start preparing meals, regardless of skill or comfort level. It's a (minor) labor of love, plain and simple.

Truly, making the baby food is the easiest part. How it's received, well, that's another matter. Don't get discouraged; your baby loves you just the same—and think of all the cute pictures you'll take in the process! Just wipe that puree off your face, head back into the kitchen, and tell yourself you'll find the right food to delight that amazing little person in the high chair who is looking at you with pure love.

The Benefits of Homemade

I choose to make my son Julian's food from scratch because I believe homemade is the best way to provide him with the most nutritious, wholesome food. Making your own food not only ensures that your baby will be eating healthy but also helps him develop tastes and habits—and maybe even the joy of cooking—that can last a lifetime. Making your own organic baby food allows you to control what is in your little one's food with room for flexibility!

I'm not saying there aren't great store-bought baby foods—there are, and I've used them. Since we can't always plan out our days perfectly, quality backups are very important. But based on my experience as a dietitian and mom, there is no more flavorful, healthy, or cost-efficient option than making your little one's meals at home.

NUTRITIONAL BENEFITS

When you cook your own food, you know exactly what's in it and where all the ingredients came from—especially when those ingredients are organic. Given our innate desire to provide our babies with the best, it makes sense that we want the highest quality for them (even if we don't typically spring for it for ourselves!). Organic homemade foods contain no unpronounceable additives, hidden sugars, or stabilizers. And if we buy produce at its peak freshness, we can guarantee very little loss of nutrients.

What you'll quickly come to realize is that once you have a heightened awareness of what you're making, you're likely to start eating healthier yourself. This might begin with snacking on the ingredients while you cook your daughter's food. As you load up your shopping cart with broccoli, quinoa, and fresh ginger to make her dinner, you'll buy extra for yourself. The process is complete when the entire family is eating the same great meal—one portion is just a bit . . . mushier!

TASTE

Have you tried the average jarred baby food? Doesn't exactly excite the senses. A jar of baby food—even if organic—is likely to have been in that jar for quite a while by the time you see it, making it impossible for it to taste fresh. This is why it's so exciting (and convenient!) that baby food companies are starting to sell refrigerated and frozen products, which do taste fantastic. But this freshness comes, literally, at a price— they're on the expensive side. That's why making your own food is good for the baby and good for the budget—it's the best-tasting, most affordable option we've got. Plus, with homemade, you can adjust flavors to your liking as you prepare it; what tastes good to you will most likely taste good to your little fella!

EASE

Cooking your own baby food isn't hard at all. Sure, it can be a little scary wondering how that first reaction to food will go and stressful knowing that you're the one responsible for what (and if) your child eats. But the actual mixing, matching, cooking, and pureeing are a cinch regardless of your comfort in the kitchen. Just follow these four easy steps:

1. Find some recipe inspiration. (Hmmm . . . where might you find that?)
2. Cook each item thoroughly. (No medium-rare here!)
3. Toss the ingredients in a blender and add liquid.
4. Blend, blend, blend. Start with a very smooth, thin consistency and work your way up to thicker, more textured purees as your baby grows.

Easy-peasy lemon squeezy! There's really not much more to it than that. With a bit of practice, you'll become a pro in no time.

TIME

Time is the second most important thing in your life right now (sorry, honey!), and of course, there is never enough of it. Laundry to do, diapers to change. . . . Add cooking to this mix, and it might feel as if there's no room in your schedule. But, really, making baby food is relatively quick and easy compared to most other kitchen undertakings. Just start by steaming a few organic apples or roasting a couple of sweet potatoes, and then turn on the blender. Yes, one ingredient, one pot and steamer insert, and one blender or food processor are all you need to begin. After cooling, the puree gets frozen and then, when it's time to feed your baby, you just defrost a portion and serve.

With a little planning, you can prepare an entire week's worth of meals in a little over an hour. Once you get the hang of cooking your own baby food and setting a plan, you'll find it doesn't take a big chunk of your time. Some of this is just getting used to the process, and you'll be glad you did because you won't waste your time with those last-minute dashes to the market.

COST SAVINGS

There's a reason the market is always jammed on Sunday mornings. People are walking the aisles, shopping lists in hand, stocking up for the week. We do this for two reasons: (1) Who has time to pick up ingredients during the work-week? (2) On a per-meal basis, cooking at home is far less expensive than eating out or takeout.

Here's an example to make it clear: At my local market, 3 pounds of organic sweet potatoes costs me about $5.99. This makes about 48 ounces of homemade puree, depending on the liquid added. But a 4-ounce jar of organic sweet potato puree costs $1.99, which is $5.16 *per pound*. When I don't have time to cook (and, believe me, there are times), I'll buy an organic

baby food pouch or jar before anything else on the shelf, but it's not hard to see how quickly it adds up on a regular basis.

Organics for Baby

So, why use organic ingredients? They're simply the healthiest option for your baby because they are grown without the use of hormones, genetically modified organisms (GMOs), or synthetic pesticides. There's no danger of these questionable or foreign substances making their way into your baby's developing body through his diet when you offer organic choices. Moreover, published research in the *British Journal of Nutrition*, as well as many other sources, now demonstrates that organic foods are higher in nutrients than their conventionally grown counterparts.

These reasons are precisely why we've seen the explosive demand for organic foods. Once only available in health food or specialty markets, organics can now be found in stores like Target, Walmart, and even Costco. According to the Organic Trade Association, as reported in the *New York Times*, sales of organic products grew 11% in 2015, "or roughly four times the growth in sales of food products over all." Demand is outpacing supply. It is because of this extreme demand and retailers' insatiable desire to acquire and keep new customers that the once lofty prices for organic foods continue to decrease. Yes, organics are still more expensive than conventional foods (about 47 percent higher), but it is more cost effective than ever to cook organic in your kitchen.

That being said, a 50-cent difference in price can be a deal breaker for a large part of the population, and while we all try to make our best effort, sometimes getting that perfect piece of organic fruit is just not in the cards. It's nothing to get discouraged about. Treat your shopping like this: Do your best to shop organic most of the time. If that's not possible due to

ORGANIC LABELING

Food labels can be a minefield. How many buzzwords can be packed into a few square inches? And what does it all mean? This is my profession, and I still often see a new term that makes zero sense to me. But many of these terms are important for making informed purchases, so let's lay it all out:

ALL NATURAL. No formal definition exists for this term, but the Food and Drug Administration (FDA) considers it to mean that nothing artificial or synthetic has been added. It is a loose definition, though, and companies can label virtually anything "natural," so I don't recommend going by this as a standard.

MADE WITH ORGANIC INGREDIENTS. This means that at least 70 percent of the product must be made with certified organic ingredients.

ORGANIC. This term indicates that at least 95 percent of the ingredients in the product are organic.

100% ORGANIC/USDA ORGANIC SEAL. A product with this label has been made entirely of organic ingredients.

NON-GMO PROJECT VERIFIED SEAL. Genetically modified organisms (GMOs) are plants or animals that have had their genetic makeup altered to exhibit traits that are not naturally theirs. They are engineered to withstand application of weed-killing toxic herbicides like glyphosate. The Non-GMO Project Verified seal assures the consumer that a product has been produced according to best practices for GMO avoidance. For a deeper discussion of what we know (and don't know) about GMOs, see page 16.

ANIMAL WELFARE APPROVED. This is a relatively new label. It holds the highest standards of any third-party auditing program, as it assures consumers that animals raised for meat, dairy, or eggs were raised on a family farm with outdoor access, with humane treatment from birth to slaughter.

For more information about labels you'll see on eggs, poultry, and beef, see chapter 2.

cost or availability, go conventional, except when it comes to the infamous "Dirty Dozen" (see page 265).

I also recommend choosing only organic options for the foods you offer your baby most consistently. So if sweet potato is a daily staple, try to use only organic sweet potatoes. Overall, the most important thing is to make sure your baby has the opportunity to eat an expansive array of foods, even if organic isn't always readily available.

Having Fun with Food

All this talk about making sure your baby gets the most nutritious, cleanest ingredients at mealtime is an important concern, but let's take a deep breath and remember that shopping and preparing food that your baby—and family—will enjoy should be fun. Yes, we must be diligent about what we put into our baby's belly, but what kind of example would we be setting if we were constantly stressed by just a glance at the apron?

A key tenet of my nutritional philosophy is having a healthy relationship with food, and it all begins with enjoying it—not only the taste of it but preparing it as well. (In my kitchen, we play music to set the mood.) The experience of eating it should be enjoyable as well. If you're having fun in the kitchen, you'll also have fun spooning your delicious concoctions into that cute little mouth.

Keep in mind that the early stages of solids are all about experimentation, for both you and your baby—but *especially* for your baby! This is probably the one time you should be happy that she's playing with her food, so let her get messy! Your baby is still getting almost all the nutrients she needs from your breast milk or formula, so not to worry if she sits there with locked jaw or if most of your carefully prepared food ends up on the floor! And when he smears that bright beet puree all over his face and your brand-new sweater, just laugh, because you'll be rewarded with the greatest gift of all: a beaming smile and giggles that would make any heart melt.

2

THE ORGANIC KITCHEN

Cooking for your little one isn't *that* different from cooking for yourself. There's just a lot more blending involved. If you've already committed to eating organic and have a well-stocked pantry, you're all set. If not, no problem! This chapter serves as a guide to eating organically and seasonally. Many of us associate organics most strongly with produce, but there is a range of foods—and a variety of food labels—to consider when shopping for the healthiest, most natural ingredients.

Once your refrigerator, freezer, and pantry are stocked, there's only the question of equipment. Fortunately, nothing special is required to make baby food, but I'll let you know which basic items are most helpful, from prepping and cooking to serving the first delicious spoonfuls.

The First Food

The time has come! Your baby is ready for that first mouthful—or, realistically, teeny tiny taste—of real food! But what to give her? Once upon a time, there was an easy answer: rice cereal. But with the American Academy of Pediatrics now recommending introducing a "wide variety of foods" with an emphasis on fruits and vegetables, which are nutritionally superior choices, a whole world of options presents itself. Instead of feeling overwhelmed by all the choices, take this as an opportunity to have fun and experiment! I chose to start my son with avocado, as its natural texture is quite amenable to those little gums. More important, avocado

THE FALL OF RICE CEREAL

Chances are, if you were born after 1950, your first food was rice cereal. In fact, until recently, rice cereal was *the* number one pediatrician-recommended first food for a variety of reasons. It's long been considered a "safe" food, meaning it has a low likelihood of causing an allergic reaction. It's also a good source of iron, which is a mineral babies need at around 6 months as their stores from birth begin to deplete.

But times are changing—and for good reason. Rice cereal lacks the important nutrients that are naturally found in fruits and vegetables. It is refined, meaning the bran and germ, which contain the most nutrients, have been removed to make the product more shelf stable. Even the benefit of its iron content (which is added) isn't superior to iron found naturally in leafy green vegetables, beans, and tofu, not to mention the iron in meat, which the body absorbs most readily.

Some parents express concern about the small amounts of arsenic in rice. Inorganic arsenic is found in our water, air, and soil and normally isn't something we really need to worry about. But because rice tends to absorb more inorganic arsenic than other food crops, the FDA advises that rice cereal shouldn't be your baby's only source of iron.

Rice cereal has fallen from its perch, but it has not disappeared, and it shouldn't. After offering vegetables and fruits first to your baby, you can easily make your own unrefined rice cereal at home, and up its iron content by adding wheat germ to it. (Don't worry too much about this, though. If you give your baby complete meals that contain iron-rich foods, he will get all the iron he needs, just like adults.) If you do offer store-bought rice cereal, make sure to buy brown rice cereal and limit it to a few times a week instead of relying on it daily.

is filled with healthy fat and plenty of important vitamins and minerals. I recommend starting with avocado or sweet potato (and then combining them!) before moving on to juicy fruits so that your baby doesn't develop that sweet tooth too quickly!

Studies show that the early exposure to flavors is key to promoting a more adventurous palate and a more varied diet later on; therefore, this stage is the perfect time to introduce more interesting, even bitter, flavors (such as onions, broccoli, and spinach) to explore. If your little one doesn't like these flavors at first (which is definitely possible), keep trying. Babies often come around and enjoy the foods they rejected the first time (or second, or third).

Eating with the Seasons

Once upon a time, strawberries were available only in certain areas from June to July, citrus couldn't be found outside the winter months, and tomatoes were a late-summer specialty. Now you can walk into any supermarket and purchase the most beautiful-looking produce any time of year. Mass-market produce has become season-less, and while that benefits millions of people who would never have access to certain fruits and vegetables in the first place, seasons still matter. I never liked tomatoes—a little bland yet overly acidic—until I tasted one in season. The clouds

THE DIRTY DOZEN

As we've discussed, it's not always possible to eat entirely organic due to a variety of factors. Sometimes things get in the way. So when you're at the market and one of those "things" pops up, just do your best and, if desired, turn to the Environmental Working Group's Dirty Dozen list to help you make your decision. Each year, this advocacy organization examines data from the FDA and USDA to create their annual Shopper's Guide to Pesticides in Produce, which includes the 12 conventionally grown (nonorganic) fruits and vegetables that contain the highest levels of pesticides—in other words, the Dirty Dozen. (Technically, it's up to 14 now.)

While the Dirty Dozen has the highest levels of pesticide residue, the Clean Fifteen lists the 15 produce items with the lowest levels. I treat these two lists as guides for which produce you should absolutely buy organic and which you can buy conventionally every now and then. Both lists appear in the back of this book (see page 265), but here are the core 12 items on the Dirty Dozen that, most of the time, you'll want to avoid buying nonorganic:

* Apples
* Celery
* Cherries
* Cherry tomatoes
* Cucumbers
* Grapes
* Nectarines

* Peaches
* Spinach
* Strawberries
* Sweet bell peppers
* Tomatoes

parted, my taste buds came alive, and I'm now a true believer in tomatoes. I had just been eating them out of season.

But seasonality is far more than just eating produce at its peak flavor. It is also the time when food is most nutritious. When food is harvested out of season, it's typically at locations far from the end consumer. Just look at the label; most of the time it reads Mexico, California, or some other warm locale. If you live in the land of eternal sunshine, great! But for those of us on the other side of the country, or in the middle, those out-of-season foods have traveled a long way before they reach our shopping bag. Farmers need to harvest these foods well before they're ripe, meaning the food ripens in transit rather than on the vine, while it's still receiving all those fantastic nutrients from the air, sun, and soil.

Eating in season is typically more affordable because the food doesn't have to travel as far to get to the grocery store, thus reducing costs. Ever notice how out-of-season asparagus is outrageously expensive? Plus, there are often sales on seasonal produce because there's simply so much of it that it will go bad if it doesn't get sold.

By purchasing local foods, you can support small family farms and most likely get produce raised with minimal pesticides. The gold standard is to get foods that are both organic *and* local. However, many small family farms cannot afford to qualify for organic certification, though they still follow very natural and healthy growing practices. So it's important to talk to the farmers the next time you stop by your farmers' market. Embrace your inner locavore!

Here is a list of my favorite foods and their seasons. Your list might vary depending where you live, but this is a good starting point.

SPRING	SUMMER	FALL	WINTER
Asparagus	Corn	Apples	Cabbage
Parsnips	Cucumbers	Brussels sprouts	Clementines
Spinach	Green beans	Celery	Cranberries
Strawberries	Peaches	Collard greens	Delicata squash
	Tomatoes	Pears	Sweet potato
	Watermelon	Pumpkins	
	Zucchini	Winter squash	

Seasonal Alternatives

I was always so envious of my friends who lived out west and had an endless supply of fresh produce year round. In New York during the winter months, it can be slim pickings, so those of us who live on the East Coast have to get creative. It is ideal to use fresh and in-season whenever possible, but when that isn't an option, there are a couple of good alternatives:

ORGANIC FROZEN PRODUCE. Take advantage of organic frozen foods. Using frozen produce cuts way down on prep time and provides the security of knowing you always have something wholesome on hand. It can even be more nutritious than out-of-season "fresh" food that has been shipped across the country. Frozen food is harvested and flash-frozen at peak freshness, locking in nutrients. Keeping a well-stocked freezer has saved me countless trips to the market. (Just remember to take out whatever you need the night before to thaw.) Also, read the labels to ensure the package contains just that particular fruit or veggie, as many frozen products contain added salt and sugar. My favorite baby-friendly frozen foods are blueberries, broccoli, cherries, edamame, kale, mangos, peaches, peas, pineapples, and spinach.

GENETICALLY MODIFIED ORGANISMS

Virtually every day there's another study or news report about genetically modified organisms (GMOs) or products that contain hormones. What's even more confusing is that every new morsel of information seems to contradict the last. Unfortunately, research on the potential effects that GMOs may have on long-term health is still in its infancy. There's speculation that GMOs can lead to inflammation, reproductive issues, allergies, and other health-related problems, but it is still too early to conclusively state that they are harmful.

Personally, I'd rather not take a risk. There is currently no requirement to label foods that contain GMOs, so the only way to ensure your food is free of GMOs is to buy organic. You can also be on the lookout for the Non-GMO Project Verified seal, which is a voluntary program. However, remember that just because something doesn't contain GMOs, it doesn't mean it's necessarily organic as well.

ORGANIC DRIED FRUIT. The next best alternative to fresh fruit is dried fruit. Have you ever rehydrated dry fruit? It's easy—just soak the fruit in water until it's plump. Your baby can enjoy a delicious plum puree in November or any time of year. Great baby-friendly dried fruits include apricots, figs, and plums (prunes). Again, check to make sure that the product contains no added sugar.

Organics Beyond Produce

We've talked a lot about organic produce, but it's important to note that the quality of the meat, poultry, and dairy you feed your little one is just as important as the fruits and vegetables you serve—if not more so. Once upon a time, going to a local butcher ensured that the meat you were getting was the best. These days, you have to do a little sleuthing yourself. Don't worry—I got you covered.

BEEF

The labels that are applied to beef are almost as numerous as those found on baby food! "Prime cut," "USDA Prime," "All Natural," "Vegetarian Diet" . . . I could go on. When it comes to beef, there are two important things to look out for:

ORGANIC. This means that the animal was raised without any hormones, antibiotics, or other things we don't want to bring anywhere near our little one. This label also ensures that everything the cows eat is also organic.

GRASS-FED. Cows naturally eat grass, and their entire digestive system is designed for that. Most conventionally raised cows are fed a mix of corn and other items to increase their fat content (flavor) and size. Nutritionally, grass-fed animals have higher levels of healthy fats like omega-3s and contain more antioxidants than animals fed a typical grain-based diet. Grass-fed beef is a bit leaner than your traditional cut, but the flavor and nutritional content are immeasurably better.

POULTRY

Look for poultry that is labeled "organic" *and* "free range." The organic label ensures that the birds were raised in an environment free of pesticides, hormones, and antibiotics, and the free range label tells you that they were allowed access to the outside. Be wary of poultry labeled free range but not organic; while these birds may have been allowed outside, there's no guarantee that they weren't raised on conventional feed rather than their natural diet. Organic and free-range chickens will be a bit leaner than their nonorganic, caged counterparts, but they're worth it.

EGGS

There are many choices when it comes to eggs. While the cage-free label (meaning, quite literally, that chickens weren't raised in a cage) is a good start, this doesn't necessarily mean they weren't raised in an overcrowded hen house; nor does it ensure their diet was all-natural. I recommend buying organic eggs from pasture-raised chickens, if possible. Chickens that are pasture raised are allowed to roam free and exist on their natural diet. You will notice a tremendous difference in flavor and in the color of the yolk (typically the yolks of organic eggs are more vibrant). The color of the shell has nothing to do with nutrition, however—brown eggs are simply from a specific breed of chicken.

There is no official regulation for using the term *pasture raised* so it's best to purchase eggs from local farmers. If you don't have access to a farmers' market or local farm, check out the website of the Cornucopia Institute (cornucopia .org) to access its Organic Egg Scorecard, which lists small farms you can review and order from.

DAIRY PRODUCTS

When you buy organic, you don't have to worry about rBST (recombinant bovine somatotropin), which is a genetically engineered hormone used to stimulate milk production in dairy cows on conventional dairy farms. And while you can be assured with organic dairy that animals were not treated with hormones or antibiotics, it's ideal (though not necessary) if you can buy organic milk, yogurt, and cheese from grass-fed animals. These products are not always easy to find, so it's important to speak to your grocer or the dairy provider at your local farmers' market to express your desire for them. Remember, a lot of small farmers raise their animals in an organic setting but cannot justify the cost of certifying it with the FDA. So have a conversation with them; they'll love that you're interested.

OILS, SPICES, AND HERBS

Aside from the primary ingredients, other ingredients that go into making delicious baby food include herbs and spices, such as basil, dill, nutmeg, and cinnamon, as well as olive oil. Organic options for these ingredients aren't always easy to find, especially when it comes to oils or dried herbs, but more and more producers are investing in organic certification. While your healthiest bet is organic, especially with fresh herbs, if the product is unattainable due to cost or scarcity, don't let that interfere with cooking a delicious meal! You will be using only very small amounts of these ingredients.

A Plentiful Pantry

Making a variety of foods is a wonderful way to introduce your baby to diverse flavors and excite her taste buds. Once you get the hang of it, you can experiment all you want with food combinations seasoned with different herbs and spices. The more flavors you offer early on, the more likely your child will enjoy a variety of foods later.

My son Julian loves foods with very strong flavors, I kid you not, and he can't get enough of anything that has onion in it! We were very quick to add herbs and spices to his food. We followed up carrots and nutmeg in week 1 with sweet potatoes and cinnamon, which is still one of his favorites. There have been plenty of times when he's looked at us blankly—or with a scowl—after we've given him something new to try, only for him to demand more the next day. Kids go through phases, especially at this age, so if at first you don't succeed, try, try again. Eventually, your child will want what you eat, so make sure that when you have mealtime together, you eat something that looks just like what your baby is biting into.

The types of herbs (whether fresh or dried) and spices you choose are up to you. Of course, you'll want to steer clear of hot spices, like cayenne, and go easy on the black pepper. However, don't let your own food quirks influence what you prepare. Lots of folks dislike the taste of cilantro, but that shouldn't interfere with giving it to your little one. While it's always easier to make food the whole family will eat, you should still work to broaden your little one's palate, even if that means making only one portion with a specific type of herb. It's a wonderful way to add flavor without having to add sugar or salt. If you keep a well-stocked pantry, it will make cooking on a regular basis much easier! Below are some of my family's favorite flavor pairings:

ALLSPICE OR CINNAMON: apples, bananas, pears, pumpkin, sweet potatoes, butternut squash, oatmeal, yogurt, beef, chicken

CUMIN: carrots, sweet potatoes, cabbage, tomatoes, beans, rice, beef, lamb

GARLIC: broccoli, cauliflower, zucchini, kohlrabi, rutabagas, quinoa, any meat

GINGER: apples, peaches, pears, squash, root vegetables, tofu, beef

MINT: broccoli, peas, zucchini, yogurt

NUTMEG: carrots, pumpkin, spinach, oatmeal, egg yolks, lamb

ONION: any vegetable, legumes, any meat

ROSEMARY: beets, squash, asparagus, mushrooms, tomatoes, chicken, fish

TARRAGON: carrots, artichokes, mushrooms, chicken, fish

THYME: beets, artichokes, potatoes, legumes, beef, chicken, fish

Essential Tools and Equipment

Cooking baby food is really pretty simple! All you need to do is make sure the food is super soft (at the start) and either puree or mash it. The tools you need to prep, cook, mash, and puree aren't really that complicated. Of course, if you have been looking for a great reason (ahem, excuse) to get a new kitchen tool (hello, Vitamix), this is the perfect time!

That said, there can be a lot of confusion about how to get started making your own baby food, and if you're like me, you want a sense of what you already have in your kitchen and what you'll need to purchase before you get started. From blenders to gadgets that will make your life easier, here are my favorite kitchen essentials:

PREP

PEELER. A sharp peeler speeds the process of peeling your fruits and vegetables. Most purees (at least at the start) are made without skin for consistency and digestive ease.

KNIVES. Every kitchen needs one good chopping knife and one good paring knife.

COOK

POTS AND STEAMERS. All early purees start here. If you already have an assortment of pots, you can just get a steamer insert to fit inside. If not, you'll want to buy a set of pots in various sizes along with steamer inserts, so you can steam more than one batch of fruits or veggies at a time.

If you want to make things super easy and are okay with having another gadget on your countertop, you can get a combination steamer-blender device. These appliances work well for produce, but they don't have the power to break down much more.

BAKING SHEETS. Baked food adds a whole new level to your baby's culinary experience. You'll want to line your baking sheets with parchment paper, so be sure to buy a few rolls of that as well.

MINI MUFFIN TIN. This is a great pan for making small portions. You'll need mini paper liners for lining the cups.

FOOD THERMOMETER. Skip it if your family doesn't eat meat, but I find this to be absolutely essential for testing when meat is ready.

BLEND

A REALLY GOOD BLENDER OR FOOD PROCESSOR. This appliance is going to be your best friend. Whether it's purees, smoothies, or soups, your blender or food processor will get a ton of use—and that's only for the little one! Invest in a good one so it lasts a long time; you'll know it was worth it when it's still working in five years. The better products on the market are very powerful, which can cut your prep time in half.

FREEZE AND THAW

SILICONE STORAGE TRAYS. These could be simple ice cube trays, or you can pay more for the fancy "baby food only" trays. Just make sure whatever you use has a cover (or create your own with plastic wrap) to protect against freezer burn.

SMALL GLASS BOWLS AND JARS. These are perfect for thawing your frozen cubes of deliciousness. Many of them fit perfectly in a bottle warmer!

STORE

SMALL GLASS LOCKABLE CONTAINERS OR MASON JARS. As food begins to take a more central role in your baby's life, you'll find her craving the real stuff at all hours of the day, so it's important to have these convenient storage and go-to containers.

STORAGE BAGS. Zip-top bags will be your second-best friend. After freezing food for about 24 hours in a storage tray, you'll pop the freezer tray cubes into these bags for longer-term storage—and don't forget to label. Frozen pea purees and frozen green bean purees don't look all that different from one another. You'll use these bags often, so consider reusable options.

SERVE

MESH FOOD FEEDERS. If you're nervous about putting even a small amount of food into your baby's mouth, try a mesh food feeder. The food (fresh or frozen) goes in the bag and your baby can suck on it, drawing out the flavors and even some nutrients, without any fear of gagging or choking. These are great developmental tools and a way for your baby to get healthy food on the go as she grows! Also, they're good for teething if you use cold produce or even ice.

SPOONS. Early on, I recommend a soft silicone-based spoon like the Beaba or OXO spoon. Both are BPA-, phthalate-, and PVC-free, and the shape of the spoon seems to make feeding a fidgety baby easier. As they get older and those teeth come in, a firmer spoon with a deeper bowl is best. I personally like Munchkin's options. They're inexpensive and do the job.

BOWLS. Part of the success of those first bites is getting your baby comfortable with the experience of eating. This means sitting down to a meal! Try to "plate" your baby's food before putting it on her tray or spooning into her open mouth, to help her get used to mealtime.

Now that you're all stocked up, in the next chapter you'll learn some basics for getting your little one started on this exciting culinary journey. While there's a lot to keep in mind and consider, what's most important is to have fun and be sure to take some videos!

3

THE FIRST FEEDING AND BEYOND

The day has come. You leave your pediatrician's office with the blessing (or advice) to start solids, and all you can think is "What do we try first?" This is one incredibly exciting step of many in your baby's development. I hope you'll dive in enthusiastically with the understanding that, like all new experiences, there will be many highs and some lows. By this point, your baby has probably put everything within reach in her cute little mouth anyway, so food is just another thing to explore. Record it, watch it later, and giggle as your child begins to express herself—scrunched-up faces with that first sour bite, a satisfying "mmm" sound as she reaches for more. There are no rules here, so buckle up and enjoy the ride!

Signs of Readiness

Babies are incredible. One day they are lying there, making cute gurgling sounds (or wailing!) and the next they are moving all over the place, laughing (or still wailing) and turning their little heads when you call their names. They give you telltale signs for every step in their development. When it comes to introducing solids, though, it can feel a bit frustrating. It's not as if your baby can look up one day and say, "Can I have a bite of that avocado?"

So when is the right time? The American Academy of Pediatrics says around 6 months; I've heard pediatricians say as early as 4 months. We introduced food just after 5 months, not because the calendar said so, but because our son was literally begging for real food. He was staring at our plates, drooling with every bite we took, and practically ripping food out of our hands if he got within reach! So one day we just knew it was time. We put the high chair together, sat him down, and spooned an avocado (mashed until incredibly smooth) into his eagerly await-ing mouth. I will never forget that first reaction (it's on video!). He crinkled his face in absolute disgust, shook his head, stared at us in disbelief, and then leaned in for more! He hasn't looked back since.

Julian has always been very clear about what he wants. Not all babies are going to make it as obvious as he did for us. Here are some of the signs to look out for.

Your baby:

* Is able to sit up without support
* Shows interest in food (grabs at your food, opens his mouth for food, stares longingly at food, and starts to mimic eating)
* Leans in for food
* Exhibits diminished tongue-thrust reflex (this enables a baby to actually swallow food, rather than push it out with his tongue)

If you're not seeing these signs yet, don't sweat it; he'll be ready when he's ready.

Structured Introductions

I spent way too much time strategizing exactly what that first bite would be; there may or may not have been a few sleepless nights. . . . Truth-fully, it doesn't much matter what you introduce first as long as it is a *single* food (one type of vegetable or fruit) and that it's a consistency your baby can eat—in other words, pureed. (I've got you covered with three chapters of recipes for purees.)

ONE AT A TIME

If you remember just one thing about introducing food, remember this: Stay with each single food for a few days before moving on to a new one. This is to ensure that your baby has no reactions; sometimes it takes a day for a rash, hive, or other sign of allergy to come out. Once you're sure everything is A-OK with that food, add a flavorful spice or herb to the mix (see page 19 for ideas). Test one spice or herb at a time, the way you would with new foods.

KEEP IT PLAYFUL

Let your baby play with his food and don't be too quick to wipe his little mouth. Know that your baby is going to make a mess, and be at peace with it. If at any time your baby turns his head, end the feeding at that point. You don't want to force it; he *will* eat when he's both ready and interested, and when he is interested, it will be so much fun. You'll be so surprised to see what your little one likes and doesn't like.

KEEP TRYING

At this stage, food is more about development than nutrition, so don't worry about how much or how little your baby eats, and keep the breast milk or formula at the same level. If your little one rejects something, try the same food again the next day. Once you do hit on a couple of purees that your baby enjoys a bit, try some combinations of those foods (for combination recommendations, see page 29). As before,

just ensure there is no reaction before moving on to the next combination. Soon enough, you'll be whipping up all sorts of baby-friendly concoctions.

The First Puree

It's time. The blender's hooked up, the food is perfectly soft, and all you need to do is press the puree button. You're ready!

THE SETUP

It's important to remember that these early days aren't just about getting the little one comfortable with food but about the entire ritual that goes into it. Essentially, teaching your baby *how* to eat is as important as *what* to eat. If he's comfortable with the process, the physical act of eating will be much easier. Make sure to put him in his high chair, pull up a seat right in front, and engage with him while he's eating. There are a lot of other seating options out there, but a high chair, which allows the baby's feet to be planted and brings him above eye level to the table, is the closest thing to sitting at the dinner table. If you ever hope to have the whole family around the dinner table, now's the time to start ingraining this idea.

We had Julian do a test run in his high chair the day before we introduced him to solid food. We put him in the high chair, made sure everything fit perfectly, and gave him some toys to play with to get comfortable in this new contraption. Then, when it came time to eat, he already knew what the first step felt like, which removed one layer of stress for Mom and Dad.

I recommend offering a feeding either an hour before or after a milk or formula feeding; that way, the baby isn't completely full or starving, but content. The ideal time is their happiest time.

THE FOOD

Okay. We know that we should serve a single-food puree first. We know to give it to him from a bowl with a spoon while he's sitting in a high chair. Now it's time to make the historic choice of what exactly to give him! In the next chapter, you'll find a host of different options for that very first bite, but if you're overwhelmed, just pick one from the list below:

AVOCADO: great texture, fun color, mild flavor, and brimming with healthy fats and over 20 different vitamins and minerals

PEAR: sweet but not too sweet, delicious both roasted and steamed, and a great source of fiber, vitamin C, and antioxidants

SWEET POTATO: creamy texture, great color for the little one to fixate on, and filled with beta-carotene (precursor for vitamin A), vitamin C, fiber, and potassium

Once you're ready to move on to the more complicated stuff, I still recommend keeping these three foods in the rotation. In the back of the book, I've put together a schedule for the first eight weeks of when to introduce different recipes (see page 263).

THE TEXTURE

I remember it perfectly: My husband and I were standing in the kitchen, an open jar of baby food that we bought in one hand and the puree we made in the other. "Is this too lumpy?" "The stuff in the jar is so smooth. . . ." We definitely focused a bit too much on the perfect texture, so let my obsession be your gain! That first bite should be very smooth and fairly thin. If a spoonful of it slides off easily, you've got yourself the ideal consistency.

It's important in the beginning to keep the texture (like the flavors and ingredients) as simple as possible. This is the first time they are ever putting food in their mouths. I recommend taking out the blender (or immersion blender) for that first puree, as it's the only way to get it super smooth. We, again being a bit hyperfocused, took out the old mortar and pestle, and my husband spent nearly 10 minutes hand-churning avocado and a bit of breast milk while our son watched in awe. (As time progresses, you'll want to start thickening things up—not blending them as finely—so your baby can get used to new textures on his way to eating whole foods.)

FOODS TO AVOID IN THE FIRST YEAR

There are loads of options for what your baby can eat in the first year, and most foods are fair game as they mature. That being said, there are a few foods to hold off on before your baby turns 1 year old:

HONEY. While we all know how baby would love this sweet deliciousness (think of the funny videos of them figuring out the sticky texture!), unfortunately, honey is a big no-no. Honey can contain *Clostridium botulinum*, which is harmless to adults but can lead to botulism in babies. Botulism is a very serious and often deadly infection, so steer clear of honey.

COW'S MILK. You want to avoid replacing your baby's breast milk or formula in the first year with cow's milk because it doesn't contain enough essential fatty acids, iron, or vitamin E; it also has too much protein, potassium, and sodium, which can cause damage to their developing kidneys. However, it is okay to include dairy products such as yogurt, butter, cheese, and milk in recipes.

FISH HIGH IN MERCURY (TUNA, KING MACKEREL, SWORDFISH, AND SHARK). While I highly encourage you to give your little one fish, stay away from those that are known to be high in mercury. His little nervous system can't handle that much.

CHOKING HAZARDS. Stay away from grapes, tough meats, bones (in fish and poultry), hot dogs, tough skins (like potato skins, eggplant skins), popcorn, small seeds, hard nuts, raisins, and lettuce.

REFINED SUGARS. I'm a dietitian, so I counsel all my clients, both adult and kids, to stay away from refined sugars. They add zero nutritional value to your meals and cause all types of problems down the road (obesity, heart disease, inflammation . . . I could go on). If your child's taste buds become accustomed to this unnatural sweetness, you'll have a hard time getting her to enjoy more wholesome foods.

TEXTURES AND PORTIONS THROUGH THE STAGES

All good things come to those who eat. It's amazing to see how my own son has progressed from his first bite of smooth avocado to pushing purees out of the way and reaching for whole pieces of chicken! Here's a breakdown of the various stages to give you an idea of texture and portion sizes. Remember, every baby is different, so use this as a guide, not a rule.

STAGE 1: 4 to 6 months

TEXTURE: smooth, watery, and thin
PORTION SIZE: 1 teaspoon up to about 2 tablespoons

STAGE 2: 7 to 9 months

TEXTURE: still primarily smooth as new flavors are combined; offer thicker purees by month 9
PORTION SIZE: ¼ cup to ½ cup per feeding, with two to three feedings per day

STAGE 3: 10 to 12 months

TEXTURE: chunky purees, whether blended or fork-mashed, as well as finely chopped foods
PORTION SIZE: ¼ cup to ½ cup per feeding, with three feedings a day plus a snack (such as banana slices, black beans, or avocado bites)

Don't be surprised if your baby gags a bit when learning to eat solid food. This is an entirely new sensation, and it's a natural reflex. That first swallow may even be a gag, and it might terrify you, but remember, it's not uncommon. There will also be times when that gag turns into a spit-up. That's not a bad thing, as it's indicating that your baby's body is doing its job and getting something out that shouldn't be in there. Maybe the puree is too chunky or the baby might have an allergy to that food (see page 36 for more on allergies). Since every baby is different, speak with your pediatrician about any concerns you might have.

Choking, however, is an entirely different matter. It's very important to remember that a baby's throat is very narrow. What might seem like a tiny piece of food to you may be too large for the baby's throat, which is why in the first couple of months of feeding your purees should be blended to ensure they are completely smooth. I encourage every soon-to-be or new parent to take an infant CPR class, especially before you introduce food. There you'll learn the signs of choking and how to respond.

THE PORTION

Don't throw out the breast milk or formula just yet! Those first few bites are literally that: *a few bites*. The amount of food you give in the beginning is very small and is not intended to influence the amount of milk or formula your baby is eating. Again, this stage is all about exploration and getting comfortable (both you and the little one) with the whole idea of eating solids. As you progress, read your child's cues. If he is leaning in with his mouth wide open, then it's safe to say you can give him a bit more. If it's the opposite reaction, don't force it. Babies are the ultimate self-regulators; at this point, everything is still an innate trait rather than a decision. I wish we kept that ability!

Start with 1 teaspoon once a day for the first few weeks, and then work up to 2 to 4 teaspoons once or twice a day.

THE REACTION

So, how'd it go? Crinkled nose? Tears of disgust? Or smiles and shouts of joy? Regardless, keep at it. There will be days when everything is perfect, and the next when your baby will reject everything you put in front of him. It can take up to 25 tries for a baby to eat a new food! If things aren't taking, try offering food at a different time of day.

Try eating with them, as babies love to mimic Mom and Dad. Patience and persistence are key here; the last thing you want is to create a stressful environment around food; they pick up on it. Keep it light and fun and know that in five years when she's sitting at the table eating with a knife and fork, you can all have a good laugh.

Great Combinations

Soon enough, both you and your baby will be old pros at feeding time. That's when the real fun begins! By this point, you're probably bored (and so is the little one) with all these single foods. Time to spice things up! Here's when you can start mixing foods together to create fun flavor profiles and, most important, nutritionally dense foods.

You'll find soon enough that there are combinations (there are dozens of different ones in part 2) that you might never have thought tasty, perhaps even leading to more adventurous eating on your own part!

If you are looking as much for inspiration as you are for recipes, I've put together this handy chart of superfoods and the foods that complement them. And if the word *superfoods* sounds familiar but you're not quite sure what they are, here's how I usually explain it: superfoods are foods that contain so many nutrients, they are considered to be especially beneficial to your health. The following chart shows you foods you can combine with superfoods for great flavor and top-notch nutrition.

SUPERFOOD COMBINATIONS

Apricots
Apples
Berries
Cinnamon
Fish
Ginger
Green beans
Pears
Peas
Poultry
Spinach

Avocados
Bananas
Beef
Black beans
Cherries
Cilantro
Cumin
Mangos
Nectarines
Peaches
Quinoa

Beets
Beef
Carrots
Fennel
Leafy greens
Parsnips
Rosemary
Tarragon
Tofu
Yogurt

Blueberries
Allspice
Avocado
Banana
Cinnamon
Fish
Melons
Poultry
Oatmeal
Other berries
Quinoa
Yogurt

Broccoli
Apples
Beef
Carrots
Cauliflower
Nutmeg
Pears
Rosemary
Thyme
Tofu

Kale
Apples
Bananas
Nutmeg
Pears
Potatoes
Poultry
Sweet potatoes
Tofu

Lentils
Cherries
Cinnamon
Figs
Kale
Plums
Quinoa
Sweet potatoes
Thyme
Tomatoes

Quinoa
Apples
Avocados
Beef
Beets
Kale
Pears
Peas
Poultry
Spinach
Winter squash

Spinach
Beef
Cauliflower
Citrus
Eggs
Fish
Garlic
Onions
Plums
Poultry
Thyme

Sweet Potatoes
Apricots
Avocados
Broccoli
Cinnamon
Ginger
Green Beans
Kale
Pears
Peas
Spinach

Winter Squash/ Pumpkins
Cranberries
Ginger
Kale
Nutmeg
Oranges
Poultry
Quinoa

Yogurt
All berries
All fruits
Beets
Cinnamon
Winter squash

Balanced Nutrition from the Beginning

Offering your baby a varied diet from all food groups is the best way to make sure she's getting everything she needs to grow strong and healthy. Here are some guidelines to keep in mind:

* FRUITS AND VEGETABLES: 6 months and up
* GRAINS: 6 months and up
* DAIRY: 8 months and up (but no cow's milk before 12 months)
* MEAT: 6 months and up

Here are some of the key nutrients you'll want to pay close attention to from ages 4 to 12 months:

FAT. The healthiest fats are found in full-fat dairy products, avocados, nut butters, and olive oil. Fat helps the body absorb fat-soluble vitamins (like A, E, D, and K), and also helps with brain and nerve development.

IRON. Stores are diminished by the time babies are 6 months old, so it is important to get this mineral through food. Key sources of iron are meat, poultry, and fish, as well as vegetarian sources like egg yolks, legumes, tofu, and green leafy vegetables.

OMEGA-3 FATTY ACIDS. This essential fatty acid is important for brain development. The best source of omega-3s is cold-water fish like wild salmon and sardines. This form of omega-3s is more readily absorbed by the body than plant-based forms like flaxseed, chia seeds, and walnuts. I recommend serving these types of fish at least twice a week.

PROBIOTICS. These are great for digestion. In this book, the probiotic source you'll see most often in the recipes is yogurt. But probiotics are found in a range of fermented foods, including kefir, miso, sauerkraut, sourdough bread, and more.

VITAMIN D. Vitamin D is found in animal products, but 20 minutes of sun exposure each day is really the best way for the body to produce enough of this vitamin. According to the American Academy of Pediatrics, breastfed babies under 12 months need to take a daily 400 IU supplement a day of vitamin D. Speak with your pediatrician about this. Vitamin D is added to formula.

ZINC. A baby's zinc stores deplete at around 6 months. Zinc is helpful for keeping baby's immune system strong and for skin healing, and is found mainly in animal products.

Skipping Purees

Babies didn't always eat purees—blenders are a relatively new invention. So what did we as humans do without our trusty Vitamix, Blendtec, Ninja, Beaba, or Cuisinart? Well, what is old is new again, and the practice of "baby-led weaning" that is so widespread in Europe has crossed the Atlantic, and is becoming increasingly popular in the United States. It has nothing to do with weaning from the breast but rather is an approach that allows your baby to feed herself whole food—in appropriately sized pieces, of course—from the start. Proponents of baby-led weaning believe this method not only gives children a more varied diet but also helps them develop essential skills and socialization much faster. It can also prevent overfeeding, as the baby is completely in charge of what (and how much) goes in her mouth.

However, since babies develop at different speeds, this approach might not be the best for everyone. It's true that those early bites are more about development than nutrition, but nutrition quickly becomes an important part of the equation if their fine-motor skills aren't developed or if they simply aren't interested in feeding themselves.

So what to do? That's up to you—and your baby. I see benefits in both approaches, so it truly depends on *your* comfort level. You can always give it a shot and have a few purees handy just in case, or do a combination. It doesn't have to be an all-or-nothing approach. Regardless, this book offers both purees and whole food recipes, so just skip to the chapter that matches your approach. If baby-led weaning appeals to you, here are a handful of great options to kick things off:

* AVOCADO: ripe, cut into sticks, and lightly coated in oat flour, for easier pickup
* BANANA: peeled halfway, with baby holding the peel and gumming the peeled banana half
* BROCCOLI: steamed and broken into large pieces; the florets are easier to gum
* CARROTS: peeled, steamed, and cut into long, thick strips
* CAULIFLOWER: steamed and broken into large pieces; the florets are easier to gum
* EGG: can be hard-boiled and halved or made into a flat "omelet"
* SWEET POTATO: steamed or roasted until very soft and served without the skin

SPOTLIGHT ON VEGETARIAN DIETS

Is it your plan to raise your child as a vegetarian? If you're thinking about it but aren't totally committed to the idea, you might want to discuss it with your pediatrician so you can make sure your baby will get enough vitamin B$_{12}$, zinc, iron, vitamin D, and protein. Knowing which vegetarian-friendly foods are good sources of these nutrients is important; you'll find a list here. For longtime vegetarians, this may be a good refresher for you. With regard to vitamin D, sunshine is really the best way to get enough, so discuss this with your pediatrician if your child doesn't eat animal products and doesn't have an opportunity to get outdoors in the sunshine for at least 20 minutes a day.

Iron
* Black beans
* Broccoli
* Dark leafy greens (kale, collard greens, etc.)
* Dried apricot
* Edamame
* Kale
* Lentils
* Oatmeal
* Parsley
* Peas
* Pinto beans
* Tofu

Zinc
* Legumes
* Eggs
* Peas
* Tofu

Vitamin B$_{12}$
* Eggs
* Hard cheese
* Milk (if over 12 months)
* Nutritional yeast

Protein
* Cheese
* Edamame
* Legumes
* Milk (if over 12 months)
* Nut butter
* Quinoa
* Tofu
* Yogurt

The Family That Eats Together

In an ideal world, we would all sit down by 7:00 p.m., baby included, and have a delicious meal over thought-provoking conversation. Problem is, a little thing called reality. We're all busy, with different jobs, schedules, and so on, so getting everyone around the table at the same time can be difficult. Throw a little one into the mix, and you're typically pushing up mealtime by an hour or so.

The key here is to try—if it doesn't work, then fake it. What does that mean? Well, when it's time for baby's dinner, try to get whoever is at home to sit at the table. It doesn't necessarily mean they have to eat. If they'd like, they can have a little snack, but the idea is to just be together. That way, your baby sees everyone who is at home sitting together at mealtime, which quickly becomes ingrained as a habit.

Having a family meal is also a way to get your baby used to grown-up food and all its varied flavors and textures. This will make it a lot easier as he transitions to eating on his own and sitting at the table. It also allows Mom and Dad to cook one meal that everyone can enjoy. Include at least one food your child likes, and expose him to the glorious foods on your plate!

This Book's Recipes

So what's to come? Part 2 includes a huge assortment of recipes for all stages—more than 200, in fact! Single ingredient and combo purees, finger foods and snacks, as well as full composed meals for toddlers and family.

I was constantly looking for new fun recipes to try, and I'm very fortunate that Julian was always eager for more! The following is a compilation of some of our favorites, with tons of variety to make sure there is something for everyone, from new and different to trusted standbys. The premise is to work toward skipping the "kid's menu" and build meals the whole family can enjoy. It's a lot easier to build good habits than it is to break bad ones.

Also, since I *am* a dietitian, it is my job to make sure foods not only taste good but are also healthy. I've worked hard to maximize both the flavor and nutritional value of each recipe. I've had a lot of fun trying out everything on my husband and, of course, on Julian!

So what do these recipes *not* include? There are no refined sugars, artificial sweeteners, or preservatives. My food philosophy focuses on the fact that everything that is not processed is allowed (because "forbidden" foods will come back to bite you in the long run). All the recipes are made with whole foods and, as you will quickly realize, I'm not shy about adding fats

ALLERGIES, INTOLERANCES, AND SENSITIVITIES

As exciting as this time can be, when introducing your baby to new foods, you may be concerned about food allergies, sensitivities, or intolerances, and that's a valid concern. Trust me, I'm right there with you. My husband and I were so worried when we saw hives break out on our son's face after eating certain foods. It wasn't until later that we learned he, in fact, has egg and nut allergies. Fortunately, there are many resources for parents and kids.

Under the guidance of the FDA, the Food Allergen Labeling and Consumer Protection Act identifies the following eight foods as major food allergens:

1. Milk
2. Eggs
3. Fish (e.g., bass, flounder, cod)
4. Crustacean shellfish (e.g., crab, lobster, shrimp)
5. Tree nuts (e.g., almonds, walnuts, pecans)
6. Peanuts
7. Wheat
8. Soybeans

But just because these foods are on the list doesn't mean you shouldn't try them, and pediatricians no longer subscribe to the notion that by avoiding them you prevent the likelihood of a child developing an allergy. Remember, you are offering only small amounts at first and watching your baby for any negative reaction to any food he eats, whether or not it's on the list. Also keep in mind that your child may be sensitive to foods that aren't on this list. If your baby doesn't have a reaction to a food, you can introduce slightly bigger portions slowly over time.

If you see any sign of an allergic reaction—including rash, hives, gastrointestinal distress like vomiting or diarrhea, teary eyes, face or tongue swelling, or difficulty breathing within minutes or up to a few hours after consuming the food—either discontinue that food or try it again under medical supervision. Get immediate medical attention for your baby if the reaction is severe.

Oftentimes, a rash can simply signal a skin irritation and could be the result of sensitive skin and not an allergy to a food she just had. If you're unsure, then definitely schedule an appointment with your pediatrician to discuss your concerns and develop a plan for reintroducing a suspect food.

to baby food, as they are necessary for proper development. So you won't find any "low-fat" options. Kids, just like adults, love fatty foods and will eat them! And they should!

But when you are cooking for your family, it is nice to control what goes into the food. You'll see healthy fats like olive oil, avocados, and nut butters. There might also be some butter, especially in the toddler section, as I am perfectly fine with a good-quality butter that comes from grass-fed cows.

Each chapter is broken down by months so you can follow along as your baby ages. Each also includes an overview of what's happening developmentally, recommended portions for each age, and a question-and-answer section.

When it comes to purees, this book assumes that you're not going to make one serving at a time but rather mash or cook and puree several servings of sweet potatoes, apples, broccoli, and so on, and freeze them for quick and easy use later. All the combination puree recipes call for freezer cubes of single-ingredient purees. If you don't happen to have the purees you'll need on hand, turn to page 261 for an at-a-glance cooking chart for making purees.

The recipes were written and designed so that you can know, at a glance, whether they're freezer friendly. This little snowflake will make it obvious. Colorful labels ensure you'll also know if the recipe conforms to your dietary restrictions. Here's what you'll see:

DF	Dairy Free
GF	Gluten Free
NF	Nut Free
V	Vegetarian
Vegan	Vegan (of course!)

Some recipes allow you to choose between two ingredients, such as whole wheat flour or almond flour. In this case, you'll see a label indicating that the recipe has a gluten-free option.

I'm excited to share my favorites, and hope your family enjoys them, too!

PART 2
RECIPES FOR
BABY & FAMILY

4

STAGE 1: SINGLE-INGREDIENT PUREES

Your baby is growing up! By introducing ingredients one at a time, you can learn your baby's likes and dislikes (as well as possible food sensitivities) while introducing different flavors and textures. Foods at this stage need to be thin, so mixing the purees with breast milk, formula, or water will help create a consistency that won't stimulate your baby's gag reflex. The foundational purees that follow offer healthy, whole foods for your baby, as well as suggested herb and spice pairings.

DEVELOPMENTALLY SPEAKING

Your baby may seem ready for foods as early as 4 months, but most pediatricians recommend waiting to start first foods until about 6 months. As I mentioned, we started my son Julian on food when he was 5 months old. To be safest, this chapter recommends starting at 6 months, but you'll know your baby is ready when you see these signs:

* Sitting up without support
* Showing interest in food by staring or grabbing at food, leaning in or opening her mouth for food, and/or mimicking eating
* Diminishing of the tongue-thrust reflex (as this reflex lessens, your baby will be able to swallow food instead of push it out)

PORTION GUIDELINES

When your baby first starts eating, she doesn't need much, so portions of solids will be very small, and you'll primarily be offering breast milk or formula supplemented by solids.

* Your baby will continue to need between 24 and 40 ounces of breast milk or formula daily.
* Initially, offer once each day about 1 teaspoon of solid food, thinned if necessary with breast milk, formula, or water until smooth at first, and later to the desired consistency. As long as your baby continues to open her mouth when offered a spoon, you can keep the feeding going.

FAQ

Q: Should my baby's first several purees come from fruits or vegetables? Should I pick something he's most likely to enjoy—and how do I know what that might be?

A: We've all been eating food for so long that it's really very hard to imagine starting with a blank slate, which is exactly the benefit your little one has. Most of us would probably prefer to eat a sweet fruit instead of a green vegetable if given the choice, but babies are highly receptive to the full spectrum of foods and their flavors—sweet, savory, umami, what have you.

There's little point in wondering what your baby will like best, since most babies tend to like *everything* initially, as long as the texture is right. I recommend starting with a slightly sweet vegetable, such as a carrot or sweet potato, or a non-sweet fruit, like an avocado. While your baby will surely love peaches and mango once they're introduced, starting with a super-sweet fruit early on may make it harder to take to vegetables. I'm not such a stickler as to recommend avoiding fruit for weeks, but it's good to offer vegetables for the first few purees, and then start to combine them. Let your baby surprise you with her love of green beans, peas, cauliflower, and more.

Avocado Puree

MAKES 15 (1-OUNCE) FREEZER TRAY CUBES

1½ pounds avocados (about 3 avocados), peeled and pitted

Thanks to their creamy texture, avocados are easy to make into an on-demand, no-cook puree. Whether you use a mortar and pestle (like we did) or immersion blender for whipping up a feeding or three, or blending several avocados to freeze multiple ounces for use in later dishes, avocado is likely to be a staple in the early months of feeding—if not early years! It's delicious on its own and adds wonderful flavor to other vegetables, legumes, and meats. Avocados are an excellent source of fiber, vitamin C, and vitamin A, as well as healthy fats.

HERBS AND SPICES *Avocados pair well with sweet and savory spices and herbs, such as grated lime or lemon zest, cilantro, garlic powder, onion powder, and ground nutmeg, cumin, and coriander.*

In a blender or food processor, combine the avocado and a pinch of an herb or spice, if using. Puree until smooth. Adjust the texture by adding a little breast milk, formula, or water to achieve the desired consistency.

STORAGE: Fill a freezer cube tray with 1-ounce portions. Freeze overnight. Store the frozen cubes in a tightly sealed zip-top bag for up to 6 months.

TIP: To cut an avocado, use a sharp knife and work your way lengthwise around the edge of the avocado. Twist to separate the halves. Use a large spoon to remove the pit, and then scoop the flesh away from the peel.

Sweet Potato, Yam, or Potato Puree

MAKES 15 (1-OUNCE) FREEZER TRAY CUBES

1½ pounds sweet potatoes, yams, or potatoes (about 3), peeled and cut into ¼-inch dice

STORAGE: Fill a freezer cube tray with 1-ounce portions. Freeze overnight. Store the frozen cubes in a tightly sealed zip-top bag for up to 6 months.

This recipe covers sweet potatoes and yams, as well as all colors of potatoes, such as white, russet, purple, and red potatoes. They're grouped here not because they're in the same vegetable family (they're not), but because the cooking methods and times are virtually identical. Sweet potatoes are an ideal first food because of their baby-friendly sweetness and nutritional profile. All vegetables in this category are starchy and high in fiber.

HERBS AND SPICES *Sweet potatoes work well with a pinch of both savory herbs such as thyme and ground cumin, and sweet spices such as ginger and cinnamon. Potatoes pair well with rosemary and thyme, as well as with onion and garlic powder.*

1. In a medium saucepan with a steamer insert, bring about 1 inch of water to a simmer. Add the potatoes. Cover and steam until tender, about 10 minutes.
2. Transfer the potatoes to a blender or food processor, along with a pinch of an herb or spice, if using. Puree until smooth. Adjust the texture by adding a little breast milk, formula, or water to achieve the desired consistency.

TIP: I love roasting these vegetables (and sweet potatoes in particular) in the oven as an alternative to steaming. To roast, preheat the oven to 400°F. Cut several slices into each sweet potato, but don't cut all the way through to the other end. Wrap the potatoes in aluminum foil and bake for 45 minutes to an hour, until the potato inside the skin is very tender and a knife can easily slide in and out. Let them cool to room temperature before scooping out the inside and pureeing. I would tend to bake several sweet potatoes for the week and puree or serve them for Julian to feed himself. I'd often include the sweet potatoes in my own meals, or just snack on them.

Banana Puree

DF GF NF Vegan

**MAKES 15 (1-OUNCE)
FREEZER TRAY CUBES**

**1½ pounds bananas
(about 3 bananas), peeled**

Bananas are incredibly popular with babies (including my own!), thanks to their sweetness and easy-to-swallow consistency. Bananas are a good source of potassium, and they're also high in immunity-boosting vitamin C and anti-oxidants. While plantains are members of the banana family, they are much starchier and require cooking before you puree them. For a recommendation on preparing plantains, see the tip.

HERBS AND SPICES *Bananas are delicious with ground nutmeg, cinnamon, allspice, or ginger.*

In a blender or food processor, combine the bananas and a pinch of spice, if using. Puree until smooth. Adjust the texture by adding a little breast milk, formula, or water to achieve the desired consistency.

STORAGE: Fill a freezer cube tray with 1-ounce portions. Freeze overnight. Store the frozen cubes in a tightly sealed zip-top bag for up to 6 months.

TIP: To make plantain puree, peel the plantains first and then follow the instructions for cooking and pureeing potatoes on page 43.

Apple or Pear Puree

DF GF NF Vegan

MAKES 15 (1-OUNCE) FREEZER TRAY CUBES

1½ pounds apples or pears (about 4 medium apples or pears), peeled, cored, and cut into ¼-inch dice

Because apples and pears have similar textures, they are interchangeable in this puree recipe. Either makes a wonderful introduction to fruit, as they're not overpoweringly sweet. Picked at the peak of ripeness in the fall, apples have a sweet-tart flavor and crisp bite, while pears are softer with a milder flavor. Both come in many varieties. Consider combining a sweet Bosc pear with a crispy Asian pear, or a sweet apple like Red Delicious with a tart Granny Smith. Both apples and pears are high in fiber and are a good source of vitamins and minerals.

HERBS AND SPICES *Apples work well with sage or rosemary, as well as with sweet spices like ground cinnamon, ginger, and nutmeg. Pears taste great with fennel and anise, as well as with spices such as ground ginger and cinnamon.*

1. In a medium saucepan with a steamer insert, bring about 1 inch of water to a simmer. Add the fruit. Cover and steam until tender, 5 to 10 minutes.
2. Transfer the fruit to a blender or food processor, along with a pinch of an herb or spice, if using. Puree until smooth. Adjust the texture by adding a little breast milk, formula, or water to achieve the desired consistency.

STORAGE: Fill a freezer cube tray with 1-ounce portions. Freeze overnight. Store the frozen cubes in a tightly sealed zip-top bag for up to 6 months.

TIP: Roasting pears brings out their sweetness even more. I would often roast pears with ginger (peeled and minced), and then enjoy one for my own dessert, or later add the pear to oatmeal or yogurt. I'd always set aside some of the roasted pear for Julian and puree it, which he loved.

Root Vegetable Puree

MAKES 15 (1-OUNCE)
FREEZER TRAY CUBES

1½ pounds root vegetables (about 5 parsnips, carrots, or turnips), peeled and cut into ½-inch cubes

Root vegetables are available seasonally in the spring through the fall, and they store well in winter cellars as well. Veggies like parsnips, carrots, and turnips all make fantastic purees. These are fairly starchy vegetables with a neutral to slightly sweet flavor. Prep is the same for all root vegetables. While it's fastest to steam root vegetables, roasting is a great option for bringing out their rich flavor. See the tip for roasting instructions.

HERBS AND SPICES *Consider pairing this puree with thyme or tarragon, which work well with earthy flavors. Alternatively, you can try sweet spices, such as ground nutmeg or allspice, which enhance the sweetness of the starch in these vegetables.*

1. In a medium saucepan with a steamer insert, bring about 1 inch of water to a simmer. Add the chopped vegetables. Cover and steam until tender, 5 to 10 minutes.
2. Transfer the steamed vegetable to a blender or food processor, along with a pinch of an herb or spice, if using. Puree until smooth. Adjust the texture by adding a little breast milk, formula, or water to achieve the desired consistency.

STORAGE: Fill a freezer cube tray with 1-ounce portions. Freeze overnight. Store the frozen cubes in a tightly sealed zip-top bag for up to 6 months.

TIP: Root vegetables develop an especially delicious flavor when roasted. They're just as easy to cook this way, but it takes longer than steaming. Preheat the oven to 400°F. Cover a baking sheet with parchment and arrange the peeled and cut vegetables on it. Place the sheet in the oven and roast the vegetables for about 30 minutes or until slightly browned, turning once after 15 minutes. When done, remove from the oven and let them come to room temperature before pureeing.

Dark Leafy Greens Puree

MAKES 15 (1-OUNCE) FREEZER TRAY CUBES

1½ pounds dark leafy greens, stemmed and chopped

Dark leafy greens include many different types, but spinach, kale, and Swiss chard are probably the ones you tend to cook most often. Consider making purees of these greens, as well as others such as collard greens, mustard greens, beet greens, purslane, and escarole, all of which are are readily available throughout the summer. Each is an excellent source of nutrients such as iron, folate, vitamin C, vitamin K, and vitamin A. Prepare greens with tough stems (like Swiss chard and kale) by cutting away the stems and using only the leaves in your puree.

HERBS AND SPICES *Rosemary is a wonderful herb to pair with these purees, but the spice options are even more extensive. I recommend ground cumin or nutmeg, or even grated orange zest. Onion and garlic powders make for deliciously savory additions, too.*

1. In a medium saucepan with a steamer insert, bring about 1 inch of water to a simmer. Add the greens. Cover and steam until tender, 5 to 10 minutes.
2. Transfer the steamed greens to a blender or food processor, along with a pinch of an herb or spice, if using. Puree until smooth. Adjust the texture by adding a little breast milk, formula, or water to achieve the desired consistency.

STORAGE: Fill a freezer cube tray with 1-ounce portions. Freeze overnight. Store the frozen cubes in a tightly sealed zip-top bag for up to 6 months.

TIP: If you don't want them to go to waste, you can chop the stems and use them in your own meals, such as in stir-fries and soups.

Green Bean Puree

MAKES 15 (1-OUNCE)
FREEZER TRAY CUBES

1½ pounds green beans
(about 5 cups), strings
and stems removed, cut
into ½-inch pieces

You may think of green beans as a green vegetable, but they're actually a member of the legume family. There are over a hundred varieties of green beans, and not all of them are green! You can also find wax beans, which are white, as well as yellow, purple, or red beans. The best-known type of this veggie is the string bean, which is typically in season from mid-spring through late summer. They are a good source of fiber, protein, and vitamin C.

HERBS AND SPICES *Green beans are delicious with a number of herbs, including tarragon, rosemary, and chives.*

1. In a medium saucepan with a steamer insert, bring about 1 inch of water to a simmer. Add the beans. Cover and steam until tender, 5 to 10 minutes.
2. Transfer the beans to a blender or food processor, along with a pinch of an herb, if using. Puree until smooth. Adjust the texture by adding a little breast milk, formula, or water to achieve the desired consistency.

STORAGE: Fill a freezer cube tray with 1-ounce portions. Freeze overnight. Store the frozen cubes in a tightly sealed zip-top bag for up to 6 months.

TIP: Trimming the ends of beans can feel like a time-consuming task when you do them one at a time. Instead, line up the beans on a cutting board and trim away the tips on both ends in batches. Then chop them into ½-inch pieces in bunches.

Summer Squash Puree

DF GF NF Vegan

MAKES 15 (1-OUNCE) FREEZER TRAY CUBES

1½ pounds summer squash (about 3 small, 1½ medium, or 1 large summer squash), peeled and cut into ¼-inch dice

As the name indicates, summer squash is abundant during the summer months, typically starting in late June. Included in this category are zucchini, yellow squash, Italian squash, pattypan squash, chayote, crookneck squash, and straightneck squash. Summer squash typically has white flesh under a colorful, edible rind. The flavor tends to be mild, so it pairs well with many other foods.

HERBS AND SPICES *Season summer squash with garlic and savory herbs like tarragon and rosemary.*

1. In a medium saucepan with a steamer insert, bring about 1 inch of water to a simmer. Add the squash. Cover and steam until tender, about 10 minutes.
2. Transfer the steamed squash to a blender or food processor, along with a pinch of an herb, if using. Puree until smooth. Adjust the texture by adding a little breast milk, formula, or water to achieve the desired consistency.

STORAGE: Fill a freezer cube tray with 1-ounce portions. Freeze overnight. Store the frozen cubes in a tightly sealed zip-top bag for up to 6 months.

TIP: You don't need to peel away much of the summer squash. Just use a vegetable peeler with light pressure to remove the fibrous outer rind.

Winter Squash Puree

DF GF NF Vegan

MAKES 15 (1-OUNCE) FREEZER TRAY CUBES

1½ pounds winter squash (about 1 small squash), rind, seeds, and pulp removed, and cut into ¼-inch dice

Winter squash starts to show up in markets in the late summer and remains available through late fall and into the winter months. It tends to have a tough outer rind, large seeds in the center, and sweet, earthy orange flesh. Types of winter squash include acorn, butternut, and spaghetti squash. It's high in vitamin C and vitamin A, which support healthy immunity.

HERBS AND SPICES Many adults like winter squash with lots of sweetness added, such as brown sugar and cinnamon, but it's equally tasty in savory applications. For babies, avoid sugar as a sweetener, and consider instead vanilla extract, grated citrus zest, spices like ground nutmeg, ginger, cinnamon, and cloves, or herbs such as tarragon, rosemary, and thyme.

1. In a medium saucepan with a steamer insert, bring about 1 inch of water to a simmer. Add the squash. Cover and steam until tender, about 10 minutes.
2. Transfer the steamed squash to a blender or food processor, along with a pinch of an herb or spice, if using. Puree until smooth. Adjust the texture by adding a little breast milk, formula, or water to achieve the desired consistency.

STORAGE: Fill a freezer cube tray with 1-ounce portions. Freeze overnight. Store the frozen cubes in a tightly sealed zip-top bag for up to 6 months.

TIP: There's no rule that says you can add only one herb or spice to a puree. If your baby has shown a tolerance for both vanilla and nutmeg after a few separate offerings of each, consider adding both to the squash puree. A pinch of nutmeg and ⅛ teaspoon of vanilla extract will nicely flavor the vegetable.

Broccoli or Cauliflower Puree

MAKES 15 (1-OUNCE) FREEZER TRAY CUBES

1½ pounds cauliflower or broccoli (about 1 head), cut into small pieces

Broccoli is one of those vegetables that, whether or not we love it, we know we should eat it. Together with cauliflower, these cruciferous vegetables have a "good for you" reputation that comes from their incredibly high amounts of vitamins C and K, not to mention the significant fiber and folate content. When it comes to preparing them, you don't need to use just the florets here; you can chop the stems into small pieces and steam them as well. That way, none of the vegetable will go to waste. As an infant, Julian loved a cauliflower puree with cumin. Now as a toddler, he enjoys the same veg + spice combo, but with the cauliflower roasted and not pureed.

HERBS AND SPICES *Ground nutmeg works well with both broccoli and cauliflower. Cauliflower is also tasty with cumin, tarragon, thyme, or garlic powder, while broccoli is delicious with rosemary.*

1. In a medium saucepan with a steamer insert, bring about 1 inch of water to a simmer. Add the cauliflower or broccoli. Cover and steam until tender, about 10 minutes.
2. Transfer the cauliflower or broccoli to a blender or food processor, along with a pinch of an herb or spice, if using. Puree until smooth. Adjust the texture by adding a little breast milk, formula, or water to achieve the desired consistency.

STORAGE: Fill a freezer cube tray with 1-ounce portions. Freeze overnight. Store the frozen cubes in a tightly sealed zip-top bag for up to 6 months.

TIP: Some babies get a little gassy from broccoli. If this is your experience, try introducing it again after a month. As your baby's intestines mature, she will be better able to handle these vegetables.

Pumpkin Puree

DF GF NF Vegan

MAKES 15 (1-OUNCE) FREEZER TRAY CUBES

1½ pounds pumpkin, rind, seeds, and pulp removed, and cut into ¼-inch dice to yield about 3 cups

Available in the fall through early winter, pumpkin has a slightly sweet and earthy flavor. You'll need to remove the rind, pulp, and seeds and cook just the fleshy part under the rind. When pumpkin is not in season, buy frozen chunks of organic pumpkin, which takes all the work out of the prep while retaining all the nutrients and flavor. Packed with vitamin A, pumpkin can help support your baby's developing eyesight. It's also a good source of fiber for intestinal health and vitamin C to boost immunity.

HERBS AND SPICES *Try pumpkin with sage or spices like ground ginger or cinnamon. You can also mix it with the go-to pumpkin spice flavoring, a combination of ground ginger, cinnamon, nutmeg, allspice, and cloves.*

1. In a medium saucepan with a steamer insert, bring about 1 inch of water to a simmer. Add the pumpkin. Cover and steam until tender, about 10 minutes.
2. Transfer the pumpkin to a blender or food processor, along with a pinch of an herb or spice, if using. Puree until smooth. Adjust the texture by adding a little breast milk, formula, or water to achieve the desired consistency.

STORAGE: Fill a freezer cube tray with 1-ounce portions. Freeze overnight. Store the frozen cubes in a tightly sealed zip-top bag for up to 6 months.

TIP: You can bake the pumpkin in the oven to make removing the rind a snap. Quarter the pumpkin with a sharp knife, then scoop out the seeds and pulp. Put the pumpkin quarters, cut-side up, on a baking sheet lined with parchment. Bake in a preheated 375°F oven for 15 minutes. Cool and peel.

Pea Puree

MAKES 15 (1-OUNCE) FREEZER TRAY CUBES

1½ pounds fresh or frozen peas (not canned)

Like green beans, peas are legumes. They're at the height of flavor and tenderness in the spring and have a slightly sweet, herbaceous flavor with a hint of earthiness. As with all legumes, they're a great source of protein. It's difficult to puree peas to complete smoothness; their texture remains a bit grainy. If your baby doesn't take well to peas alone, try reintroducing them a little later with another vegetable, such as carrots. While peas go well with many herbs and spices, my son's favorite is peas with mint.

HERBS AND SPICES *Seasonings that go well with peas include grated citrus zest, mint, basil, and ground cumin and coriander.*

1. In a medium saucepan with a steamer insert, bring about 1 inch of water to a simmer. Add the peas. Cover and steam until tender, about 5 minutes

2. Transfer the peas to a blender or food processor, along with a pinch of an herb or spice, if using. Puree until as smooth as possible. Adjust the texture by adding a little breast milk, formula, or water to achieve the desired consistency.

STORAGE: Fill a freezer cube tray with 1-ounce portions. Freeze overnight. Store the frozen cubes in a tightly sealed zip-top bag for up to 6 months.

Asparagus Puree

MAKES 15 (1-OUNCE) FREEZER TRAY CUBES

1½ pounds asparagus, stalks trimmed and cut into ½-inch pieces

In the spring, you can find tender, thin stalks of asparagus that work perfectly for baby food purees. This vegetable contains essential nutrients for bone development, including calcium and magnesium, as well as nutritious vitamins like folate, vitamin C, and vitamin A to support your baby's overall health.

HERBS AND SPICES *Asparagus is delicious with mint, tarragon, lemon, grated lemon zest, or garlic.*

1. In a medium saucepan with a steamer insert, bring about 1 inch of water to a simmer. Add the asparagus. Cover and steam until tender, 5 to 10 minutes.
2. Transfer the asparagus to a blender or food processor, along with a pinch of an herb, if using. Puree until smooth. Adjust the texture by adding a little breast milk, formula, or water to achieve the desired consistency.

STORAGE: Fill a freezer cube tray with 1-ounce portions. Freeze overnight. Store the frozen cubes in a tightly sealed zip-top bag for up to 6 months.

TIP: To trim the asparagus, hold the end of each piece and bend gently until the tough, woody end of the stalk breaks off.

Berry Puree

MAKES 15 (1-OUNCE) FREEZER TRAY CUBES

1½ pounds berries (about 2 cups), hulled if necessary (see tip) and cut into pieces if fruit is larger than ¾ inch

There's no denying that all berries have sweet, juicy flavors that babies just love. While it's likely blueberries, strawberries, and raspberries will be the berries you offer most often, don't discount blackberries, tayberries (which taste like a combination of raspberry and blackberry), and marionberries (a type of blackberry) to really give your baby a variety of flavors. Berries are in season from June through late summer, depending on the variety, and taste the very best during these months. Fortunately, organic frozen berries are widely available, making it possible for your baby and you to enjoy them year-round. Berries are an excellent source of antioxidants and nutrients.

I recommend steaming blueberries, because without that step their skins will not become completely smooth when blending. If you wait to offer blueberries until you're not concerned about offering a completely smooth puree, there's no need to steam them; just blend them fresh or after thawing, if frozen.

HERBS AND SPICES *Try savory herbs like thyme or rosemary, or spices such as ground cinnamon, ginger, or allspice. Blackberries and thyme or blueberries and rosemary are interesting combinations that your baby may love, even if you wouldn't normally think to combine them.*

1. If using blueberries, in a medium saucepan with a steamer insert, bring about 1 inch of water to a simmer. (If using any other type of berry, skip to step 2.) Add the blueberries. Cover and steam for 5 minutes.
2. Transfer the berries to a blender or food processor, along with a pinch of an herb or spice, if using. Puree until smooth. Adjust the texture by adding a little breast milk, formula, or water to achieve the desired consistency.

STORAGE: Fill a freezer cube tray with 1-ounce portions. Freeze overnight. Store the frozen cubes in a tightly sealed zip-top bag for up to 6 months.

TIP: Unlike other berries, strawberries need hulling. The quickest way to hull a strawberry is to grasp just under the stem and use your thumbnail to scoop out the hull as you remove the stem.

Stone Fruit Puree

MAKES 15 (1-OUNCE) FREEZER TRAY CUBES

1½ pounds stone fruits (about 5 peaches, nectarines, plums, or apricots, or 3 cups of cherries)

TIP: You can also remove the pit and peel before steaming, which makes it easier to process the fruit after it is steamed. Use a sharp knife to cut away the tough outer peel, and then halve the fruit to remove the pit. Cut into small cubes and steam in a steamer insert for about 5 minutes.

Stone fruits are juicy, sweet fruits available at the height of summer. Included in this family are peaches, nectarines, plums, cherries, apricots, and other fruit with pits. They are fantastic by themselves and are wonderful vehicles for delivering vitamins C and K, beta carotene, and potassium to your baby. While ripe fruit may seem soft enough to simply mash before offering, I recommend removing their skins (with the exception of cherries—can you imagine?) for initial feedings. The cooking method used in this recipe allows you to remove the tough peels to make the puree as smooth as possible.

HERBS AND SPICES *Stone fruits are surprisingly good with a hint of savory flavors, such as basil, mint, thyme, rosemary, and even onion powder. For a sweeter note, consider ground cloves or nutmeg. Some specific combinations to try include peaches and nutmeg, apricots and basil, cherries and thyme, and plums and rosemary.*

1. In a medium saucepan, bring about 1 inch of water to a simmer. Carve an X into the side of each piece of stone fruit with a sharp paring knife, which makes it easier to peel them after steaming. Place the fruits in the water, X-side down.
2. Cover and steam the fruit until tender, about 5 minutes for smaller fruits like cherries or up to 10 minutes for large fruits like peaches or nectarines. Remove the fruit from the boiling water and allow it to cool until you can handle it.
3. Starting at the X, remove the peel of the fruit. Pull the flesh away from the pits and discard the pits.
4. Transfer the steamed fruit to a blender or food processor, along with a pinch of an herb or spice, if using. Puree until smooth. Adjust the texture by adding a little breast milk, formula, or water to achieve the desired consistency.

STORAGE: Fill a freezer cube tray with 1-ounce portions. Freeze overnight. Store the frozen cubes in a tightly sealed zip-top bag for up to 6 months.

Dried Fruit Puree

MAKES 15 (1-OUNCE) FREEZER TRAY CUBES

12 ounces dried fruit (about 2 cups)

When fresh fruits aren't in season, you can still make a flavorful fruit puree by using reconstituted dried fruits. Dried fruits to try include prunes (dried plums), figs, dates, cranberries, cherries, apricots, and raisins. You'll need to soak the fruits in hot water before pureeing them to achieve the desired consistency.

HERBS AND SPICES *The herb or spice you choose depends on the fruit. Rosemary is excellent with figs. Prunes are tasty with a pinch of thyme. Apricots pair well with ground ginger. Cranberries go quite naturally with ground cinnamon. Dates with ground nutmeg make a flavorful combination.*

1. Put the dried fruit in a large bowl and pour in enough boiling water to cover. Cover the bowl and allow the fruit to soak until it is plump and soft, about 20 minutes. Drain.
2. Transfer the fruit to a blender or food processor, along with a pinch of an herb or spice, if using. Puree until smooth. Adjust the texture by adding a little breast milk, formula, or water to achieve the desired consistency.

STORAGE: Fill a freezer cube tray with 1-ounce portions. Freeze overnight. Store the frozen cubes in a tightly sealed zip-top bag for up to 6 months.

TIP: Prune puree is a tried-and-true folk remedy for constipation. If your baby is having problems with constipation, offer a prune puree or one mixed in with oatmeal or yogurt.

Mango or Papaya Puree

MAKES 15 (1-OUNCE) FREEZER TRAY CUBES

1 ½ pounds mango (about 2 mangos) or papaya (about 1 ½ papayas), peeled and pitted

A mango or papaya at the height of ripeness tastes more like a dessert than a fruit! These delightfully sweet tropical fruits can add variety to your baby's diet while providing a whole host of nutrients. Mangos are a good source of folate as well as vitamins A and C. Papayas are rich in enzymes that can help with your baby's digestion and also contain vitamin C, vitamin A, and magnesium. These juicy fruits are big on flavor that stands up well on its own, but they also pair well with other produce, herbs, and spices.

HERBS AND SPICES *Add a pinch of sweeter spices such as ground cinnamon, ginger, allspice, or nutmeg to bring out the best in tropical fruits. Warm, savory spices such as ground cumin or coriander work well, too.*

In a blender or food processor, combine the mango or papaya and a pinch of spice, if using. Puree until smooth. Adjust the texture by adding a little breast milk, formula, or water to achieve the desired consistency.

STORAGE: Fill a freezer cube tray with 1-ounce portions. Freeze overnight. Store the frozen cubes in a tightly sealed zip-top bag for up to 6 months.

Melon Puree

DF GF NF Vegan

MAKES 15 (1-OUNCE) FREEZER TRAY CUBES

1½ pounds melon (about 1 small melon), rind, seeds, and pulp removed, and cut into chunks

Melon is sweet and juicy. Depending on the variety, melon begins to reach its peak ripeness in late spring and continues through late summer, when ripe, juicy watermelon is available. Varieties of melon include honeydew, cantaloupe, casaba, watermelon, Crenshaw, muskmelon, and many others. Most melons have a tough rind you'll need to remove, as well as seeds and pulp in the middle. If using watermelon, make sure to choose a seedless variety, or you'll need to pick out the seeds.

HERBS AND SPICES *Mint and rosemary pair very well with melon, as do ground cloves and ginger.*

In a blender or food processor, combine the melon and a pinch of an herb or spice, if using. Puree until smooth. Adjust the texture by adding a little breast milk, formula, or water to achieve the desired consistency.

STORAGE: Fill a freezer cube tray with 1-ounce portions. Freeze overnight. Store the frozen cubes in a tightly sealed zip-top bag for up to 6 months.

TIP: With its tough outer rind, it may be difficult to tell if a melon is ripe. Try this: Tap the melon and listen for a hollow sound. If it passes that test, sniff the melon near the stem. It should have a sweet, pleasant aroma. If so, you're good to go.

Cranberry Puree

MAKES 15 (1-OUNCE) FREEZER TRAY CUBES

1½ pounds fresh cranberries (about 6 cups)

1 cup water

Cranberries have a delightfully tart flavor with just a hint of sweetness. The berries are grown in bogs and harvested in the fall, so you can find them in the produce section of the grocery store or at farmers' markets and farm stands during this season. They are a low-sugar fruit and an excellent source of antioxidants and vitamin C, which can help build your baby's immune system.

HERBS AND SPICES *Cranberries pair with both savory herbs and sweet spices. Try rosemary or thyme, or ground cinnamon, ginger, allspice, cloves, or nutmeg.*

1. In a medium saucepan, bring the cranberries and water to a simmer over medium-high heat. Cook, stirring frequently, for about 5 minutes, until the cranberries pop (you'll actually hear them popping).
2. Transfer the cranberries to a blender or food processor, along with the cooking liquid, plus a pinch of an herb or spice, if using. Puree until smooth. Adjust the texture by adding a little breast milk, formula, or water to achieve the desired consistency.

STORAGE: Fill a freezer cube tray with 1-ounce portions. Freeze overnight. Store the frozen cubes in a tightly sealed zip-top bag for up to 6 months.

TIP: You can store fresh cranberries in their packaging in your refrigerator for about 3 weeks.

Beet Puree

MAKES 15 (1-OUNCE) FREEZER TRAY CUBES

1½ pounds beets (about 4 or 5), peeled and chopped into ½-inch cubes

Beets are a wonderful way to sweeten up baby food purees without adding any sugars or sweeteners, and they're packed with antioxidants. Beets come in more varieties than just the bright red color most of us associate with them. Feel free to try golden beets, white beets, or many of the other beet varieties available at your farmers' market. Not only are they just as delicious, you won't have to worry about the mess that red beets tend to make, which I learned the hard way. Julian always enjoyed golden beets, in particular, prepared with fennel.

HERBS AND SPICES *For herb pairings, try rosemary or tarragon, which complement the sweet flavor of the beets. Sweeter spices make nice complements, too; choose ground cinnamon, allspice, ginger, or nutmeg.*

1. In a medium saucepan with a steamer insert, bring about 1 inch of water to a simmer. Add the chopped beets. Cover and steam until tender, 5 to 10 minutes.
2. Transfer the steamed beets to a blender or food processor, along with a pinch of an herb of spice, if using. Puree until smooth. Adjust the texture by adding a little breast milk, formula, or water to achieve the desired consistency.

STORAGE: Fill a freezer cube tray with 1-ounce portions. Freeze overnight. Store the frozen cubes in a tightly sealed zip-top bag for up to 6 months.

Edamame Puree

**MAKES 15 (1-OUNCE)
FREEZER TRAY CUBES**

**1½ pounds
shelled edamame**

Edamame are young soybeans. These soft beans grow in fibrous pods and are available either shelled or in the pod. If yours are in the pod, you'll need to shell them and discard the pods. Edamame is a complete source of protein and also provides fiber and iron for your growing baby.

HERBS AND SPICES *Edamame have a fresh flavor that works well with basil, thyme, garlic powder, and onion powder.*

1. In a medium saucepan with a steamer insert, bring about 1 inch of water to a simmer. Add the edamame. Cover and steam for 5 minutes.
2. Transfer the edamame to a blender or food processor, along with a pinch of an herb, if using. Puree until smooth. Adjust the texture by adding a little breast milk, formula, or water to achieve the desired consistency.

STORAGE: Fill a freezer cube tray with 1-ounce portions. Freeze overnight. Store the frozen cubes in a tightly sealed zip-top bag for up to 6 months.

TIP: It may be difficult to find fresh edamame, but frozen edamame will work equally well. Thaw overnight in the refrigerator before steaming.

Bell Pepper Puree

DF GF NF Vegan

MAKES 15 (1-OUNCE) FREEZER TRAY CUBES

1½ pounds bell peppers (about 6 peppers), seeded and chopped

Bell peppers, also known as sweet peppers, come in a variety of colors including red, yellow, orange, green, brown, and purple. They have a slightly sweet, mildly peppery flavor that isn't too spicy. For single-ingredient purees, you'll probably want to stick to red, yellow, or orange bell peppers, which are sweeter than their green counterparts. Bell peppers deliver vitamin C, vitamin B$_6$, and vitamin A.

HERBS AND SPICES *Bell peppers pair well with warm spices, such as ground cumin or coriander.*

1. In a medium saucepan with a steamer insert, bring about 1 inch of water to a simmer. Add the peppers. Cover and steam until tender, about 10 minutes.
2. Transfer the steamed peppers to a blender or food processor, along with a pinch of spice, if using. Puree until smooth. Adjust the texture by adding a little breast milk, formula, or water to achieve the desired consistency.

STORAGE: Fill a freezer cube tray with 1-ounce portions. Freeze overnight. Store the frozen cubes in a tightly sealed zip-top bag for up to 6 months.

TIP: While bell peppers don't have the heat that hot peppers do, removing the seeds and ribs eliminates any bitter flavors and makes for a smoother puree.

Artichoke Heart Puree

MAKES 15 (1-OUNCE) FREEZER TRAY CUBES

3 large artichokes, stems and tops trimmed

If you've only eaten jarred artichoke hearts, forget everything you remember about their taste and give steamed artichokes a chance. Their flavor is rich, unique, and decidedly addictive. In this recipe you'll cook the fresh artichokes whole and then peel away the leaves and the choke, leaving only the heart. Even though you won't offer the leaves to your baby, save them for yourself. The tender base is edible and delicious. If you can't find fresh artichokes, which are available in spring, you can use frozen artichoke hearts. Fresh or frozen, artichokes contain fiber, iron, folate, and other essential nutrients. They are an excellent source of folate for your baby's brain development. They also contain fiber, iron, and other essential nutrients. You can cook fresh artichokes whole and then peel away the leaves and the choke, leaving only the heart.

HERBS AND SPICES *Artichokes are delicious with grated lemon zest, thyme, or parsley.*

1. Place the artichokes in a large pot of water, cover, and bring to a boil. Cook, covered, until the hearts are soft, about 1 hour.
2. Allow the artichokes to cool until you can handle them. Trim away any extra stem. Pull off the leaves. Use the edge of a large spoon to remove the choke from the heart and discard.
3. Transfer the artichoke hearts to a blender or food processor, along with a pinch of an herb, if using. Puree until smooth. Adjust the texture by adding a little breast milk, formula, or water to achieve the desired consistency.

STORAGE: Fill a freezer cube tray with 1-ounce portions. Freeze overnight. Store the frozen cubes in a tightly sealed zip-top bag for up to 6 months.

TIP: If using frozen artichoke hearts, use about 5 hearts and steam them in a pot with a steamer insert until tender, about 10 minutes.

Cereal

MAKES 15 (1-OUNCE) FREEZER TRAY CUBES

½ cup whole grain, such as barley, oats, or brown rice

2 cups breast milk, formula, or water (or a combination)

The way to introduce babies to grains is by making cereal—grinding grains and then cooking them with a hot liquid. You can choose from a variety of whole grains for your cereal. Brown rice and quinoa are nutritious, naturally gluten-free options. If gluten is something you want to avoid, make sure to look for oats (both rolled or steel cut) that are labeled as gluten free, which ensures that they were not packaged in factory with gluten-containing grains. If gluten is not a concern, barley and farro are other wonderful whole grains. Cereals are a good source of fiber and vitamin E, and when combined with legumes such as black beans or lentils, they make for powerhouse plant-based protein sources. Other good add-ins to boost protein include ground flaxseed, hemp seed, and wheat germ. All cereals mix well with fruit or vegetable purees.

1. In a food processor or blender, process the grain into a fine powder, about 1 minute.

2. In a saucepan, bring the liquid to a simmer. Stir in the ground grain. Cook, stirring constantly, until the cereal is soft, about 10 minutes.

STORAGE: Fill a freezer cube tray with 1-ounce portions. Freeze overnight. Store the frozen cubes in a tightly sealed zip-top bag for up to 6 months.

TIP: If you're not inclined to fill up your freezer with cereal purees, you can store the dry processed grains in your pantry in a tightly sealed container for up to 6 months. When ready to use, cook them with hot liquid at a ratio of 1 part cereal to 4 parts liquid.

Bean or Lentil Puree

DF GF NF Vegan

**MAKES 15 (1-OUNCE)
FREEZER TRAY CUBES**

**1 cup dried beans
or lentils**

Beans and lentils are versatile legumes that tend to have a neutral flavor, which makes them ideal for pairing with a large number of other ingredients and flavors. This recipe will work for all dried beans, such as black beans, kidney beans, white beans, navy beans, garbanzo beans (chickpeas), and lentils. Packed with protein and high in fiber, legumes are a great go-to baby food because they're so nutritious and easy to eat and enjoy.

HERBS AND SPICES *The sky is the limit. Try warm spices like ground cumin or coriander, or herbs like cilantro, chives, or even a bay leaf (just don't forget to remove the bay leaf before pureeing!). Lentils are especially delicious with woody herbs like rosemary or thyme.*

1. In a bowl, cover the beans or lentils with enough water to reach an inch above their surface. Cover the bowl and soak overnight. Drain and rinse.
2. Transfer the beans or lentils to a large pot and pour in enough fresh water to cover them. Add a bay leaf or a pinch of an herb or spice, if using. Bring to a boil. Cook, covered, until the legumes are soft, about 30 minutes for lentils, about 60 minutes for black beans, and 90 minutes or longer for larger beans. Drain, and remove the bay leaf, if using.
3. In a blender or food processor, puree the legumes until smooth. Adjust the texture by adding a little breast milk, formula, or water to achieve the desired consistency.

STORAGE: Fill a freezer cube tray with 1-ounce portions. Freeze overnight. Store the frozen cubes in a tightly sealed zip-top bag for up to 6 months.

TIP: To save time, you can use canned beans. Bring the beans (undrained) to a simmer in a saucepan. Cook for 5 minutes. Drain and puree with water, breast milk, or formula to achieve the desired consistency.

Tofu Puree

**MAKES 15 (1-OUNCE)
FREEZER TRAY CUBES**

**12 ounces silken
tofu, drained**

Tofu is super easy to make into a baby food puree. It provides an excellent source of plant-based protein and has an extremely neutral flavor, which means it takes on the flavor of whatever you add to it or combine with it. And do combine it! While toddlers often take a liking to uncooked cubes of tofu, the best way to introduce it to a baby is with another fruit or vegetable he already enjoys. Even if you've never tried or enjoyed tofu, don't necessarily discount it for your baby. Using tofu is a great way to make a hearty, nutritious combination puree.

HERBS AND SPICES *Use sweet spices, warm spices, woody herbs, pungent herbs, or minty herbs—pretty much any flavor—with tofu to create different tastes for your baby to explore.*

In a blender or food processor, puree the tofu along with ⅛ teaspoon of any dried herb or spice, if using, until smooth. Adjust the texture by adding a little breast milk, formula, or water to achieve the desired consistency.

STORAGE: It's so quick and easy to puree tofu that you may not wish to bother storing it in freezer tray cubes. But it does freeze well. To freeze, fill a freezer cube tray with 1-ounce portions. Freeze overnight. Store the frozen cubes in a tightly sealed zip-top bag for up to 6 months.

TIP: When you blend tofu with vegetables or fruits, I recommend not adding herbs or spices. Leave it neutral so the full flavor of the complementary food comes through.

Fish Puree

MAKES 15 (1-OUNCE) FREEZER TRAY CUBES

1½ pounds fish, bones and skin removed and cut into ½-inch pieces

Ever heard someone refer to fish as "brain food"? Fish are high in omega-3 fatty acids, which are wonderful for brain development. So don't shy away from offering certain types of fish to your baby. They also make for an excellent source of protein, and most have a mild flavor that works well with many fruits, vegetables, and grains. For first fish introductions, use a mild, white-fleshed fish such as halibut, cod, or snapper. Or you can try a fresh-water fish like trout, or a pink-fleshed fish like salmon. Avoid fish with a high mercury content, such as marlin, swordfish, tuna, or tilefish.

HERBS AND SPICES *Try grated lemon zest, garlic, tarragon, or fennel.*

1. In a medium saucepan with a steamer insert, bring about 1 inch of water to a simmer. Add the fish. Cover and steam until cooked through, 5 to 10 minutes.
2. Transfer the fish to a blender or food processor, along with a pinch of an herb, if using. Puree until smooth. Adjust the texture by adding a little breast milk, formula, or water to achieve the desired consistency.

STORAGE: Fill a freezer cube tray with 1-ounce portions. Freeze overnight. Store the frozen cubes in a tightly sealed zip-top bag for up to 6 months.

TIP: Though there's no such thing as organic fish, wild-caught fish might be the closest thing because it tends to have fewer contaminants than farmed fish. When you select fish, it should have a briny, but not fishy, odor.

Poultry Puree

MAKES 15 (1-OUNCE) FREEZER TRAY CUBES

1½ pounds boneless, skinless poultry breasts and thighs, cut into ¼-inch dice

Poultry is a good first animal protein for babies in omnivorous families. It has a mild flavor, and you can adjust the texture as much as you need to with liquid or other purees so that it's just right for your baby. It's also packed with healthy B vitamins (including vitamin B_{12} for energy), zinc, and iron, as well as plenty of protein to support growing bodies. Try turkey, chicken, duck, or any other poultry that's available.

HERBS AND SPICES *Poultry pairs well with sage, thyme, rosemary, and garlic powder.*

1. In a medium saucepan with a steamer insert, bring about 1 inch of water to a simmer. Add the poultry. Cover and steam until cooked through, 10 to 15 minutes.
2. Transfer the poultry to a blender or food processor, along with a pinch of an herb, if using. Puree until smooth. Adjust the texture by adding a little breast milk, formula, or water to achieve the desired consistency.

STORAGE: Fill a freezer cube tray with 1-ounce portions. Freeze overnight. Store the frozen cubes in a tightly sealed zip-top bag for up to 6 months.

TIP: The smaller you cut the pieces of poultry, the quicker it will steam (the same goes for hard vegetables). Making the dice small ensures that you will get the poultry well done within the time specified.

Meat Puree

DF GF NF

MAKES 15 (1-OUNCE) FREEZER TRAY CUBES

1½ pounds boneless cuts of meat, trimmed of fat and cut into ¼-inch dice

Pureed meat . . . doesn't exactly excite the palate, does it? As with the other excellent protein sources covered in the preceding pages (such as tofu, fish, and poultry) meat purees are best offered initially with another fruit or vegetable that your baby likes, or even an herb or spice that your baby has tried previously. Meat has a bold flavor that is most appealing, at least initially, along with other flavors. Sometimes, meat purees are a bit thick to start, so be sure to thin the puree to the consistency your baby needs. For the healthiest meals, choose meat from animals that have been grass-fed (pastured), rather than grain-fed. Pastured animal products tend to be higher in omega-3 fatty acids, which help fight inflammation and support healthy immune function.

HERBS AND SPICES *Consider trying garlic, rosemary, sage, or thyme, or ground cumin or coriander. Beef and rosemary make for an excellent combination. Pork and sage is a classic pairing. When you're ready to try offering lamb, ground cumin or coriander are my go-to recommendations.*

1. In a medium saucepan with a steamer insert, bring about 1 inch of water to a simmer. Add the meat. Cover and steam until cooked through, 10 to 15 minutes.
2. Transfer the meat to a blender or food processor, along with a pinch of an herb or spice, if using. Adjust the texture by adding a little breast milk, formula, or water to achieve the desired consistency.

STORAGE: Fill a freezer cube tray with 1-ounce portions. Freeze overnight. Store the frozen cubes in a tightly sealed zip-top bag for up to 6 months.

TIP: Choose lean cuts of meat whenever possible and trim the fat off the meat before steaming it. You can also brown ground meat in a sauté pan on the stove top (without oil) and puree it.

5

STAGE 2: SMOOTH COMBINATION PUREES

With a bunch of single-ingredient purees in your arsenal, it's time to have fun with combinations. No rule says you must offer single-ingredient purees for an extended period of time. If your baby has tried two different purees separately a few times and not reacted to either, you can mix them up. Some of Julian's favorite combinations included banana and avocado, sweet potato and spinach, and white beans and leeks. As you approach the 8-month mark, experiment with slightly less smooth purees. It's so rewarding to watch them advance as little eaters.

DEVELOPMENTALLY SPEAKING

At this age, your baby's primary source of nutrition is still breast milk or formula. Solid foods offered in small amounts one or two times a day make for a wonderful supplement. Don't worry too much if your baby isn't very interested in food, or if she eats it only with the nanny or in day care. Oftentimes, breastfed babies in particular are good solid food eaters for everyone but Mom.

If you are bottle feeding, your baby might be able to hold his own bottle by 7 or 8 months, and he's developing a pincer grasp that will help him grasp soft solid foods. Your baby will also be able to sit unaided during this stage, and he may show interest in feeding himself by grabbing for the spoon as you feed him (keep in mind that his interest exceeds his skill!). Most of the food your baby feeds himself will wind up mashed in his hand—or hair—rather than in his mouth, so offer more food than you think he'll need. At this juncture, a mess is okay, since we want to encourage our little ones to explore food and see what it's like to (attempt to) feed themselves.

PORTION GUIDELINES

Your baby's portions will increase as he grows. From the age of 6 to 8 months:

* Continue to offer breast milk or formula first. Your baby will likely consume 24 to 40 ounces throughout the course of a day.

* Offer two to three solid-food meals per day of 1 to 2 tablespoons of food, diluted as necessary to the desired consistency with breast milk, formula, or water.

FAQ

Q: When should I introduce a sippy cup to my baby? Can I offer breast milk or formula in it?

A: When you start your baby on solids (typically, around 6 months of age), that's a good time to introduce the sippy. Before 12 months of age, I recommend it just for water. Keep breast milk and formula feedings limited to the breast or bottle. And don't be tempted to offer juice in the sippy. The purpose at the start is not to find out what your baby might like drinking best, but rather for her to learn to grasp the cup and pull it up to her mouth. In reality, she's likely to swallow only a minimal amount. But even still, always offer water after a feeding, not before, to ensure she doesn't start to fill up on liquid before solids.

The first few (or possibly several) times, you'll probably need to help her tip the cup to the right angle. I started with soft, silicone spouts that fit right on the Philips Avent bottles I used with Julian, and then transitioned to a straw-based sippy cup a few months later.

Avocado and Banana Puree

MAKES 2 (2-OUNCE) SERVINGS

3 (1-ounce) freezer tray cubes avocado puree (page 42), thawed

1 (1-ounce) freezer tray cube banana puree (page 44), thawed

Pinch ground cloves, nutmeg, ginger, or cinnamon

This is one of Julian's absolute favorite purees, and there's no wonder why—the blend of creamy, rich avocado with sweet banana is pretty much irresistible. We continue to serve it to him as he grows, building on it to make smoothies. On the nutritional side, this powerhouse combo delivers healthy fat, potassium, and vitamin C.

1. Combine the thawed purees in a small bowl. Add one of the recommended spices. Mix well with a spoon. If needed, thin the puree with breast milk, formula, or water to achieve the desired consistency.
2. Store any unoffered puree in the refrigerator for up to 2 days. Do not refreeze.

Sweet Potato and Spinach Puree

MAKES 2 (2-OUNCE) SERVINGS

3 (1-ounce) freezer tray cubes sweet potato puree (page 43), thawed

1 (1-ounce) freezer tray cube spinach puree (page 47), thawed

Pinch ground cloves

Sweet potatoes (or yams) and spinach are both superfoods, so combining them in this puree provides a nutrition-packed meal for your baby. The combination is rich in iron, calcium, vitamins, and antioxidants.

1. Combine the thawed purees in a small bowl. Add the cloves. Mix well with a spoon. If needed, thin the puree with breast milk, formula, or water to achieve the desired consistency.
2. Spoon the portion you plan to serve to your baby into a small pot. Return the rest of the puree to the refrigerator, where it can be stored for up to 3 days. Do not refreeze.
3. Gently warm the puree on the stove top over low heat before serving. Discard any uneaten puree.

Pumpkin and Apple Puree

MAKES 2 (2-OUNCE) SERVINGS

2 (1-ounce) freezer tray cubes pumpkin puree (page 53), thawed

2 (1-ounce) freezer tray cubes apple puree (page 45), thawed

Pinch ground cloves

Pumpkins and apples are in season in the fall, making this an ideal puree for that time of year. If you don't have pumpkin puree ready to go in your freezer and aren't inclined to make it from scratch, you can use canned organic pumpkin. Just check the ingredients list to make sure there aren't any additives.

1. Combine the thawed purees in a small bowl. Add the cloves. Mix well with a spoon. If needed, thin the puree with breast milk, formula, or water to achieve the desired consistency.

2. Spoon the portion you plan to serve to your baby into a small pot. Return the rest of the puree to the refrigerator, where it can be stored for up to 3 days. Do not refreeze.

3. Gently warm the puree on the stove top over low heat before serving. Discard any uneaten puree.

Asparagus and Tofu Puree

MAKES 2 (2-OUNCE) SERVINGS

2 (1-ounce) freezer tray cubes asparagus puree (page 55), thawed

2 (1-ounce) freezer tray cubes tofu puree (page 70), thawed

Pinch ground coriander or cumin

This puree is a great source of protein to support growth. The full flavor of the asparagus will come out here, as the tofu is so mild. Make your puree using asparagus when it's in season in March and April, or buy it frozen for peak flavor out of season.

1. Combine the thawed purees in a small bowl. Add the coriander or cumin. Mix well with a spoon. If needed, thin the puree with breast milk, formula, or water to achieve the desired consistency.

2. Spoon the portion you plan to serve to your baby into a small pot. Return the rest of the puree to the refrigerator, where it can be stored for up to 3 days. Do not refreeze.

3. Gently warm the puree on the stove top over low heat before serving. Discard any uneaten puree.

Green Bean and Sweet Potato Puree

MAKES 2 (2-OUNCE) SERVINGS

2 (1-ounce) freezer tray cubes green bean puree (page 48), thawed

2 (1-ounce) freezer tray cubes sweet potato puree (page 43), thawed

You don't have to wait until November to introduce your baby to these classic flavors of Thanksgiving. At any time of year, this palate pleaser is likely to become a favorite.

1. Combine the thawed purees in a small bowl. Mix well with a spoon. If needed, thin the puree with breast milk, formula, or water to achieve the desired consistency.
2. Spoon the portion you plan to serve to your baby into a small pot. Return the rest of the puree to the refrigerator, where it can be stored for up to 3 days. Do not refreeze.
3. Gently warm the puree on the stove top over low heat before serving. Discard any uneaten puree.

TIP: Try stirring in a pinch each of grated orange zest and ground nutmeg to make the flavors in the vegetables pop.

Black Bean and Mango Puree

MAKES 2 (2-OUNCE) SERVINGS

3 (1-ounce) freezer tray cubes black bean puree (page 69), thawed

1 (1-ounce) freezer tray cube mango puree (page 60), thawed

Pinch ground cumin

Protein never tasted so good. The juicy mango cuts the starchiness of the black beans, giving this combination puree a satisfying sweetness and silky texture.

1. Combine the thawed purees in a small bowl. Add the cumin. Mix well with a spoon. If needed, thin the puree with breast milk, formula, or water to achieve the desired consistency.
2. Spoon the portion you plan to serve to your baby into a small pot. Return the rest of the puree to the refrigerator, where it can be stored for up to 3 days. Do not refreeze.
3. Gently warm the puree on the stove top over low heat before serving. Discard any uneaten puree.

Broccoli and Pear Puree

MAKES 2 (2-OUNCE) SERVINGS

2 (1-ounce) freezer tray cubes broccoli puree (page 52), thawed

2 (1-ounce) freezer tray cubes pear puree (page 45), thawed

Mellow yet sweet pear tones down the flavor of broccoli in this combination to make it one your baby will continue to open his mouth for. Both ingredients are fiber rich, so this is a good option if your baby is experiencing constipation.

1. Combine the thawed purees in a small bowl. Mix well with a spoon. If needed, thin the puree with breast milk, formula, or water to achieve the desired consistency.

2. Spoon the portion you plan to serve to your baby into a small pot. Return the rest of the puree to the refrigerator, where it can be stored for up to 3 days. Do not refreeze.

3. Gently warm the puree on the stove top over low heat before serving. Discard any uneaten puree.

Blueberry and Yogurt Puree

MAKES 2 (2-OUNCE) SERVINGS

1 (1-ounce) freezer tray cube blueberry puree (page 56), thawed

3 ounces plain full-fat yogurt

Your baby will love this creamy, slightly tangy puree. With their high level of antioxidants, blueberries bring more than just sweetness to this puree. The yogurt is an excellent source of probiotics to support your baby's digestive health as well as calcium for healthy bone development.

1. Combine the thawed puree and the yogurt in a small bowl. Mix well with a spoon. If needed, thin the puree with breast milk, formula, or water to achieve the desired consistency.

2. Store any unoffered puree in the refrigerator for up to 3 days. Do not refreeze.

Butternut Squash and Swiss Chard Puree

MAKES 2 (2-OUNCE) SERVINGS

3 (1-ounce) freezer tray cubes butternut squash puree (page 51), thawed

1 (1-ounce) freezer tray cube Swiss chard puree (page 47), thawed

Pinch ground nutmeg

By the time butternut squash is in season in late summer, chard is abundant. This puree is relatively mild with a slight sweetness, so it's a highly palatable early combination. As your baby grows, feel free to sauté the chard in a little olive oil and roast the squash before pureeing to enrich the flavors of each vegetable.

1. Combine the thawed purees in a small bowl. Add the nutmeg. Mix well with a spoon. If needed, thin the puree with breast milk, formula, or water to achieve the desired consistency.

2. Spoon the portion you plan to serve to your baby into a small pot. Return the rest of the puree to the refrigerator, where it can be stored for up to 3 days. Do not refreeze.

3. Gently warm the puree on the stove top over low heat before serving. Discard any uneaten puree.

TIP: Try combining purees of other starchy orange veggies and greens in the same proportions, such as sweet potato and kale, acorn squash and spinach, or pumpkin and collard greens.

Pea and Carrot Puree

MAKES 2 (2-OUNCE) SERVINGS

2 (1-ounce) freezer tray cubes pea puree (page 54), thawed

2 (1-ounce) freezer tray cubes carrot puree (page 46), thawed

There's a reason this veggie combo is an American classic: It's high in protein and fiber for healthy muscle growth and digestion, and it contains vitamins A, B, and C.

1. Combine the thawed purees in a small bowl. Mix well with a spoon. If needed, thin the puree with breast milk, formula, or water to achieve the desired consistency.
2. Spoon the portion you plan to serve to your baby into a small pot. Return the rest of the puree to the refrigerator, where it can be stored for up to 3 days. Do not refreeze.
3. Gently warm the puree on the stove top over low heat before serving. Discard any uneaten puree.

TIP: For minty pea and carrot puree, add ⅛ teaspoon minced fresh mint.

Edamame and Apricot Puree

MAKES 2 (2-OUNCE) SERVINGS

3 (1-ounce) freezer tray cubes edamame puree (page 64), thawed

1 (1-ounce) freezer tray cube apricot puree (page 58), thawed

Pinch ground allspice

Edamame are an excellent source of protein and fiber, while the apricot delivers antioxidants—particularly vitamin A—and a nice sweet flavor to this combo.

1. Combine the thawed purees in a small bowl. Add the allspice. Mix well with a spoon. If needed, thin the puree with breast milk, formula, or water to achieve the desired consistency.
2. Store any unoffered puree in the refrigerator for up to 3 days. Do not refreeze.

TIP: If you don't have edamame puree on hand, you can replace it with 3 freezer tray cubes of tofu puree.

Zucchini and Brown Rice Cereal Puree

MAKES 2 (2-OUNCE) SERVINGS

2 (1-ounce) freezer tray cubes zucchini puree (page 83), thawed

2 (1-ounce) freezer tray cubes brown rice cereal (page 68), thawed

⅛ teaspoon dried oregano

Zucchini and brown rice are both very mild, so if you really want to ease your baby's palate into combinations, this puree (minus the oregano) might be the one you feel most comfortable starting with. The oregano does give it a little kick to introduce your baby to a classic Mediterranean flavor.

1. Combine the thawed purees in a small bowl. Add the oregano. Mix well with a spoon. If needed, thin the puree with breast milk, formula, or water to achieve the desired consistency.

2. Spoon the portion you plan to serve to your baby into a small pot. Return the rest of the puree to the refrigerator, where it can be stored for up to 3 days. Do not refreeze.

3. Gently warm the puree on the stove top over low heat before serving. Discard any uneaten puree.

Broccoli and Pinto Bean Puree

MAKES 1 (5-OUNCE) SERVING

3 (1-ounce) freezer tray cubes broccoli puree (page 52), thawed

2 (1-ounce) freezer tray cubes pinto bean puree (page 69), thawed

Pinch garlic powder

Broccoli on its own can be surprisingly light, so pairing it with pinto beans makes a more satisfying, protein-rich meal for your little one.

1. Combine the thawed purees in a small bowl. Add the garlic powder. Mix well with a spoon. If needed, thin the puree with breast milk, formula, or water to achieve the desired consistency.

2. Spoon the portion you plan to serve to your baby into a small pot. Return the rest of the puree to the refrigerator, where it can be stored for up to 3 days. Do not refreeze.

3. Gently warm the puree on the stove top over low heat before serving. Discard any uneaten puree.

Chickpea and Mango Puree

DF GF NF Vegan

MAKES 2 (2-OUNCE) SERVINGS

3 (1-ounce) freezer tray cubes chickpea puree (page 69), thawed

1 (1-ounce) freezer tray cube mango puree (page 60), thawed

Pinch ground ginger

Chickpeas and mango come together here in a tasty marriage of sweet and earthy. Chickpeas are a fiber-rich food, so this is a great puree for your baby if other solid foods have led to some irregularity or constipation.

1. Combine the thawed purees in a small bowl. Add the ginger. Mix well with a spoon. If needed, thin the puree with breast milk, formula, or water to achieve the desired consistency.

2. Store any unoffered puree in the refrigerator for up to 3 days. Do not refreeze.

Kale and Banana Puree

DF GF NF Vegan

MAKES 2 (2-OUNCE) SERVINGS

2 (1-ounce) freezer tray cubes kale puree (page 47), thawed

2 (1-ounce) freezer tray cubes banana puree (page 44), thawed

Pinch ground nutmeg

This kale and banana puree is a nutritional powerhouse, packed with antioxidants that contribute to a baby's growth, good health, and immunity. Loaded with vitamin A, this puree also supports your baby's eyesight.

1. Combine the thawed purees in a small bowl. Add the nutmeg. Mix well with a spoon. If needed, thin the puree with breast milk, formula, or water to achieve the desired consistency.

2. Store any unoffered puree in the refrigerator for up to 2 days. Do not refreeze.

TIP: If you don't have kale puree available, substitute any dark leafy green, such as Swiss chard puree, spinach puree, or collard greens puree.

Oat and Pear Puree

DF GF option NF Vegan

MAKES 2 (2-OUNCE) SERVINGS

3 (1-ounce) freezer tray cubes oat cereal (page 68), thawed

1 (1-ounce) freezer tray cube pear puree (page 45), thawed

Pears add a wonderfully mild sweetness to the blank slate of oat cereal. To boot, pears are a great source of fiber to keep your baby regular.

1. Combine the thawed purees in a small bowl. Mix well with a spoon. If needed, thin the puree with breast milk, formula, or water to achieve the desired consistency.
2. Store any unoffered puree in the refrigerator for up to 3 days. Do not refreeze.

TIP: Ginger combines well with pears. Try adding a pinch of ground ginger or ⅛ teaspoon grated fresh ginger to the puree before you mix it.

Cauliflower and Broccoli Puree

DF GF NF Vegan

MAKES 3 (1-OUNCE) SERVINGS

2 (1-ounce) freezer tray cubes cauliflower puree (page 52), thawed

1 (1-ounce) freezer tray cube broccoli puree (page 52), thawed

This puree will help you fill your baby's tummy with healthy, high-fiber veggies, which are a rich source of nutrients for growing bodies.

1. Combine the thawed purees in a small bowl. Mix well with a spoon. If needed, thin the puree with breast milk, formula, or water to achieve the desired consistency.
2. Spoon the portion you plan to serve to your baby into a small pot. Return the rest of the puree to the refrigerator, where it can be stored for up to 3 days. Do not refreeze.
3. Gently warm the puree on the stove top over low heat before serving. Discard any uneaten puree.

TIP: Cumin goes well with broccoli and cauliflower. Add just a pinch right before mixing.

Sweet Potato and Cherry Puree

MAKES 2 (2-OUNCE) SERVINGS

3 (1-ounce) freezer tray cubes sweet potato puree (page 43), thawed

1 (1-ounce) freezer tray cube cherry puree (page 58), thawed

Pinch ground cinnamon

The slightly sweet taste and starchy texture of the sweet potatoes blends well with the juiciness of the cherries for a flavorful puree.

1. Combine the thawed purees in a small bowl. Add the cinnamon. Mix well with a spoon. If needed, thin the puree with breast milk, formula, or water to achieve the desired consistency.
2. Store any unoffered puree in the refrigerator for up to 3 days. Do not refreeze.

TIP: Sweet potatoes blend well with other stone fruits as well.

Oat and Banana Puree

MAKES 2 (2-OUNCE) SERVINGS

3 (1-ounce) freezer tray cubes oat cereal (page 68), thawed

1 (1-ounce) freezer tray cube banana puree (page 44), thawed

Pinch ground allspice

Sweeten your baby's oat cereal naturally with banana. This simple puree makes a nutritious breakfast or tasty snack and has a sweet, slightly nutty flavor.

1. Combine the thawed purees in a small bowl. Add the allspice. Mix well with a spoon. If needed, thin the puree with breast milk, formula, or water to achieve the desired consistency.
2. Store any unoffered puree in the refrigerator for up to 2 days. Do not refreeze.

TIP: You can also make this puree with fresh banana: Puree a quarter of a peeled banana in the food processor or blender and mix well with the oat cereal.

Broccoli and Potato Puree

MAKES 2 (2-OUNCE)
SERVINGS

2 (1-ounce) freezer tray
cubes broccoli puree
(page 52), thawed

2 (1-ounce) freezer tray
cubes potato puree
(page 43), thawed

⅛ teaspoon dried
tarragon or thyme, or
¼ teaspoon minced
fresh tarragon or thyme

Think of this puree as a baby's version of a baked potato with broccoli. Here you start your little one off with a standard flavor pairing that you'll build on as she grows and eventually enjoys loaded baked potatoes with the entire family.

1. Combine the thawed purees in a small bowl. Add the tarragon. Mix well with a spoon. If needed, thin the puree with breast milk, formula, or water to achieve the desired consistency.

2. Spoon the portion you plan to serve to your baby into a small pot. Return the rest of the puree to the refrigerator, where it can be stored for up to 3 days. Do not refreeze.

3. Gently warm the puree on the stove top over low heat before serving. Discard any uneaten puree.

Fish and Peach Puree

MAKES 2 (2-OUNCE)
SERVINGS

3 (1-ounce) freezer
tray cubes fish puree
(page 71), thawed

1 (1-ounce) freezer
tray cube peach puree
(page 58), thawed

Pinch garlic powder

If you like grilled fish with a fruit-based salsa, you can imagine why this mellow yet sweet puree would appeal to a little one.

1. Combine the thawed purees in a small bowl. Add the garlic powder. Mix well with a spoon. If needed, thin the puree with breast milk, formula, or water to achieve the desired consistency.

2. Spoon the portion you plan to serve to your baby into a small pot. Return the rest of the puree to the refrigerator, where it can be stored for up to 3 days. Do not refreeze.

3. Gently warm the puree on the stove top over low heat before serving. Discard any uneaten puree.

Pea and Butternut Squash Puree

MAKES 2 (2-OUNCE) SERVINGS

2 (1-ounce) freezer tray cubes pea puree (page 54), thawed

2 (1-ounce) freezer tray cubes butternut squash puree (page 51), thawed

Pinch ground turmeric

Peas and butternut squash is a popular ingredient pairing, and adult meals typically feature it in everything from pasta to soup to curries. Here the pairing is complemented by turmeric, a spice becoming ever more common due to its potent anti-inflammatory power.

1. Combine the thawed purees in a small bowl. Add the turmeric. Mix well with a spoon. If needed, thin the puree with breast milk, formula, or water to achieve the desired consistency.

2. Spoon the portion you plan to serve to your baby into a small pot. Return the rest of the puree to the refrigerator, where it can be stored for up to 3 days. Do not refreeze.

3. Gently warm the puree on the stove top over low heat before serving. Discard any uneaten puree.

TIP: Any of the winter squash purees, like acorn squash or spaghetti squash, can be used in place of the butternut squash in this recipe.

Chickpea and Artichoke Puree

DF GF NF Vegan

MAKES 2 (2-OUNCE) SERVINGS

2 (1-ounce) freezer tray cubes chickpea puree (page 69), thawed

2 (1-ounce) freezer tray cubes artichoke puree (page 67), thawed

⅛ teaspoon dried oregano

Mild yet hearty is the name of the game with this ingredient pairing. The oregano adds a bit of a kick, which your baby may or may not like. Feel free to try any other savory herb you have on hand in its place.

1. Combine the thawed purees in a small bowl. Add the oregano. Mix well with a spoon. If needed, thin the puree with breast milk, formula, or water to achieve the desired consistency.

2. Spoon the portion you plan to serve to your baby into a small pot. Return the rest of the puree to the refrigerator, where it can be stored for up to 3 days. Do not refreeze.

3. Gently warm the puree on the stove top over low heat before serving. Discard any uneaten puree.

TIP: If you don't have artichoke puree, you can puree 2 canned or jarred artichoke hearts, which are already cooked. Drain them before pureeing.

Sweet Potato and Cranberry Puree

 DF GF NF Vegan

MAKES 2 (2-OUNCE) SERVINGS

3 (1-ounce) freezer tray cubes sweet potato puree (page 43), thawed

1 (1-ounce) freezer tray cube cranberry puree (page 62), thawed

Pinch ground cinnamon

Cranberries and sweet potatoes is a popular fall combo, and your baby is sure to love the sweet-tart flavor of the cranberries.

1. Combine the thawed purees in a small bowl. Add the cinnamon. Mix well with a spoon. If needed, thin the puree with breast milk, formula, or water to achieve the desired consistency.

2. Spoon the portion you plan to serve to your baby into a small pot. Return the rest of the puree to the refrigerator, where it can be stored for up to 3 days. Do not refreeze.

3. Gently warm the puree on the stove top over low heat before serving. Discard any uneaten puree.

Chicken and Pea Puree

MAKES 2 (2-OUNCE) SERVINGS

2 (1-ounce) freezer tray cubes chicken puree (page 72), thawed

2 (1-ounce) freezer tray cubes pea puree (page 54), thawed

Pinch garlic powder

Babies need protein for growth and development, and this puree delivers it in a delicious combo. The peas add an earthy herbal flavor to the chicken.

1. Combine the thawed purees in a small bowl. Add the garlic powder. Mix well with a spoon. If needed, thin the puree with breast milk, formula, or water to achieve the desired consistency.

2. Spoon the portion you plan to serve to your baby into a small pot. Return the rest of the puree to the refrigerator, where it can be stored for up to 3 days. Do not refreeze.

3. Gently warm the puree on the stove top over low heat before serving. Discard any uneaten puree.

Swiss Chard, Cherry, and Tofu Puree

MAKES 5 (1-OUNCE) SERVINGS

3 (1-ounce) freezer tray cubes Swiss chard puree (page 47), thawed

1 (1-ounce) freezer tray cube cherry puree (page 58), thawed

1 (1-ounce) freezer tray cube tofu puree (page 70), thawed

Your baby will get the antioxidants vitamin A and C along with bone-building nutrients potassium and magnesium in this puree. The sweetness of the cherries reduces the slightly bitter bite of the chard. Tofu doesn't affect the flavor but adds nutrition and makes the puree more filling.

1. Combine the thawed purees in a small bowl. Mix well with a spoon. If needed, thin the puree with breast milk, formula, or water to achieve the desired consistency.

2. Spoon the portion you plan to serve to your baby into a small pot. Return the rest of the puree to the refrigerator, where it can be stored for up to 3 days. Do not refreeze.

3. Gently warm the puree on the stove top over low heat before serving. Discard any uneaten puree.

TIP: Add a pinch of ground ginger or 1/8 teaspoon grated fresh ginger to boost flavor.

Avocado, Black Bean, and Brown Rice Cereal Puree

DF GF NF Vegan

MAKES 2 (2-OUNCE) SERVINGS

2 (1-ounce) freezer tray cubes avocado puree (page 42), thawed

1 (1-ounce) freezer tray cube black bean puree (page 69), thawed

1 (1-ounce) freezer tray cube brown rice cereal (page 68), thawed

⅛ teaspoon grated lime zest

Pinch ground cumin

Consider this puree to be a baby's introduction to the flavor she's likely to enjoy later in life in the form of burritos. A great source of protein for muscle and tissue building, this puree is also packed with fiber and important vitamins and minerals to support your baby's growth and development.

1. Combine the thawed purees in a small bowl. Add the lime zest and cumin. Mix well with a spoon. If needed, thin the puree with breast milk, formula, or water to achieve the desired consistency.

2. Spoon the portion you plan to serve to your baby into a small pot. Return the rest of the puree to the refrigerator, where it can be stored for up to 3 days. Do not refreeze.

3. Gently warm the puree on the stove top over low heat before serving. Discard any uneaten puree.

TIP: If you don't have avocado puree on hand, you can mash half of an avocado until smooth and stir it in after the puree has been gently warmed.

Melon, Yogurt, and Prune Puree

DF option | GF | NF | V | Vegan option

MAKES 3 (2-OUNCE) SERVINGS

2 (1-ounce) freezer tray cubes cantaloupe puree (page 61), thawed

3 ounces plain full-fat yogurt (nondairy if desired)

1 (1-ounce) freezer tray cube prune puree (page 59), thawed

Pinch ground allspice

Your baby will love this creamy and sweet puree, which is high in calcium, magnesium, and iron for strong bones, as well as being an excellent source of protein to support growing bodies.

1. Combine the thawed purees and the yogurt in a small bowl. Add the allspice. Mix well with a spoon. If needed, thin the puree with breast milk, formula, or water to achieve the desired consistency.
2. Store any unoffered puree in the refrigerator for up to 3 days. Do not refreeze.

TIP: Other dried fruit purees, such as cranberry or date, can be used in place of the prune puree.

Quinoa, Kale, and Apple Puree

DF | GF | NF | Vegan

MAKES 5 (1-OUNCE) SERVINGS

2 (1-ounce) freezer tray cubes quinoa cereal (page 68), thawed

2 (1-ounce) freezer tray cubes kale puree (page 47), thawed

1 (1-ounce) freezer tray cube apple puree (page 45), thawed

Pinch ground cloves

Both quinoa and kale are superfoods. The apple adds just enough sweetness to ensure this nutritious meal is yummy, too.

1. Combine the thawed purees in a small bowl. Add the cloves. Mix well with a spoon. If needed, thin the puree with breast milk, formula, or water to achieve the desired consistency.
2. Spoon the portion you plan to serve to your baby into a small pot. Return the rest of the puree to the refrigerator, where it can be stored for up to 3 days. Do not refreeze.
3. Gently warm the puree on the stove top over low heat before serving. Discard any uneaten puree.

TIP: You can replace the kale puree with any dark leafy greens puree for a similar nutritional profile.

Pumpkin and Brown Rice Cereal Puree

MAKES 2 (2-OUNCE) SERVINGS

2 (1-ounce) freezer tray cubes pumpkin puree (page 53), thawed

2 (1-ounce) freezer tray cubes brown rice cereal (page 68), thawed

Pinch ground allspice or pumpkin pie seasoning

This is the perfect puree for autumn, when pumpkins are in season and plentiful. With its slightly sweet, earthy flavor, pumpkin is loaded with antioxidants for a healthy immune system.

1. Combine the thawed purees in a small bowl. Add the allspice or pumpkin pie seasoning. Mix well with a spoon. If needed, thin the puree with breast milk, formula, or water to achieve the desired consistency.

2. Store any unoffered puree in the refrigerator for up to 3 days. Do not refreeze.

TIP: For babies 8 months and up, you can stir in 1 tablespoon ¼-inch-diced steamed apple for a chunky puree.

Green Bean, Avocado, and Pear Puree

MAKES 2 (2-OUNCE) SERVINGS

2 (1-ounce) freezer tray cubes green bean puree (page 48), thawed

1 (1-ounce) freezer tray cube avocado puree (page 42), thawed

1 (1-ounce) freezer tray cube pear puree (page 45), thawed

This puree is an excellent source of fiber for healthy digestion; it also contains folate for baby's brain development. The pear adds mild sweetness, while the avocado makes for a creamy texture.

1. Combine the thawed purees in a small bowl. Mix well with a spoon. If needed, thin the puree with breast milk, formula, or water to achieve the desired consistency.

2. Store any unoffered puree in the refrigerator for up to 3 days. Do not refreeze.

TIP: Add a pinch of ground ginger to this puree before mixing for a little extra flavor.

Carrot, Quinoa Cereal, and Black Bean Puree

MAKES 3 (2-OUNCE) SERVINGS

2 (1-ounce) freezer tray cubes carrot puree (page 46), thawed

2 (1-ounce) freezer tray cubes quinoa cereal (page 68), thawed

2 (1-ounce) freezer tray cubes black bean puree (page 69), thawed

The combination of quinoa and black beans provides your baby with a balanced plant-based source of protein and fiber, and the carrots add not only sweetness to the mix but also plenty of vitamins and minerals. In place of the carrot puree, you can also try spinach, broccoli, or cauliflower.

1. Combine the thawed purees in a small bowl. Mix well with a spoon. If needed, thin the puree with breast milk, formula, or water to achieve the desired consistency.
2. Spoon the portion you plan to serve to your baby into a small pot. Return the rest of the puree to the refrigerator, where it can be stored for up to 3 days. Do not refreeze.
3. Gently warm the puree on the stove top over low heat before serving. Discard any uneaten puree.

Turkey, Apple, and Spinach Puree

MAKES 3 (2-OUNCE) SERVINGS

2 (1-ounce) freezer tray cubes turkey puree (page 72), thawed

2 (1-ounce) freezer tray cubes apple puree (page 45), thawed

2 (1-ounce) freezer tray cubes spinach puree (page 47), thawed

Pinch dried sage

Fresh apples and spinach are both available in the fall, which is a great time to offer your baby this puree. It's an excellent source of lean protein, fiber, and vitamins and minerals.

1. Combine the thawed purees in a small bowl. Add the sage. Mix well with a spoon. If needed, thin the puree with breast milk, formula, or water to achieve the desired consistency.
2. Spoon the portion you plan to serve to your baby into a small pot. Return the rest of the puree to the refrigerator, where it can be stored for up to 3 days. Do not refreeze.
3. Gently warm the puree on the stove top over low heat before serving. Discard any uneaten puree.

Apple and Brown Rice Cereal Puree

MAKES 2 (2-OUNCE)
SERVINGS

2 (1-ounce) freezer
tray cubes apple puree
(page 45), thawed

2 (1-ounce) freezer tray
cubes brown rice cereal
(page 68), thawed

Pinch ground cinnamon

Pinch ground ginger

Here's a simple combination with a sweet flavor your baby will love. When making your apple puree, choose sweet-tart apples, such as Honeycrisp or Pink Lady, or try a combination of sweet and tart apples like Golden Delicious and Granny Smith.

1. Combine the thawed purees in a small bowl. Add the cinnamon and ginger. Mix well with a spoon. If needed, thin the puree with breast milk, formula, or water to achieve the desired consistency.

2. Store any unoffered puree in the refrigerator for up to 3 days. Do not refreeze.

TIP: Add even more nutrients by replacing 1 freezer tray cube of the rice cereal with 1 freezer tray cube of leafy greens puree such as spinach or kale.

Spinach, Plum, and Oat Cereal Puree

MAKES 3 (2-OUNCE)
SERVINGS

2 (1-ounce) freezer tray
cubes spinach puree
(page 47), thawed

1 (1-ounce) freezer
tray cube plum puree
(page 58), thawed

3 (1-ounce) freezer
tray cubes oat cereal
(page 68), thawed

Pinch ground cloves

This puree is an excellent source of fiber and potassium. It's also high in vitamin K, which supports healthy blood clotting. The iron and vitamin C content work synergistically to help your baby build red blood cells.

1. Combine the thawed purees in a small bowl. Add the cloves. Mix well with a spoon. If needed, thin the puree with breast milk, formula, or water to achieve the desired consistency.

2. Spoon the portion you plan to serve to your baby into a small pot. Return the rest of the puree to the refrigerator, where it can be stored for up to 3 days. Do not refreeze.

3. Gently warm the puree on the stove top over low heat before serving. Discard any uneaten puree.

TIP: Cherry or prune puree makes a great substitute for the plum puree here.

Lentil, Swiss Chard, and Date Puree

DF **GF** **NF** **Vegan**

MAKES 3 (2-OUNCE) SERVINGS

3 (1-ounce) freezer tray cubes lentil puree (page 69), thawed

2 (1-ounce) freezer tray cubes Swiss chard puree (page 47), thawed

1 (1-ounce) freezer tray cube date puree (page 59), thawed

Pinch ground nutmeg

This puree practically screams healthy with most of its punch coming from the greens and legumes, then sweetened naturally with dates. If you don't have frozen purees on hand, consider sautéing the chard for your own meal and adding lentils cooked with low-sodium vegetable broth, then pureeing it all for your baby with the addition of dates.

1. Combine the thawed purees in a small bowl. Add the nutmeg. Mix well with a spoon. If needed, thin the puree with breast milk, formula, or water to achieve the desired consistency.
2. Spoon the portion you plan to serve to your baby into a small pot. Return the rest of the puree to the refrigerator, where it can be stored for up to 3 days. Do not refreeze.
3. Gently warm the puree on the stove top over low heat before serving. Discard any uneaten puree.

Quinoa Cereal, Apricot, and Spinach Puree

DF **GF** **NF** **Vegan**

MAKES 3 (2-OUNCE) SERVINGS

2 (1-ounce) freezer tray cubes quinoa cereal (page 68), thawed

2 (1-ounce) freezer tray cubes apricot puree (page 58), thawed

2 (1-ounce) freezer tray cubes spinach puree (page 47), thawed

⅛ teaspoon minced fresh thyme

Apricot and spinach balance each other well in this naturally grain-free cereal combination, which gets a protein boost from the quinoa. It's also high in antioxidants and contains plenty of fiber.

1. Combine the thawed purees in a small bowl. Add the thyme and mix well with a spoon. If needed, thin the puree with breast milk, formula, or water to achieve the desired consistency.
2. Spoon the portion you plan to serve to your baby into a small pot. Return the rest of the puree to the refrigerator, where it can be stored for up to 3 days. Do not refreeze.
3. Gently warm the puree on the stove top over low heat before serving. Discard any uneaten puree.

TIP: Try other dried fruit purees in place of the apricot, such as cranberry or date.

Sweet Potato, Kale, and Zucchini Puree

MAKES 3 (2-OUNCE) SERVINGS

3 (1-ounce) freezer tray cubes sweet potato (page 43), thawed

2 (1-ounce) freezer tray cubes kale puree (page 47), thawed

1 (1-ounce) freezer tray cube zucchini puree (page 49), thawed

This vegetable trio combines sweet and savory to give your baby a flavorful, nutrition-packed puree.

1. Combine the thawed purees in a small bowl. Mix well with a spoon. If needed, thin the puree with breast milk, formula, or water to achieve the desired consistency.
2. Spoon the portion you plan to serve to your baby into a small pot. Return the rest of the puree to the refrigerator, where it can be stored for up to 3 days. Do not refreeze.
3. Gently warm the puree on the stove top over low heat before serving. Discard any uneaten puree.

TIP: Add some sweetness by stirring in a pinch each of ground allspice and ground ginger.

Oat Cereal, Apple, and Edamame Puree

MAKES 3 (2-OUNCE) SERVINGS

3 (1-ounce) freezer tray cubes oat cereal (page 68), thawed

2 (1-ounce) freezer tray cubes apple puree (page 45), thawed

1 (1-ounce) freezer tray cube edamame puree (page 64), thawed

Pinch ground ginger

We all know that apples and oatmeal make a perfect pair, but edamame? For all you doubters, remember that edamame is very mild, so it doesn't really alter the flavor profile, but it does add a protein-rich punch.

1. Combine the thawed purees in a small bowl. Add the ginger. Mix well with a spoon. If needed, thin the puree with breast milk, formula, or water to achieve the desired consistency.
2. Spoon the portion you plan to serve to your baby into a small pot. Return the rest of the puree to the refrigerator, where it can be stored for up to 3 days. Do not refreeze.
3. Gently warm the puree on the stove top over low heat before serving. Discard any uneaten puree.

6

9 TO 12 MONTHS

STAGE 3: CHUNKY COMBINATION PUREES

When your baby starts to scarf down thicker purees and makes good chewing motions when she eats, you can introduce chunkier purees. The purees in this chapter have small chunks and interesting textures. Foods such as cooked lentils, bits of rice, and chunks of soft fruits ensure easy chewing and swallowing. As you offer chunkier textures, you can also dilute foods less, or you can leave the foods undiluted altogether. Likewise, you can offer small bits of single ingredients, such as chopped bananas or avocados, whole lentils, and other foods of similar textures.

DEVELOPMENTALLY SPEAKING

By the age of about 8 or 9 months, babies tend to master a firm pincer grasp, which allows them to pick up small objects, including soft foods. Of course, your child may not have great control over what's now in her hand, or the textures of the food may fascinate her, so prepare for lots of squishing between little fingers as she attempts to feed, or simply entertain, herself. When she is this age, you can still offer to spoon-feed your baby, although she may show interest in feeding herself, an experiment you can allow her to try if you're not afraid of a little mess. A combination of small bits of soft foods your baby can feed herself supplemented with spoonfuls of chunky purees you offer is a good balance that ensures at least some food goes into your baby's mouth, and not all of it winds up squished behind her ear. With Julian, we would often give him pieces of soft foods like fish, avocado, soft fruit, and veggies along with smoother purees to develop a balanced meal of protein, veggies, and carbohydrates.

PORTION GUIDELINES

By now, your baby should be eating three solid meals per day, as well as continuing with breast milk or formula.

* Offer 24 to 40 ounces of breast milk or formula per day.
* Offer 1 to 2 ounces (or more depending on appetite) of solid foods at each feeding.

FAQS

Q: I have a lot of smooth purees remaining in my freezer. Do I need to discard these now that I want to offer more textured purees?

A: There's no need to discard earlier purees that aren't chunky. Mix them with a little wheat germ, flaxseed, chia seeds, or undiluted cereal to thicken, and add small chunks of soft fruits and vegetables, legumes, and other healthy soft whole foods.

Q: My baby seems more interested in playing with his food than eating it. Should I be worried?

A: Your baby enjoys tactile experiences, and food offers this. Lay something under the high chair that you don't mind throwing in the washing machine, and let your baby go to town. The more concern you express, or the more you try to stop the play, the less likely he is to enjoy the experience. And enjoying the entire meal experience is key to enjoying food! As long as you're continuing to offer food and your baby doesn't seem hungry, chances are he's eating the right amount of food for him.

Pear and Carrot Puree

DF GF NF Vegan

MAKES 2 (2-OUNCE) SERVINGS

½ pear, peeled, cored, and cut into ¼-inch dice

3 (1-ounce) freezer tray cubes carrot puree (page 46), thawed

⅛ teaspoon dried thyme or ¼ teaspoon minced fresh thyme

A mildly sweet vegetable and a mildly sweet fruit come together here in a delicious, easily digestible, and quite pretty puree. It is a great source of vitamins A and C, which will provide your baby with a healthy and flavorful dose of antioxidants.

1. In a medium saucepan with a steamer insert, bring about 1 inch of water to a simmer. Steam the pear, covered, until tender, about 6 minutes.
2. Add the pear, carrot puree, and thyme to a sauté pan or small pot. Mix until combined and gently warm the puree on the stove top over low heat before serving. Discard any uneaten puree.

TIP: Apple puree can be substituted for the pear puree. You can also try using other root vegetables in place of the carrots. To customize this puree, simply use 3 freezer tray cubes of any root veggie puree with 1 freezer tray cube of any fruit puree.

Lentil, Red Pepper, and Coconut Puree

DF GF NF Vegan

MAKES 8 (2-OUNCE) SERVINGS

1 cup cooked lentils, drained if canned

1 red bell pepper stemmed, seeded, and cut into ¼-inch dice

¼ cup coconut milk

¼ cup water

¼ teaspoon nutmeg

Rich coconut milk and the sweet tang of red bell peppers nicely flavor the ultra-healthy lentils in this combination. This is a hearty meal that makes a great offering for the last solid feeding of the day.

1. In a medium saucepan, bring the lentils, red pepper, coconut milk, water, and nutmeg to a simmer, stirring occasionally. Simmer until the red peppers are soft, about 6 minutes.

2. Transfer half of the mixture to a blender or food processor and puree until smooth. If needed, thin the puree with breast milk, formula, or water to achieve the desired consistency.

3. Stir the pureed mixture back into the remaining unpureed ingredient mixture. Cool slightly before serving. Store any unoffered puree in the refrigerator for up to 3 days or in the freezer for up to 6 months.

White Bean and Leek Puree

MAKES 4 (2-OUNCE) SERVINGS

1 tablespoon olive oil

1 leek, white and green parts chopped

3 (2-ounce) freezer tray cubes white bean puree (page 69), thawed

If your little one has shown an early liking for savory purees, here's the next winner for you to try. Julian absolutely loved this puree, and I can't even count how many times we made it for him. If you don't happen to have a leek on hand, feel free to substitute 2 tablespoons chopped onions or shallots, prepared the same way as the leek.

1. In a large sauté pan, heat the olive oil on medium-high heat until it shimmers. Add the chopped leek and cook, stirring occasionally, until it's soft, 5 to 7 minutes.

2. Add the thawed white bean puree to the sauté pan and mix the ingredients together. Continue cooking until just warmed. Store any unoffered puree in the refrigerator for up to 3 days. Do not refreeze.

TIP: Leeks often hold dirt between the layers, so thorough washing is necessary. Chop the leeks and put them in a bowl full of cold water. Move the leeks around with your hands and allow the dirt to fall to the bottom of the bowl. Scoop out the leeks with a slotted spoon and empty the water, rinsing away any dirt. Return the leeks to the bowl, fill it with water again, and repeat the process until there's no dirt at the bottom of the bowl.

Sweet Potato, Chickpea, and Quinoa Puree

MAKES 8 (2-OUNCE)
SERVINGS

**2 cups canned
chickpeas, drained**

**⅛ teaspoon ground
cinnamon**

**½ sweet potato, peeled
and cut into ¼-inch dice,
or 2 (2-ounce) freezer
tray cubes sweet potato
puree (page 43), thawed**

½ cup cooked quinoa

Chickpeas have a soft texture that mashes really well, and it serves as the pureed base for this toothsome meal. Freezing cooked quinoa in 2-ounce servings allows you to pull this meal together in a snap. Sweet potatoes add a light sweetness to the earthier flavors of the quinoa and chickpeas. You can also add greens to the chickpea puree, such as a green bean or spinach puree.

1. In a blender or food processor, puree the chickpeas and cinnamon until smooth. If needed, thin the puree with breast milk, formula, or water to achieve the desired consistency.

2. If using thawed sweet potato, jump to step 3. If using fresh sweet potatoes, bring about 1 inch of water to a simmer in a small saucepan with a steamer insert. Place the sweet potatoes in the steamer insert. Cover and steam until tender, about 5 minutes. Allow to cool slightly.

3. In a small bowl, combine the pureed chickpeas, sweet potato, and quinoa. If you like, gently warm a single serving of the mixture. Store any unoffered puree in the refrigerator for up to 3 days or in the freezer for up to 6 months. Do not refreeze if using frozen sweet potato puree.

TIP: You can substitute any canned legume here, such as kidney beans or black beans. They all make a smooth pureed base for your baby's meal.

Spinach, Black Bean, and Parsnip Puree

MAKES 4 (2-OUNCE) SERVINGS

1 parsnip, peeled and cut into ¼-inch dice

1 cup canned black beans, drained

3 (1-ounce) freezer tray cubes spinach puree (page 47), thawed

¼ cup cooked brown rice

Cutting parsnips (or any other root vegetable) into tiny, bite-size pieces and steaming them until they are soft adds chunkiness to this puree, while the smooth black beans and spinach are a great source of protein and antioxidants.

1. In a blender or food processor, add the black beans and the thawed spinach puree. Puree until smooth.
2. In a small saucepan with a steamer insert, bring about 1 inch of water to a simmer. Add the parsnip. Cover and steam until tender, about 5 minutes. Turn off the heat and remove the steamer insert with the parsnip. Pour out the cooking water, reserving it.
3. To the saucepan, add the parsnip, bean, and spinach puree mixture, and brown rice. Stir to combine and heat on low until the puree is warmed throughout. Thin, if necessary, with the reserved cooking water. Store any unoffered puree in the refrigerator for up to 3 days. Do not refreeze.

Cranberry and Ground Beef Puree

MAKES 3 (2-OUNCE) SERVINGS

3 ounces ground beef

⅛ teaspoon dried thyme

3 (1-ounce) freezer tray cubes cranberry puree (page 62), thawed

Cooking ground beef into small crumbles is a great way to introduce texture to your baby's stage 3 purees. If the crumbles of ground beef are too big, pulse them three or four times in a food processor or blender to break them up. To save time, cook up to a pound of ground beef ahead of time and freeze ¼-cup portions in zip-top bags for up to 6 months.

1. In a small sauté pan, cook the ground beef over medium-high heat, crumbling it with a spoon, until brown, about 6 minutes. Add the thyme. Allow to cool slightly.
2. Stir the thawed cranberry puree into the beef. Store any unoffered puree in the refrigerator for up to 3 days. Do not refreeze.

Pea, Quinoa, and Ground Turkey Puree

MAKES 8 (2-OUNCE) SERVINGS

½ cup quinoa

1 cup water

½ cup fresh or frozen peas

½ teaspoon minced fresh basil

4 ounces ground turkey

While this recipe calls for fresh peas, you can use 4 (1-ounce) freezer tray cubes of pea puree instead. However, if you do use the frozen pea puree, you cannot refreeze this dish.

1. Using a fine-mesh sieve, run the quinoa under cold water to rinse. Drain.
2. In a small saucepan, bring the quinoa and 1 cup of water to a boil. Cover, reduce the heat to medium-low, and simmer for 12 minutes. Add the peas and simmer for 3 minutes more. Fluff with a fork and cool slightly.
3. Transfer half of the mixture to a food processor or blender. Add the basil and puree until smooth. If needed, thin the puree with breast milk, formula, nondairy milk, or water to achieve the desired consistency.
4. In a small sauté pan, cook the ground turkey over medium-high heat, crumbling it with a spoon, until brown, about 6 minutes. Allow to cool slightly.
5. Transfer the pea and quinoa mixture, the puree, and the ground turkey to a medium bowl and stir to mix. Store any unoffered puree in the refrigerator for up to 3 days or in the freezer for up to 6 months.

TIP: To save time, cook up to 1 pound of ground turkey ahead of time and freeze ¼-cup portions in zip-top bags for up to 6 months. Do not refreeze cooked ground turkey once it is thawed.

Banana and Mango Puree

MAKES 4 (2-OUNCE) SERVINGS

1 banana, peeled

1 mango, peeled, pitted, and cut into ¼-inch pieces

This sweet and juicy puree uses fresh bananas and fresh mangos, so you can freeze additional portions as needed. Your baby will love the sweet tropical flavors associated with the fruits.

1. In a small bowl, mash the banana with a fork, thinning with breast milk, formula, or water as needed.
2. Stir in the mango pieces. Store any unoffered puree in the refrigerator for up to 3 days or in the freezer for up to 6 months.

TIP: For extra flavor, stir in ⅛ teaspoon ground allspice when you mash the bananas.

Parsnip, Carrot, and Lentil Puree

MAKES 4 (2-OUNCE) SERVINGS

3 (1-ounce) freezer tray cubes parsnip puree (page 46), thawed

3 (1-ounce) freezer tray cubes carrot puree (page 46), thawed

½ cup precooked lentils, drained if canned

¼ teaspoon dried tarragon

Lentils are the perfect size for babies learning to chew on textured foods. If you don't have the frozen vegetable purees on hand, use fresh carrots and parsnips (about 2 each) and roast them. It's more than you'll need for the puree, but the extras are for you to snack on. Peel and quarter each vegetable into sticks and lightly coat them with olive oil before adding to an oven preheated to 400°F. Roast for about 30 minutes.

1. Combine the thawed purees in a small saucepan. Add the lentils and the tarragon and mix well with a spoon.
2. Gently warm the puree on the stove top over low heat. Store any unoffered puree in the refrigerator for up to 3 days. Do not refreeze.

TIP: Cooked peas make a great substitute for lentils in this puree.

Zucchini, Yellow Squash, and Chicken Puree

DF GF NF

MAKES 4 (2-OUNCE) SERVINGS

¼ cup peeled diced zucchini (¼-inch dice)

3 (1-ounce) freezer tray cubes summer squash puree (page 49), thawed

2 (1-ounce) freezer tray cubes chicken puree (page 72), thawed

This is a great puree for summer, when you can make the most of abundant summer squash such as zucchini and yellow squash. Here the zucchini is offered in little chunks, mixed in with the chicken and yellow squash purees. As your baby grows, substitute cooked vegetables and chicken for the purees. The diced zucchini give this chunky puree some chewiness, and your baby will love the sweetness of the butternut squash. This puree is a great source of fiber, protein, and vitamin A.

1. Combine the thawed purees in a small saucepan. Mix well with a spoon. Gently warm the puree over low heat.
2. In another small saucepan with a steamer insert, bring about 1 inch of water to a boil. Add the zucchini. Cover and simmer for 5 minutes.
3. Add the zucchini to the puree and mix well with a spoon. Store any unoffered puree in the refrigerator for up to 3 days. Do not refreeze.

TIP: If you like, you can add ⅛ teaspoon of either dried sage or ground nutmeg.

Apricot, Sweet Potato, and Turkey Puree

MAKES 4 (2-OUNCE) SERVINGS

4 (1-ounce) freezer tray cubes sweet potato puree (page 43), thawed

2 (1-ounce) freezer tray cubes apricot puree (page 58), thawed

⅛ teaspoon ground ginger

2 ounces ground turkey

Turkey and sweet potato is a classic combination, and adding apricot here brings out the sweetness of the sweet potato, which perfectly complements the flavors in the puree. This puree is a great source of vitamin A, which will support your baby's developing eyesight.

1. Combine the thawed purees in a small saucepan. Add the ginger. Mix well with a spoon. Gently warm the puree over low heat.
2. In a small sauté pan, cook the ground turkey, crumbling it with a spoon, until brown, about 6 minutes.
3. Add the turkey to the puree and mix well with a spoon. Store any unoffered puree in the refrigerator for up to 3 days. Do not refreeze.

Blueberry, Cottage Cheese, and Oat Cereal Puree

GF option NF V

MAKES 3 (2-OUNCE) SERVINGS

2 (1-ounce) freezer tray cubes blueberry puree (page 56), thawed

¼ cup cottage cheese

2 (1-ounce) freezer tray cubes oat cereal (page 68), thawed

⅛ teaspoon ground cinnamon

Cottage cheese is the perfect food for babies just entering the chunky puree stage. It gives your baby something to chew and is a good source of protein. Blueberries are loaded with antioxidants, and oats are a high-quality source of whole grains. If you are avoiding gluten, look for oats that are labeled gluten free.

In a small bowl, stir all the ingredients together until well combined. Store any unoffered puree in the refrigerator for up to 3 days. Do not refreeze.

TIP: For a nondairy option, replace the cottage cheese with plain nondairy yogurt. To add chunkiness, use ¼ cup cooked steel-cut oats, cooled, in place of the oat cereal.

Apple, Parsnip, and Spinach Puree

MAKES 4 (2-OUNCE) SERVINGS

½ apple, peeled, cored, and cut into ¼-inch dice

½ parsnip, peeled and cut into ¼-inch dice

4 (1-ounce) freezer tray cubes spinach puree (page 47), thawed

¼ teaspoon ground cinnamon

Apples and parsnips go well together whether you eat them raw (for the older kids), steamed (as this recipe instructs), or roasted. They slightly sweeten the larger helping of spinach for a tasty, healthful puree.

1. In a saucepan with a steamer insert, bring about 1 inch of water to a simmer. Steam the apple and parsnip until very tender, about 10 minutes.
2. In a small bowl, combine the spinach puree with the apples, parsnips, and cinnamon.
3. If desired, gently warm one serving of the puree on the stove top over low heat. Store any unoffered puree in the refrigerator for up to 3 days. Do not refreeze.

Cherry, Fig, and Salmon Puree

**MAKES 4 (2-OUNCE)
SERVINGS**

2 ounces skinless salmon,
cut into small pieces

¼ teaspoon minced fresh
tarragon

1 fig, cut into ¼-inch dice

6 (1-ounce) freezer tray
cubes cherry puree
(page 58), thawed

Cherries and figs are delicious with salmon, which is an excellent source of protein and omega-3 fatty acids. This puree is also a good source of vitamin B₁₂ for energy and plenty of antioxidants. Fresh figs are available in June and again in August or September.

1. Sprinkle the salmon with the tarragon.
2. In a small saucepan with a steamer insert, bring about 1 inch of water to a boil. Add the salmon and the figs. Steam until the fish is opaque, about 6 minutes.
3. Transfer the salmon and figs to a small bowl. Add the thawed cherry puree. Mix well with a spoon to combine. Store any unoffered puree in the refrigerator for up to 3 days. Do not refreeze.

TIP: If fresh figs aren't available, make a puree from reconstituted dried figs using the recipe for dried fruit on page 59. Then mix two 1-ounce servings of the dried fig puree with the cherry puree, steaming the salmon by itself.

Ground Pork and Apple Puree

MAKES 4 (2-OUNCE)
SERVINGS

2 ounces ground pork

⅛ teaspoon dried sage

6 (1-ounce) freezer
tray cubes apple puree
(page 45), thawed

Pork, apple, and sage are a classic fall flavor combination. When cooking the ground pork, crumble it with a spoon so the pieces are the desired size. You can also pulse the cooked ground pork a few times in the food processor or blender if the pieces are too big.

1. Sprinkle the pork with the sage.
2. In a small sauté pan, cook the ground pork over medium-high heat, crumbling it with a spoon, until brown, about 6 minutes.
3. Transfer the pork to a small bowl and add the thawed apple puree. Mix well with a spoon to combine. Store any unoffered puree in the refrigerator for up to 3 days. Do not refreeze.

TIP: Cranberries add a nice touch of flavor and a good dose of antioxidants here. If desired, replace 2 cubes of apple puree with 2 cubes of cranberry puree.

Beef, Blackberry, and Brown Rice Puree

MAKES 4 (2-OUNCE)
SERVINGS

3 (1-ounce) freezer tray
cubes blackberry puree
(page 56), thawed

2 (1-ounce) freezer
tray cubes beef puree
(page 73), thawed

¼ cup cooked brown rice

¼ teaspoon dried thyme

Juicy blackberry tastes really good with beef and a pinch of dried thyme. You can buy precooked organic rice in either the freezer or rice section of your grocery store, and that speeds up cooking times substantially. Alternatively, freeze cooked rice in ¼-cup portions in zip-top bags for up to 6 months.

1. Combine the thawed purees in a small bowl. Add the rice and thyme. Mix well with a spoon.
2. Gently warm a single serving of the mixture. Store any unoffered puree in the refrigerator for up to 3 days. Do not refreeze.

TIP: For a green boost, replace 1 cube of blackberry puree with 1 cube of pureed greens, such as kale or spinach.

Broccoli, Onion, and Quinoa Puree

MAKES 4 (2-OUNCE) SERVINGS

1 tablespoon olive oil

½ onion, minced

4 (1-ounce) freezer tray cubes broccoli puree (page 52), thawed

¼ cup cooked quinoa

Having cooked quinoa on hand makes it easy to make purees like this. You can thaw the quinoa alongside the purees in the refrigerator, gently rewarming it all as a unit.

1. In a medium sauté pan, heat the olive oil on medium-high heat until it shimmers. Add the onion and cook, stirring occasionally, until soft, about 7 minutes.

2. Add the broccoli puree and quinoa and mix all of the ingredients. Continue cooking until the mixture is warm, 2 to 3 minutes. Store any unoffered puree in the refrigerator for up to 3 days. Do not refreeze.

TIP: Nutmeg goes well with cruciferous veggies like broccoli. Stir ⅛ teaspoon ground nutmeg into the mixture if you'd like.

Cod, Green Bean, and Plum Puree

MAKES 4 (2-OUNCE) SERVINGS

4 (1-ounce) freezer tray cubes green bean puree (page 48), thawed

2 (1-ounce) freezer tray cubes cod puree (page 71), thawed

⅛ teaspoon ground allspice

1 plum, peeled, pitted, and cut into ¼-inch dice

Little chunks of plum provide sweet surprises for your baby as he chews on this flavorful chunky puree. The cod is a wonderful source of lean protein, and the beans add fiber.

1. Combine the thawed purees in a small saucepan. Add the allspice and mix well with a spoon. Gently warm the mixture over low heat.

2. Add the plums and mix well with a spoon to combine. Store any unoffered puree in the refrigerator for up to 3 days. Do not refreeze.

TIP: Other soft stone fruits, such as 1 cup peeled diced cherries, peaches, or nectarines, can be used in place of the plums in this puree.

Cranberry, Sweet Potato, and Turkey Puree

**MAKES 4 (2-OUNCE)
SERVINGS**

**3 (1-ounce) freezer tray
cubes cranberry puree
(page 62), thawed**

**3 (1-ounce) freezer tray
cubes turkey puree
(page 72), thawed**

**⅛ teaspoon
ground ginger**

**¼ cup diced sweet
potato (¼-inch dice)**

This is a great puree to offer your baby when the rest of the family digs into Thanksgiving dinner, and it works equally well for any other meal. It's a great source of antioxidants, fiber, and protein for your baby's growing body.

1. Combine the thawed purees in a small saucepan. Add the ginger. Mix well with a spoon. Gently warm the mixture over low heat.

2. In another small saucepan with a steamer insert, bring about 1 inch of water to a boil. Add the sweet potato. Cover and steam until tender, about 5 minutes.

3. Add the sweet potato to the puree and mix well with a spoon. Store any unoffered puree in the refrigerator for up to 3 days. Do not refreeze.

TIP: If you like, ¼ cup diced winter squash works as a great substitute for the sweet potato here. You can also use a white potato in place of the sweet potato.

Potato, Lentil, and Pear Puree

MAKES 4 (2-OUNCE) SERVINGS

4 (1-ounce) freezer tray cubes potato puree (page 43), thawed

2 (1-ounce) freezer tray cubes pear puree (page 45), thawed

¼ cup canned lentils, drained

⅛ teaspoon ground cinnamon

The potato and pear combo provides a nice backdrop for the chunky lentils in this puree. Cinnamon adds a hint of spice and sweetness.

1. Combine the thawed purees in a small saucepan. Add the lentils and cinnamon and mix well with a spoon.
2. Gently warm the mixture over low heat. Store any unoffered puree in the refrigerator for up to 3 days. Do not refreeze.

TIP: You can also make and freeze dried lentils ahead of time. To cook dried lentils, bring 1 cup of lentils and 3 cups of water to a boil. Reduce the heat to medium-low. Cover and simmer until tender, about 15 minutes.

Butternut Squash, Kale, and Lentil Puree

MAKES 4 (2-OUNCE) SERVINGS

4 (1-ounce) freezer tray cubes kale puree (page 47), thawed

2 (1-ounce) freezer tray cubes butternut squash puree (page 51), thawed

¼ cup canned lentils, drained

⅛ teaspoon nutmeg

Kale makes up the bulk of this puree, with a little butternut squash to add sweetness, and protein-packed lentils to give your baby something to chew on.

1. Combine the thawed purees in a small saucepan. Add the lentils and nutmeg and mix well with a spoon.
2. Gently warm the mixture over low heat. Store any unoffered puree in the refrigerator for up to 3 days. Do not refreeze.

TIP: If your baby is ready for some bigger chunks, use ¼ cup drained canned pinto beans in place of the lentils.

Oat, Strawberry, and Fig Puree

MAKES 4 (2-OUNCE) SERVINGS

4 (1-ounce) freezer tray cubes oat cereal (page 68), thawed

3 (1-ounce) freezer tray cubes strawberry puree (page 56), thawed

1 fig, cut into ¼-inch dice

Oatmeal gets a sweet makeover here with the addition of a swirled strawberry puree and little bits of juicy figs that also add texture. Figs are in season in early and late summer; if they're hard to come by in your area, replace them with ¼ cup of ripe cherries, pitted and finely chopped, as shown on the next page.

1. Combine the thawed purees in a small bowl. Mix well with a spoon.
2. Add the fig and mix well with a spoon. Store any unoffered puree in the refrigerator for up to 3 days. Do not freeze.

Cottage Cheese, Avocado, and Banana Puree

MAKES 4 (2-OUNCE) SERVINGS

½ banana, peeled

½ avocado, peeled and pitted

¼ teaspoon ground cinnamon

½ cup cottage cheese

This puree isn't freezer friendly, but it comes together quickly. It's rich in potassium, calcium, and protein.

1. In a blender or food processor, puree the banana and avocado with the cinnamon until smooth, adding breast milk, formula, or water to achieve the desired consistency.
2. Combine the puree and the cottage cheese in a small bowl and mix well with a spoon. Store any unoffered puree in the refrigerator for up to 3 days. Do not freeze.

TIP: To keep the banana and avocado from browning when you store it, cover the surface of the puree with plastic wrap, sealing it tightly around the edges.

Spinach, Apple, and Yogurt Puree

DF option | GF | NF | V | Vegan option

MAKES 4 (2-OUNCE) SERVINGS

¼ cup peeled diced apple (¼-inch dice)

2 (1-ounce) freezer tray cubes spinach puree (page 47), thawed

½ cup plain full-fat yogurt (nondairy if desired)

⅛ teaspoon ground cloves

This puree will give your baby a healthy dose of calcium, potassium, magnesium, iron, vitamin C, and protein. For a nondairy alternative, I like using yogurt made from coconut milk or almond milk.

1. In a small saucepan with a steamer insert, bring about 1 inch of water to a boil. Add the apple. Cover and steam until tender, about 5 minutes. Allow to cool slightly.

2. Combine the apple, thawed puree, yogurt, and cloves in a small bowl. Mix well with a spoon. Store any unoffered puree in the refrigerator for up to 3 days. Do not refreeze.

TIP: You can use a half banana in place of the apple in this puree. In a bowl, mash the peeled banana, spinach, and yogurt together, leaving the banana slightly chunky.

Pea, Peach, and Yogurt Puree

DF option   GF   NF   V   Vegan option

MAKES 4 (2-OUNCE) SERVINGS

¼ cup fresh or frozen peas

2 (1-ounce) freezer tray cubes peach puree (page 58), thawed

½ cup plain full-fat yogurt (nondairy if desired)

¼ teaspoon minced fresh mint

Small chunks of peach add a sweet flavor to nutritious yogurt and peas. This puree is a great source of protein, and adding just a hint of mint will tickle your baby's taste buds and keep her reaching for more.

1. In a small saucepan with a steamer insert, bring about 1 inch of water to a boil. Add the peas. Cover and steam until tender, about 5 minutes. Allow to cool slightly.
2. Combine the thawed puree, yogurt, peas, and mint in a small bowl. Mix well with a spoon. Store any unoffered puree in the refrigerator for up to 3 days. Do not refreeze.

TIP: If you don't have mint, ¼ teaspoon minced fresh basil is a good substitute here.

Cottage Cheese and Carrot Puree

GF   NF   V

MAKES 4 (2-OUNCE) SERVINGS

5 (1-ounce) freezer tray cubes carrot puree (page 46), thawed

¼ cup cottage cheese

The curds in cottage cheese are the perfect texture as your baby progresses to chunkier purees. This simple puree comes together quickly if you have the carrot puree on hand.

Combine the thawed puree and cottage cheese in a small bowl. Mix well with a spoon. Store any unoffered puree in the refrigerator for up to 3 days. Do not refreeze.

TIP: Ginger goes well with carrots. You can stir in ⅛ teaspoon ground ginger if you'd like.

Swiss Chard, Mango, and Black Bean Puree

DF **GF** **NF** **Vegan**

MAKES 4 (2-OUNCE) SERVINGS

4 (1-ounce) freezer tray cubes Swiss chard puree (page 47), thawed

2 (1-ounce) freezer tray cubes mango puree (page 60), thawed

¼ cup canned black beans, drained

⅛ teaspoon ground cumin

Well-cooked black beans are small and soft, so they're ideal as your baby is practicing with chunkier purees. The mango nicely sweetens the earthy flavor of the chard.

1. Combine the thawed purees in a small saucepan. Add the black beans and cumin. Mix well with a spoon.
2. Gently warm the mixture over low heat. Store any unoffered puree in the refrigerator for up to 3 days. Do not refreeze.

TIP: If you don't have black beans, you can substitute the same amount of drained canned lentils or pinto beans, which are a bit chunkier than black beans. If you are concerned about the texture, lightly mash the pinto beans.

Prune, Parsnip, and Ground Beef Puree

 DF **GF** **NF**

MAKES 4 (2-OUNCE) SERVINGS

2 (1-ounce) freezer tray cubes prune puree (page 59), thawed

4 (1-ounce) freezer tray cubes parsnip puree (page 46), thawed

2 ounces ground beef

Prunes add sweetness, while parsnips bring a mild earthy flavor. The finely ground beef gives your baby something to chew on and adds plenty of protein to support her growing body.

1. Combine the thawed purees in a small bowl. Mix well with a spoon.
2. In a small sauté pan, cook the beef over medium-high heat, crumbling it with a spoon, until brown, about 6 minutes.
3. Add the beef to the purees and mix well with a spoon. Store any unoffered puree in the refrigerator for up to 3 days. Do not refreeze.

TIP: Garlic and thyme will add more flavor to this dish. As the beef cooks, stir in ⅛ teaspoon garlic powder and ¼ teaspoon dried thyme.

Peach, Ground Turkey, and Quinoa Puree

MAKES 6 (2-OUNCE) SERVINGS

1 peach, pitted and peeled, or 4 (1-ounce) freezer tray cubes peach puree (page 58), thawed

3 ounces ground turkey

¼ cup cooked quinoa

Your baby will love the sweetness of the peach puree with little chunky bits of ground turkey and quinoa. If you make the peach puree fresh, you can freeze this chunky puree in the freezer for up to 6 months.

1. If using a fresh peach, cut it into cubes and puree it in a blender or food processor until smooth.

2. In a small sauté pan, cook the ground turkey over medium-high heat, crumbling it with a spoon, until brown, about 6 minutes.

3. In a small saucepan, combine the turkey, peach puree, and quinoa. Mix well with a spoon. Gently warm the mixture over low heat, stirring frequently, for about 1 minute. Store any unoffered puree in the refrigerator for up to 3 days or in the freezer for up to 6 months. Do not refreeze if using frozen peach puree.

TIP: Ginger adds great flavor here. Add ¼ teaspoon grated fresh ginger to the turkey as it cooks.

Oat, Yogurt, and Prune Puree

MAKES 4 (2-OUNCE) SERVINGS

¼ cup cooked steel-cut oats (gluten-free if desired)

¼ cup plain full-fat yogurt (nondairy if desired)

2 (1-ounce) freezer tray cubes prune puree (page 59), thawed

Pinch ground cinnamon

Prune puree and yogurt make a sweet, slightly tangy, creamy base for this puree. Cooking oatmeal adds small chunks that give your baby something to chew on. If your baby is sensitive to gluten, be sure to choose oats processed in a gluten-free facility.

Combine all the ingredients in a small bowl and mix well with a spoon. Store any unoffered puree in the refrigerator for up to 3 days. Do not refreeze.

TIP: You can make a big batch of oats ahead of time and freeze ¼-cup portions in zip-top bags. To make oats, use a 3:1 ratio of water to oats. Bring the water to a rolling boil, stir in the oats, and reduce the heat to low. Cover and simmer until the liquid is absorbed and the oats are soft, 10 to 15 minutes.

Black Bean, Apple, and Brown Rice Puree

MAKES 4 (2-OUNCE) SERVINGS

4 (1-ounce) freezer tray cubes black bean puree (page 69), thawed

2 (1-ounce) freezer tray cubes apple puree (page 45), thawed

¼ cup cooked brown rice

Beans and rice is a food combination popular with vegetarians and omnivores alike. Apple may seem like a funny addition, but think of it more like a salsa.

1. Combine the thawed purees in a small saucepan. Add the rice and mix well with a spoon.
2. Gently warm the mixture over low heat. Store any unoffered puree in the refrigerator for up to 3 days. Do not refreeze.

TIP: Add ¼ teaspoon of ground allspice or ground ginger as you warm the puree for added flavor.

Pea, Potato, and Ground Beef Puree

MAKES 8 (2-OUNCE) SERVINGS

1 cup fresh or frozen peas

1 white potato, peeled and cut into ¼-inch dice

4 ounces ground beef

½ teaspoon dried tarragon

Give your baby his very own version of shepherd's pie, with tasty ground beef, tender peas, and pureed potatoes. While you can use frozen purees if you have them, making this fresh allows you to freeze it for a tasty on-demand meal.

1. In a small saucepan with a steamer insert, bring about 1 inch of water to a boil. Add the peas and potatoes. Cover and steam until tender, about 5 minutes.

2. Transfer the potatoes and peas to a blender or food processor and puree until smooth, thinning as needed with breast milk, formula, or water.

3. In a small sauté pan, cook the ground beef and tarragon, crumbling the beef with a spoon, until brown, about 6 minutes.

4. Transfer the pea and potato puree and the ground beef to a medium bowl, and mix well with a spoon. Store any unoffered puree in the refrigerator for up to 3 days or in the freezer for up to 6 months.

TIP: Sweet potato is a good alternative for the white potato here.

Salmon, Spinach, and Apple Puree

**MAKES 8 (2-OUNCE)
SERVINGS**

1 apple, peeled, cored,
and cut into ¼-inch dice

2 cups spinach, torn into
small pieces

4 ounces skinless salmon

1 teaspoon olive oil

¼ teaspoon minced fresh
dill (optional)

This is a great puree for the freezer, so you can make a large batch and freeze it in single-serving portions. The salmon is an excellent source of healthy omega-3 fatty acids, while spinach is loaded with vitamin C, iron, and antioxidants.

1. Preheat the broiler. Place a rack on a baking sheet.

2. In a small saucepan with a steamer insert, bring about 1 inch of water to a boil. Add the apple and spinach. Cover and steam until tender, 5 to 10 minutes.

3. Transfer the apple and spinach to a food processor or blender. Puree until smooth, adding breast milk, formula, or water to achieve the desired consistency.

4. Brush the salmon with the olive oil and sprinkle it with the dill, if desired. Place it on the rack on the baking sheet. Broil until opaque, 3 to 5 minutes.

5. Cut the salmon (or flake it with a fork) into tiny pieces. Transfer the puree and the salmon to a medium bowl, and mix well with a spoon. Store any unoffered puree in the refrigerator for up to 3 days or in the freezer for up to 6 months.

TIP: You can use any type of white fish in place of the salmon, if you wish. Likewise, trout makes a good substitute here.

Pea, Carrot, and Cod Puree

DF GF NF

MAKES 8 (2-OUNCE) SERVINGS

½ cup fresh or frozen peas

1 carrot, peeled and cut into ¼-inch dice

4 ounces cod

1 teaspoon olive oil

¼ teaspoon grated lemon zest

½ teaspoon dried oregano

Peas and cod are both excellent sources of protein for your baby. Carrots add sweetness and plenty of nutrients to help support your baby's growth.

1. Preheat the broiler. Place a rack on a baking sheet.
2. In a small saucepan with a steamer insert, bring about 1 inch of water to a boil. Add the peas and carrots. Cover and steam until tender, 5 to 10 minutes.
3. Transfer the peas and carrots to a food processor or blender and puree until smooth, adjusting the texture as needed with breast milk, formula, or water.
4. Brush the cod with the olive oil and sprinkle it with the lemon zest and oregano. Place it on the rack. Broil until the fish is opaque, about 10 minutes. Allow to cool slightly.
5. Use a fork to create small flakes of the cooked cod. Transfer the puree and the fish to a medium bowl, and mix well with a spoon. Store any unoffered puree in the refrigerator for up to 3 days or in the freezer for up to 6 months.

TIP: In place of the cod, any white fish, such as halibut or turbot, works well in this recipe, as does salmon.

Pea and Ham Puree

MAKES 8 (2-OUNCE) SERVINGS

2 cups fresh or frozen peas

6 ounces cooked ham, cut into ¼-inch dice

¼ teaspoon ground allspice

Use natural, uncured ham in this puree. Be sure to look for brands that don't have any artificial ingredients, such as additives and preservatives. Applegate Farms is one good choice.

1. In a small saucepan with a steamer insert, bring about 1 inch of water to a boil. Add the peas. Cover and steam until tender, 5 to 10 minutes.
2. Transfer the peas to a food processor or blender. Puree until smooth, thinning as needed with breast milk, formula, or water.
3. Add the ham and allspice to the food processor or blender. Pulse five times, or until the ham is finely chopped but not pureed. Store any unoffered puree in the refrigerator for up to 3 days or in the freezer for up to 6 months.

TIP: This recipe works well with asparagus in place of the peas. Steam 2 cups of asparagus tips and replace the allspice with an equal amount of dried tarragon.

Kale, Pear, and Cottage Cheese Puree

GF NF V

MAKES 8 (2-OUNCE) SERVINGS

1 cup stemmed and chopped kale

1 pear, peeled, cored, and cut into ¼-inch dice

1 cup cottage cheese

¼ teaspoon ground nutmeg

Cottage cheese is a great source of protein and calcium to support your baby's forming bones and growing body. The kale and pear offer your baby immune-supporting vitamins, minerals, and antioxidants.

1. In a small saucepan with a steamer insert, bring about 1 inch of water to a boil. Add the kale and pear. Cover and steam until tender, 5 to 10 minutes. Allow to cool slightly.

2. Transfer the kale and pear to a blender or food processor and puree until smooth, adding breast milk, formula, or water as needed to achieve the desired consistency.

3. Combine the puree, cottage cheese, and nutmeg in a small bowl and mix well with a spoon. Store any unoffered puree in the refrigerator for up to 3 days or in the freezer for up to 6 months.

TIP: If you'd prefer to use fresh cottage cheese each time you offer your baby this treat, you can freeze the puree in 1-ounce portions and thaw 2 freezer tray cubes per ¼ cup cottage cheese. Don't refreeze if using the freezer tray cubes.

Apple, Lentil, and Quinoa Puree

DF GF NF Vegan

MAKES 10 (2-OUNCE) SERVINGS

2 apples, peeled, cored, and cut into ¼-inch dice

¼ teaspoon grated fresh ginger or ¼ teaspoon ground ginger

1 cup cooked lentils, drained if canned

1 cup cooked quinoa

Lentils and quinoa provide all the amino acids necessary to create a complete source of vegetarian protein to support your baby's growing body. The apple puree adds sweetness and creates a smooth base for the chunky lentils and quinoa.

1. In a small saucepan with a steamer insert, bring about 1 inch of water to a boil. Add the apples. Cover and steam until tender, 5 to 10 minutes.

2. Transfer the apples to a food processor or blender. Add the ginger. Puree until smooth, adding breast milk, formula, or water to achieve the desired consistency.

3. Gently warm the lentils and quinoa in a medium saucepan over low heat. Add the apple puree and mix well with a spoon. Store any unoffered puree in the refrigerator for up to 3 days or in the freezer for up to 6 months.

TIP: If you'd like a slightly less chunky puree, blend the lentils along with the apples, but leave the quinoa whole.

Green Bean, Sweet Potato, and Ground Turkey Puree

MAKES 8 (2-OUNCE) SERVINGS

1 cup green beans, cut into ¼-inch pieces

1 sweet potato, peeled and cut into ¼-inch dice

4 ounces ground turkey

Ground turkey adds texture to this puree of sweet potatoes and green beans. The sweet potatoes have a delicate flavor that complements the taste of the beans. This recipe is also loaded with protein and plenty of vitamins and minerals.

1. In a small saucepan with a steamer insert, bring about 1 inch of water to a boil. Add the green beans and sweet potato. Cover and steam until tender, 5 to 10 minutes.

2. Transfer the beans and sweet potato to a food processor or blender. Puree until smooth, adding breast milk, formula, or water to achieve the desired consistency.

3. In a small sauté pan, cook the ground turkey over medium-high heat, crumbling it with a spoon, until brown, about 6 minutes.

4. Transfer the puree and the turkey to a medium bowl, and mix well with a spoon. Store any unoffered puree in the refrigerator for up to 3 days or in the freezer for up to 6 months.

TIP: For more flavor, add ¼ teaspoon each garlic powder and onion powder to the turkey as it cooks.

TIP: The secret to crumbling ground meats when you cook them is to use the side of a wooden spoon to keep breaking the meat into smaller and smaller pieces. If, when the meat is cooked, the pieces still seem too large, you can pulse them briefly in the food processor or blender to chop them more finely.

Banana, Quinoa Cereal, and Blueberry Puree

MAKES 4 (2-OUNCE) SERVINGS

½ banana, peeled

Pinch ground allspice

4 (1-ounce) freezer tray cubes quinoa cereal (page 68), thawed

2 (1-ounce) freezer tray cubes blueberry puree (page 56), thawed

With antioxidants, potassium, and protein, this tasty treat for your baby also helps meet his nutritional needs. Add even more protein and calcium by stirring in a few tablespoons of plain yogurt to each portion, if you wish.

In a small bowl, mash the banana and allspice, leaving the texture slightly chunky. Add the purees and mix well with a spoon. Store any unoffered puree in the refrigerator for up to 3 days. Do not freeze.

TIP: Any berry or stone fruit puree that you have in the freezer will work in this recipe, so feel free to mix it up based on what you have available.

Spaghetti Squash, Spinach, Pear, and Lentil Puree

DF GF NF Vegan

MAKES 10 (2-OUNCE) SERVINGS

½ spaghetti squash, halved lengthwise and seeded

1½ teaspoons olive oil

2 cups spinach, cut into pieces

1 pear, peeled, cored, and cut into ¼-inch dice

¼ teaspoon ground allspice

1 cup cooked lentils, drained if canned

Lentils are a great source of plant-based protein, while spinach and squash are loaded with antioxidants. The pear brings a mild sweetness your baby will enjoy. This puree is also high in fiber.

1. Preheat the oven to 375°F. Line a baking sheet with parchment.
2. Brush the cut side of the spaghetti squash with the olive oil. Place the squash, cut-side down, on the prepared baking sheet. Bake until soft, about 40 minutes. Allow to cool slightly so it is easier to handle.
3. Use a spoon to scoop the flesh of the squash from the rind and set it aside.
4. In a small saucepan with a steamer insert, bring about 1 inch of water to a boil. Add the spinach and pear. Cover and steam until tender, 5 to 10 minutes.
5. Transfer the squash, pear, and spinach to a food processor or blender. Add the allspice. Puree until smooth, adding breast milk, formula, or water as needed to achieve the desired consistency.
6. Gently warm the lentils in a medium saucepan over low heat. Add the puree and mix well with a spoon. Store any unoffered puree in the refrigerator for up to 3 days or in the freezer for up to 6 months.

TIP: You can also use other winter squashes here, baking them in the oven in the same way and for the same amount of time as the spaghetti squash.

Acorn Squash and Chicken Puree

MAKES 8 (2-OUNCE) SERVINGS

2 cups acorn squash, peeled, seeded, and cut into ¼-inch dice

¼ teaspoon ground sage

1 cup rotisserie chicken, cut into ¼-inch dice

Chicken and squash is a tasty combination, and it's loaded with plenty of vitamin A and protein to support your baby's developing eyesight and growing body. Babies love the sweetness of the winter squash and the slight chewiness of the chicken.

1. In a small saucepan with a steamer insert, bring about 1 inch of water to a boil. Add the acorn squash. Cover and steam until tender, 5 to 10 minutes.

2. Transfer the squash to a food processor or blender. Add the sage. Puree until smooth, adding breast milk, formula, or water as needed to achieve the desired consistency.

3. Add the chicken to the blender or food processor. Pulse 5 or 10 times, until the chicken is finely chopped but not pureed. Store any unoffered puree in the refrigerator for up to 3 days or in the freezer for up to 6 months.

TIP: While using rotisserie chicken is a great time-saver, you can also cook your own. Brush a boneless, skinless chicken breast or thigh with a little olive oil and broil it for about 15 minutes, turning occasionally. Cut the chicken into small pieces before adding it to the food processor or blender.

7

10 MONTHS AND UP

SMOOTHIES AND FINGER FOODS

Your baby has fully moved into eating solid foods now, and she can likely feed herself bites of egg, banana, or even very tender meat, and drink from a sippy cup with (relatively) minimal mess. Now is the time to start offering even more healthy, fun foods that your baby can feed herself. This chapter is filled with foods that are packed with nutrition and offer your baby a wide range of flavors and textures to help her develop a taste for nutritious, wholesome foods. Smoothies are an especially tantalizing offering that you and your baby can enjoy together. In addition to several smoothie recipes, see page 138 for a guide to creating your own smoothies.

DEVELOPMENTALLY SPEAKING

Because babies develop at different rates, age isn't the only indicator of readiness for finger foods. Look for these signs:

* He sits without support for longer periods.
* He uses his teeth to chew purees.
* He can eat thick purees.
* He is able to grab small bites of food and pull them toward his mouth (and, sometimes, succeeds in getting them in his mouth).
* He attempts to take the spoon from you as you feed him.

PORTION GUIDELINES

Your baby is growing, but she still doesn't need a lot of food. Offer solids three times per day and supplement with breast milk or formula.

* Offer ¼ cup to ½ cup of solid food for breakfast, midday, and evening meals.
* Supplement food with 24 to 32 ounces of breast milk or formula daily.

FAQ

Q: I know I shouldn't give my daughter cow's milk before she turns 1 year old, but I'm also not producing enough breast milk to use in smoothies. Is it okay to introduce nut-based milk to my 10-month-old?

A: Absolutely! Because of my son's allergies, we used hemp milk galore! You can certainly introduce nuts and seeds at this stage, and these milks make a nice base. While nuts are a good source of fiber and protein, the liquid made from the nuts contains very little of either, so I recommend adding a protein and fat source in your child's smoothie (see the next page for recommendations). If you purchase a nut-based milk, be on the lookout in the ingredients list for carrageenan, a preservative used as a thickening agent and stabilizer, which you'll want to avoid. Choose the unsweetened versions and rotate between the various nut milk options! I also recommend trying to make your own. It's actually quite simple and provides more nutrition and flavor. The Vitamix website offers one basic recipe for almond or cashew milk. For the sweetener, I always recommend raw honey or pure maple syrup, not sugar.

ANATOMY OF A SMOOTHIE

I always encourage a little experimentation in the kitchen. If you generally go by the (recipe) book, smoothies are the perfect departure for winging it with confidence. Every great smoothie starts with a liquid and fresh or frozen organic produce. It's only improved by the additions of protein and healthy fat (which make an ideal base), and a superfood or two.

FOR A STARTER SMOOTHIE, choose one ingredient from the liquid and base columns, and one to three ingredients from the fruit column.

FOR A GREEN SUPER SMOOTHIE, choose one ingredient from the liquid, base, and greens columns. Feel free to use a combination of fruits and more than one add-in.

LIQUID	+	BASE	+	FRUIT	+	GREENS	+	SUPERFOOD ADD-INS
1 cup		**1–2 tablespoons**		**1–2 cups**		**1 handful**		**1-2 tablespoons (seeds)** **¼ teaspoon (herbs and spices)**
Breast milk or formula		Nut butters		Banana		Kale		Chia seeds
Cow's milk		Yogurt or Kefir		Berries		Spinach		Flax seeds
Nondairy milk (coconut, almond, rice, etc.)		Avocado		Pear		Chard		Hemp seeds
		Tofu		Mango				Wheat germ
Water or coconut water				Cherries				Mint
				Pineapple				Basil
				Your choice!				Ginger
								Turmeric

Save That Smoothie

TOO THICK: Add more liquid. Start with ¼ cup and add in ¼-cup increments.

TOO THIN: Add more fruit or yogurt.

TOO BITTER: Sweeten by adding 1 Medjool date or 1 teaspoon of raw honey, pure maple syrup, or pure vanilla extract.

TOO WARM: Add a handful of ice.

NOT BLENDING WELL: Blend in batches in this order: liquid, greens, fruit, add-ins.

Yogurt Berry Smoothie

DF option | GF | NF | V | Vegan option

2 (1-CUP) SERVINGS

3 (1-ounce) freezer tray cubes berry puree (page 56), thawed, or 3 ounces berries of your choice

2 (1-ounce) freezer tray cubes spinach or kale puree (page 47), thawed

2 ounces plain full-fat yogurt (nondairy if desired)

3 ounces breast milk, formula, or any nondairy milk

1/8 teaspoon ground cinnamon

Smoothies are an excellent vehicle for serving nutritious meals to your baby in the form of tasty drinks. This classic smoothie is fabulous in the spring when berries are in season, but you can also use any berry puree cubes you have in the freezer. The yogurt is a great source of protein.

In a blender, combine all the ingredients. Process until the mixture is smooth. Store any unoffered smoothie in the refrigerator for up to 3 days. When serving the remaining smoothie, adjust the consistency with a little extra liquid as needed and blend again before serving.

TIP: You can replace the yogurt with tofu or with an extra scoop of infant formula or an organic whey protein powder without any additives.

Carrot Cake Smoothie

DF GF Vegan

MAKES 2 (1-CUP) SERVINGS

1 cup breast milk, formula, or any nondairy milk

½ frozen banana

½ cup sliced carrot

1 medjool date, pitted

1 tablespoon nut butter of choice

1 teaspoon chia seeds

1 teaspoon cinnamon

This dessert favorite is reinvented here as a creamy and smooth drink. The color has a nice peachy richness and the sweetness of the date makes added sugars totally unnecessary. Enjoy this any time of the day!

In a blender, combine all the ingredients. Process until smooth. Store any unoffered smoothie in the refrigerator for up to 3 days. When serving the remaining smoothie, adjust the consistency with a little extra liquid as needed and blend again before serving.

TIP: This recipe is really a starter version for your little one that I encourage you to modify from time to time. The classic flavor of a carrot cake comes from its spices, so experiment by adding ground nutmeg and ginger, too. Other ingredients to consider adding include shredded, unsweetened coconut and chopped walnuts in place of the nut butter (if you've got a powerful blender).

Fruity Spinach and Avocado Smoothie

MAKES 2 (1-CUP) SERVINGS

4 ounces breast milk, formula, or any nondairy milk

1 kiwi, peeled

2 (1-ounce) freezer tray cubes pear puree (page 45), thawed

4 (1-ounce) freezer tray cubes spinach puree (page 47), thawed, or 4 ounces frozen spinach

½ avocado, pitted

1 tablespoon fresh mint or basil (optional)

This juicy smoothie brings the nutritional powerhouse spinach to a sweetly flavored beverage. Spinach is high in vitamin A, vitamin B$_6$, vitamin C, and iron, while kiwi is a great source of fiber and vitamin C. The pear adds a mellow sweetness to the smoothie.

In a blender, combine all the ingredients. Process until smooth. Store any unoffered smoothie in the refrigerator for up to 3 days. When serving the remaining smoothie, adjust the consistency with a little extra liquid as needed and blend again before serving.

TIP: Experiment away with substitutions. You can add an equal amount of kale or Swiss chard puree, or try banana or mango in place of the pear.

Banana Cream Pie Smoothie

DF option GF NF Vegan option

MAKES 2 (1-CUP) SERVINGS

4 ounces breast milk, formula, or any nondairy milk

1 cup plain yogurt (nondairy if desired) or unsweetened kefir

1 small frozen banana

½ teaspoon pure vanilla extract

1 teaspoon ground turmeric

1 teaspoon allspice or nutmeg

¼ cup ice

Sure to become a family favorite, this naturally sweet blend pairs frozen banana with vanilla and nutmeg to create a wonderfully rich flavor. The turmeric adds an anti-inflammatory kick while the kefir provides protein and probiotics.

In a blender, combine all the ingredients. Process until smooth. Store any unoffered smoothie in the refrigerator for up to 3 days. When serving the remaining smoothie, adjust the consistency with a little extra liquid as needed and blend again before serving.

Mixed Berry Smoothie Bowl

`DF` `GF` `NF` `Vegan option`

MAKES 2 (1-CUP) SERVINGS

FOR THE SMOOTHIE

2 ounces breast milk, formula, or any nondairy milk

½ cup frozen blueberries

½ cup frozen strawberries

1 cup plain yogurt (nondairy if desired)

¾ cup crushed ice

FOR THE TOPPINGS

(choose 1 or more)

2 to 3 raspberries, quartered

4 to 5 blueberries, quartered

2 strawberries cut into ¼-inch dice

2 slices peach cut into ¼-inch dice

½ tablespoon chia seeds

Smoothie bowls are incredibly popular with adults right now, but they're also perfect for babies who don't have the hang of sucking through a straw yet. Juicy berries and yogurt form the base of the smoothie, and a handful of toppings give your baby more flavors to chew on. Feel free to mix in toppings that you have on hand and know your baby can successfully chew and swallow.

1. In a blender, combine all the ingredients. Process until the mixture is smooth and thick. Set aside any unoffered puree before adding the toppings. Top with the your choice of cut raspberries, blueberries, strawberries, peach, and chia seeds.

2. The unoffered smoothie can be stored in the refrigerator for up to 3 days. Adjust the consistency with a little more ice to thicken it up and blend again before serving.

Pumpkin Smoothie

DF GF NF Vegan

MAKES 2 (1-CUP) SERVINGS

6 ounces breast milk, formula, or any nondairy milk

1 cup pumpkin puree (page 53), thawed, or canned pumpkin

¼ cup crushed ice

½ teaspoon pumpkin pie seasoning

1 tablespoon hemp seeds

Using canned pumpkin makes this smoothie super easy and no-cook, but, by all means, if you still have pumpkin puree in your freezer, use it up! Hemp seeds are a great protein source, but if you don't have them, you can replace them with 1 cup of yogurt. This smoothie offers the comforting taste of pumpkin pie at any time of year.

In a blender, combine all the ingredients. Process until smooth. Store any unoffered smoothie in the refrigerator for up to 3 days. When serving the remaining smoothie, adjust the consistency with a little extra liquid as needed and blend again before serving.

TIP: If you don't have pumpkin pie seasoning, add a pinch each of ground ginger, nutmeg, allspice, and cinnamon.

Almond Butter and Cherry Smoothie

DF GF Vegan

MAKES 2 (1-CUP) SERVINGS

6 ounces breast milk, formula, or any nondairy milk

2 tablespoons almond butter

4 (1-ounce) freezer tray cubes cherry puree (page 58), thawed

Think of this smoothie as an elevated PB&J, substituting almonds for the standard peanuts and fresh cherries for jam. It's hearty and sweet, and your baby won't need a glass of fresh (nondairy) milk on the side, as it goes right into the smoothie.

In a blender, combine all the ingredients. Process until smooth. Store any unoffered smoothie in the refrigerator for up to 3 days. When serving the remaining smoothie, adjust the consistency with a little extra liquid as needed and blend again before serving.

TIP: Berry puree makes a good substitute here for the cherry puree, and if you wish, you can replace the almond butter with any other nut butter.

Banana and Avocado Superfood Smoothie

MAKES 2 (1-CUP) SERVINGS

6 ounces breast milk, formula, or any nondairy milk

2 tablespoons chia seeds

4 (1-ounce) freezer tray cubes kale puree (page 47), thawed

½ banana, peeled

½ avocado, pitted

Here's an amped-up version of Julian's favorite puree, reborn as a smoothie. His beloved banana and avocado combination gets a superfood kick from chia seeds and a healthy dose of kale.

In a blender, combine all the ingredients. Process until smooth. Store any unoffered smoothie in the refrigerator for up to 3 days. When serving the remaining smoothie, adjust the consistency with a little extra liquid as needed and blend again before serving.

TIP: Add ¼ teaspoon ground nutmeg to this smoothie for a little sweet spice.

Strawberry and Cucumber Smoothie

MAKES 2 (1-CUP) SERVINGS

4 ounces breast milk, formula, or any nondairy milk

¼ cup plain yogurt

½ cup strawberries

½ Persian cucumber, unpeeled, cut into large chunks, or ½ English cucumber, seeds removed, cut into large chunks

1 to 2 medjool dates, pitted

¼ teaspoon minced, peeled fresh ginger

Smoothies tend to be rich. In the warmer months of summer and the early fall, I opt for this refreshing, lighter recipe featuring fresh strawberries and cucumber.

In a blender, combine all the ingredients. Process until smooth. Store any unoffered smoothie in the refrigerator for up to 3 days. When serving the remaining smoothie, adjust the consistency with a little extra liquid as needed and blend again before serving.

Protein Power Smoothie

MAKES 2 (1-CUP) SERVINGS

6 ounces breast milk, formula, or any nondairy milk

2 ounces tofu

2 (1-ounce) freezer tray cubes butternut squash puree (page 51), thawed

½ banana, peeled

¼ teaspoon ground ginger

Your local smoothie place might add a protein powder "boost" to your smoothie, but this recipe calls for just a couple of ounces of tofu to pack in the protein without affecting the taste. The sweet banana pairs well with the butternut squash, delivering a tasty and nutritious fruit and veggie combo for your little one.

In a blender, combine all the ingredients. Process until smooth. Store any unoffered smoothie in the refrigerator for up to 3 days. When serving the remaining smoothie, adjust the consistency with a little extra liquid as needed and blend again before serving.

TIP: There are many suitable replacements for the butternut squash puree depending on what you have in your freezer. Try pumpkin, sweet potato, apricot, or any other winter squash.

Kale and Mango Smoothie

MAKES 2 (1-CUP) SERVINGS

6 ounces breast milk, formula, or any nondairy milk

½ mango, peeled, pitted, and cut into cubes

3 (1-ounce) freezer tray cubes kale puree (page 47), thawed

¼ teaspoon ground allspice

Cutting up a mango is sometimes a challenge, with the juicy fruit and the large pit in the center. To cut a mango, peel it with a vegetable peeler and then slice lengthwise around the pit, separating the flesh into two halves. Next, cut the flesh into cubes around the pit.

In a blender, combine all the ingredients. Process until smooth. Store any unoffered smoothie in the refrigerator for up to 3 days. When serving the remaining smoothie, adjust the consistency with a little extra liquid as needed and blend again before serving.

TIP: Coconut milk complements the flavor of mango, so consider it if you'd like to use a nondairy milk.

Plum and Chard Smoothie

DF GF NF Vegan

**MAKES 2 (1-CUP)
SERVINGS**

6 ounces breast
milk, formula, or any
nondairy milk

3 (1-ounce) freezer tray
cubes Swiss chard puree
(page 47), thawed

3 (1-ounce) freezer
tray cubes plum puree
(page 58), thawed

¼ teaspoon
ground ginger

Smoothies are a great use for frozen puree cubes as your baby gets older, and this smoothie will ensure she gets plenty of nutritious dark leafy greens. For a hit of added protein, add 1 tablespoon nut butter, ¼ cup plain yogurt, or ¼ cup tofu.

In a blender, combine all the ingredients. Process until smooth. Store any unoffered smoothie in the refrigerator for up to 3 days. When serving the remaining smoothie, adjust the consistency with a little extra liquid as needed and blend again before serving.

TIP: If you don't have plum puree, you can use prune, date, or cherry puree instead.

Orange Dream Smoothie

DF option GF NF V Vegan option

**MAKES 2 (1-CUP)
SERVINGS**

6 ounces breast
milk, formula, or any
nondairy milk

¼ cup plain full-fat yogurt
(nondairy if desired)

4 (1-ounce) freezer tray
cubes sweet potato
puree (page 43), thawed

¼ teaspoon
ground ginger

This orange smoothie is a great way for your baby to get the nutrients he needs for his developing bones and muscles, including protein, calcium, magnesium, fiber, and antioxidants.

In a blender, combine all the ingredients. Process until smooth. Store any unoffered smoothie in the refrigerator for up to 3 days. When serving the remaining smoothie, adjust the consistency with a little extra liquid as needed and blend again before serving.

TIP: To pump up the antioxidant content and add a little sweetness, consider adding ¼ cup frozen berries or 2 freezer tray cubes berry puree.

Broccoli Bites with Cottage Cheese and Chive Dip

MAKES 4 SERVINGS

FOR THE
BROCCOLI BITES

1 cup broccoli florets

1 egg

1 tablespoon
minced onion

⅓ cup grated
Cheddar cheese

¼ cup wheat germ

FOR THE COTTAGE
CHEESE DIP

¼ cup cottage cheese

2 tablespoons plain
full-fat yogurt

¼ teaspoon
onion powder

¼ teaspoon garlic powder

1 teaspoon chopped
fresh chives

These cheesy broccoli bites are tender on the inside with lots of savory flavor. They are easy for your baby to chew, and she'll love dipping them in the creamy cottage cheese dip, which is full of calcium and protein. Wheat germ is a great addition to any meal. It is extremely high in B vitamins, Vitamin E, and minerals such as zinc and magnesium.

TO MAKE THE BROCCOLI BITES

1. Preheat the oven to 400°F. Line a baking sheet with parchment.
2. In a small saucepan with a steamer insert, bring about 1 inch of water to a boil. Add the broccoli florets. Cover and steam for 1 minute. Chop the steamed broccoli into very small pieces.
3. Beat the egg in a small bowl. Add the broccoli, onion, cheese, and wheat germ. Mix well with a spoon.
4. Form the mixture into ½-inch balls. Place on the prepared baking sheet.
5. Bake for 20 minutes. Store unoffered broccoli bites in the refrigerator for up to 3 days or in the freezer for up to 6 months.

TO MAKE THE COTTAGE CHEESE DIP

In a blender or food processor, combine all the ingredients. Blend until smooth. Store unoffered portions in the refrigerator for up to 3 days.

TIP: Make this gluten free by replacing the wheat germ with gluten-free rolled oats you've pulsed in the food processor 10 times.

Fruity Tofu Bites with Apple Yogurt Dip

DF option GF V

MAKES 4 SERVINGS

Tasty and filled with protein and calcium for growing bodies, this fruity snack will be one your baby loves. Cut the tofu into small cubes your baby can easily grasp and dunk into the creamy dip.

FOR THE FRUITY TOFU BITES

¼ cup dried
banana pieces

¼ teaspoon ground
cinnamon

¼ cup almond flour

4 ounces extra firm tofu,
cut into ½-inch cubes

1 egg, beaten

FOR THE APPLE YOGURT DIP

2 (1-ounce) freezer
tray cubes apple puree
(page 45), thawed

¼ cup plain full-fat yogurt
(nondairy if desired)

¼ teaspoon ground
cinnamon

TO MAKE THE FRUITY TOFU BITES

1. Preheat the oven to 375°F. Line a baking sheet with parchment.
2. In a blender or food processor, process the bananas and cinnamon until they are finely ground. Transfer to a small bowl and stir in the almond flour.
3. Dip the pieces of tofu into the egg, and then coat each piece on all sides with the banana-almond flour mixture.
4. Arrange the coated tofu pieces on the prepared baking sheet and bake until the coating is golden brown, 10 to 15 minutes. Store any unoffered tofu bites in the refrigerator for up to 3 days or in the freezer for up to 6 months.

TO MAKE THE APPLE YOGURT DIP

In a blender or food processor, combine all the ingredients. Puree until smooth. Store unoffered portions in the refrigerator for up to 3 days.

TIP: Before cooking tofu, it's a good idea to press out the excess water first. To do this, cut the tofu into ½-inch slices. Put the tofu in a colander and put a weighted plate on top. Allow it to sit for 20 minutes to press out the water. Continue cutting the tofu into cubes.

Vanilla Butternut Squash Bites

MAKES 4 SERVINGS

1 cup butternut squash, cut into ¼-inch dice

1 tablespoon olive oil

¼ teaspoon pure vanilla extract

¼ teaspoon ground nutmeg

Vanilla and nutmeg bring out the flavors in butternut squash (or other winter squash, such as acorn). Roasting the squash gives it a savory, caramelized flavor your baby will enjoy.

1. Preheat the oven to 450°F. Line a baking sheet with parchment.
2. In a small bowl, toss the squash with the olive oil, vanilla, and nutmeg.
3. Place the squash in a single layer on the prepared baking sheet and bake, stirring once or twice, until browned, 15 to 20 minutes. Store any unoffered squash bites in the refrigerator for up to 3 days or in the freezer for up to 6 months.

TIP: You can also use the seeds from half a vanilla bean in place of the extract, if you'd like. To gather the vanilla bean seeds, split the bean lengthwise with a sharp knife. Using the tip of the knife, scrape down the inside of the bean, gathering the seeds on the knife's tip.

Baked Apple Bites

DF GF NF V

MAKES 4 SERVINGS

¼ cup flaxseed

¼ teaspoon ground cinnamon

Pinch ground ginger

1 apple, peeled, cored, and cut into ½-inch pieces

1 egg, beaten

The natural health benefits of apples are kicked up a notch with a dusting of flaxseed and spices. Flaxseed is a good source of dietary fiber, which can help keep your baby regular. It's also high in omega-3 fatty acids, which help keep inflammation at bay and offer lifelong heart benefits.

1. Preheat the oven to 375°F. Line a baking sheet with parchment.

2. In a blender or food processor, process the flaxseed, cinnamon, and ginger to make a powder. Transfer the powder to a small bowl.

3. Dip the pieces of apple into the egg, and then coat each piece on all sides with the flaxseed powder.

4. Arrange the pieces on the prepared baking sheet and bake until the apples are soft, 20 to 25 minutes. Store any unoffered baked apple in the refrigerator for up to 3 days or in the freezer for up to 6 months.

TIP: To extend the life of your flaxseed, store it in the refrigerator in a zip-top bag.

Tropical Fruit and Black Bean Salad

MAKES 4 SERVINGS

¼ cup peeled mango cubes (¼-inch cubes)

¼ cup peeled papaya cubes (¼-inch cubes)

¼ cup peeled peach cubes (¼-inch cubes)

¼ cup canned black beans, drained

½ teaspoon minced fresh cilantro

Flavor-wise, black beans and tropical fruit are a heavenly match. This salad is tasty enough that you can make a big batch and serve it to your entire family, or use it as a salsa for fish or poultry.

In a small bowl, combine all the ingredients and toss to mix. Store any unoffered salad in the refrigerator for up to 3 days or in the freezer for up to 6 months.

TIP: If your baby doesn't like cilantro, omit it, or replace it with mint.

Shoestring Potatoes

MAKES 4 SERVINGS

1 russet potato, peeled and cut into ¼-inch shoestrings

1 tablespoon olive oil

¼ teaspoon garlic powder

¼ teaspoon onion powder

¼ teaspoon dried thyme

There are plenty of ways to cut your potatoes into shoestrings. The method requiring the least equipment is to use a knife to cut them in small, thin strips. You can also use a spiralizer, a julienne peeler, or a mandoline to create ¼-inch-thick shoestrings.

1. Preheat the oven to 450°F. Line a baking sheet with parchment.
2. In a small bowl, combine all the ingredients and toss to mix.
3. Place the potatoes in a single layer on the prepared baking sheet. Bake, flipping halfway through, until browned, 25 to 30 minutes. Store any unoffered potatoes in the refrigerator for up to 3 days.

TIP: You can also make shoestrings with other root veggies in this recipe, such as 3 carrots, 3 parsnips, or 1 celery root.

Winter Squash Fries with Hummus

MAKES 4 SERVINGS

**FOR THE
SQUASH FRIES**

1 cup acorn squash,
peeled, seeded, and cut
into ¼-inch matchsticks

1 tablespoon olive oil

¼ teaspoon garlic powder

¼ teaspoon
sweet paprika

FOR THE HUMMUS

1 cup canned
chickpeas, drained

1 tablespoon tahini

1 teaspoon olive oil

½ teaspoon grated
lemon zest

1 small garlic
clove, peeled

Winter squash makes tasty bite-size fries, and your baby will love dipping them in this flavorful chickpea dip. It's a high-fiber treat with lots of nutrients, perfect for growing bodies and grasping fingers.

TO MAKE THE SQUASH FRIES

1. Preheat the oven to 450°F. Line a baking sheet with parchment.
2. In a small bowl, combine all the ingredients and toss to mix.
3. Place the squash fries in a single layer on the prepared baking sheet. Bake until the squash starts to brown and is tender, about 15 minutes. Store any unoffered fries in the refrigerator for up to 3 days.

TO MAKE THE HUMMUS

In a blender or food processor, combine all the ingredients. Blend until smooth. Store any unoffered hummus in the refrigerator for up to 3 days.

TIP: Butternut squash also works well here. Alternatively, if it's in season, use chayote, which has a mild flavor similar to a potato.

Spiced Sweet Potato Fries with Apricot Yogurt Dip

DF option **GF** **NF** **V** **Vegan option**

MAKES 4 SERVINGS

FOR THE SWEET POTATO FRIES

1 sweet potato, peeled and cut into ¼-inch matchsticks

1 tablespoon olive oil

Pinch ground allspice

Pinch ground ginger

FOR THE APRICOT YOGURT DIP

¼ cup plain full-fat yogurt (nondairy if desired)

1 (1-ounce) freezer tray cube apricot puree (page 58), thawed

Sweet spices are tasty on sweet potatoes, and your baby will love picking up the soft fries and dipping them in yummy yogurt. The yogurt is a great source of protein and calcium to support your baby's healthy growth.

TO MAKE THE SWEET POTATO FRIES

1. Preheat the oven to 450°F. Line a baking sheet with parchment.
2. In a small bowl, combine all the ingredients and toss to mix.
3. Place the sweet potatoes in a single layer on the prepared baking sheet. Bake, flipping halfway through, until browned, 25 to 30 minutes. Store any unoffered fries in the refrigerator for up to 3 days.

TO MAKE THE APRICOT YOGURT DIP

In a small bowl, mix the yogurt and apricot puree until well blended. Store any unoffered dip in the refrigerator for up to 3 days.

TIP: If you don't have apricot puree, you can use any fruit puree you have in the freezer to sweeten and flavor this yogurt dip. Try peaches, nectarines, pears, or prunes.

Roasted Root Vegetable Cubes

MAKES 4 SERVINGS

1 carrot, peeled and cut into ¼-inch cubes

1 parsnip, peeled and cut into ¼-inch cubes

1 to 2 beets, peeled and cut into ¼-inch cubes

1 tablespoon olive oil

½ teaspoon ground cumin

¼ teaspoon onion powder

Cumin adds subtle spice to root veggies. While this recipe calls for specific root vegetables, you can use any that are seasonally available. Other vegetables to try include daikon radish, celery root, jicama, or turnip.

1. Preheat the oven to 450°F. Line a baking sheet with parchment.
2. In a small bowl, combine all the ingredients and toss to mix.
3. Place the vegetables in a single layer on the prepared baking sheet. Bake, stirring halfway through, until browned, 25 to 30 minutes. Store any unoffered vegetable cubes in the refrigerator for up to 3 days or in the freezer for up to 6 months.

TIP: You can replace the cumin with ½ teaspoon of a dried herb, such as tarragon, oregano, thyme, or Italian seasoning blend.

Sautéed Asparagus Tips

MAKES 4 SERVINGS

1 tablespoon olive oil

1 cup asparagus tips, cut in half

¼ teaspoon grated orange zest

¼ teaspoon dried tarragon

The tender tops of asparagus make a terrific, easily chewable food for your baby. Here they are flavored with just a touch of orange zest and dried tarragon, which has a slight licorice flavor.

1. In a small sauté pan, heat the olive oil over medium-high heat until it shimmers.

2. Add the asparagus, orange zest, and tarragon. Cook, stirring occasionally, until the tips begin to brown, 5 to 7 minutes. Store any unoffered asparagus in the refrigerator for up to 3 days or in the freezer for up to 6 months.

TIP: Since you're using just the asparagus tips in this recipe, cut the leftover asparagus stalks into pieces, steam them, and make asparagus puree or use them as a base for asparagus soup.

Mini Green Bean Fries

MAKES 4 SERVINGS

2 tablespoons grated Parmesan cheese

2 tablespoons wheat germ or almond flour

¼ teaspoon garlic powder

1 cup green bean pieces (1-inch pieces)

1 egg, beaten

Babies are sure to love this easy-to-grasp and healthy snack! The preparation here ensures the vegetables will develop a crispy, flavorful coating of wheat germ, Parmesan cheese, and garlic powder. Resist the temptation to eat them yourself, or there might be none left for your little one.

1. Preheat the oven to 425°F. Line a baking sheet with parchment.

2. In a small bowl, combine the cheese, wheat germ or almond flour, and garlic powder and mix well with a spoon.

3. Dredge the green beans in the egg and then in the wheat germ mixture. Arrange the green beans in a single layer on the prepared baking sheet. Bake until the beans are crisp, 12 to 15 minutes. Store any unoffered green beans in the refrigerator for up to 3 days.

Baked Falafel with Tahini Yogurt Dip

DF option | GF option | NF | V | Vegan option

MAKES 4 SERVINGS

Falafel is typically deep fried, but this recipe allows you to bake it into soft balls your baby will enjoy. The balls and dip are full of folate, vegetarian protein, fiber, and calcium to support your baby's growing body.

FOR THE FALAFEL

1 cup canned chickpeas, drained

½ onion, finely chopped

2 tablespoons chopped fresh parsley

½ teaspoon ground cumin

½ teaspoon garlic powder

½ cup whole wheat flour or oat flour

1 tablespoon olive oil

FOR THE TAHINI YOGURT DIP

¼ cup plain full-fat yogurt

1 tablespoon tahini

¼ teaspoon grated lemon zest

¼ teaspoon garlic powder

TO MAKE THE FALAFEL

1. Preheat the oven to 375°F. Line a baking sheet with parchment.
2. In a blender or food processor, combine the chickpeas, onion, parsley, cumin, garlic powder, and flour and process until smooth.
3. Form the mixture into ½-inch balls. Place them on the prepared baking sheet and gently flatten them with the back of a spoon.
4. Brush the balls with the olive oil. Bake until browned, about 10 minutes per side. Store any unoffered falafel in the refrigerator for up to 3 days or in the freezer for up to 6 months.

TO MAKE THE DIP

In a small bowl, mix all the ingredients until well blended. Store any unoffered dip in the refrigerator for up to 3 days.

TIP: For a nondairy version of the tahini yogurt dip, substitute nondairy yogurt or smooth, blended silken tofu for the plain yogurt.

Cauliflower Tots with Avocado Dipping Sauce

MAKES 4 SERVINGS

FOR THE TOTS

1 egg, beaten

1 cup cauliflower florets, grated on the large holes of a box grater

½ teaspoon onion powder

1 teaspoon whole wheat flour

FOR THE AVOCADO DIPPING SAUCE

½ avocado, peeled and pitted

1 teaspoon lime juice

¼ teaspoon minced garlic

These tots aren't made from taters—they're made from nutritious cauliflower, and you bake them in the oven instead of frying them. Avocado with a little garlic and lime offers a flavor combination that no one, not even a baby, is likely to turn down!

TO MAKE THE TOTS

1. Preheat the oven to 350°F. Line a baking sheet with parchment.
2. Beat the egg in a small bowl. Add the cauliflower, onion powder, and flour. Mix well with a spoon.
3. Form the mixture into ½-inch balls. Place them on the prepared baking sheet. Bake until browned, about 20 minutes per side. Store any unoffered tots in the refrigerator for up to 3 days or in the freezer for up to 6 months.

TO MAKE THE AVOCADO DIPPING SAUCE

1. In a small bowl, combine all the ingredients. Mash the avocado with a fork, making sure to incorporate the juice and the garlic.
2. Add a little water, a teaspoon at a time, if necessary to adjust the consistency. Store any unoffered dipping sauce in the refrigerator for up to 3 days. To keep the dip from browning when you store it, cover the surface with plastic wrap, sealing it tightly around the edges.

TIP: You can use a box grater to grate the cauliflower, or pulse it in a food processor until it is very finely chopped.

Blueberry Flaxseed Mini Muffins

MAKES 18 MUFFINS

2 cups almond flour

2 tablespoons ground flaxseed

¼ teaspoon baking soda

⅛ teaspoon sea salt

¼ cup honey or pure maple syrup

2 tablespoons unsalted butter, melted

2 eggs, beaten

1 cup dairy or nondairy milk

½ cup blueberries

These gluten-free mini muffins freeze well, so it's easy to make a batch and have quick snacks on the go. If you'd like to make these muffins dairy-free, you can replace the butter with olive oil.

1. Preheat the oven to 350°F. Line a mini muffin tin with paper liners.
2. In a medium bowl, whisk together the almond flour, ground flaxseed, baking soda, and salt.
3. In a separate bowl, whisk together the honey, butter, eggs, and milk.
4. Add the wet ingredients to the dry ingredients, using a spatula to gently fold the mixture in until just combined. Fold in the blueberries.
5. Fill each muffin cup three-quarters full.
6. Bake until the muffins are set, 13 to 15 minutes. Store the muffins in the refrigerator for up to 3 days or in the freezer for up to 6 months.

TIP: You can replace the blueberries in this recipe with ½ cup chopped dried fruits, such as cranberries, prunes, or raisins.

Black Bean Cakes with Lime Yogurt Dipping Sauce

DF option GF V

MAKES 4 SERVINGS

FOR THE CAKES

1 cup canned black beans, drained

½ cup grated sweet potato

½ teaspoon onion powder

¼ teaspoon ground cumin

¼ cup almond flour

1 egg, beaten

FOR THE LIME YOGURT DIPPING SAUCE

¼ cup plain full-fat yogurt (nondairy if desired)

¼ teaspoon grated lime zest

1 teaspoon lime juice

1 teaspoon chopped fresh cilantro

These soft, tasty cakes are the perfect finger food for your baby, and she'll love dipping them in the tangy sauce. Black beans are an excellent source of iron to support healthy blood production, and they are also a good source of vegetarian protein.

TO MAKE THE CAKES

1. Preheat the broiler. Line a baking sheet with parchment.
2. In a small bowl, mash the black beans. Add the sweet potato, onion powder, cumin, almond flour, and egg. Mix well with a spoon to combine.
3. Form the mixture into ½-inch balls. Place the balls on the prepared baking sheet and gently flatten them with the back of a spoon.
4. Broil until golden brown, about 10 minutes. Flip and broil until browned on the other side, another 2 to 3 minutes. Store any unoffered cakes in the refrigerator for up to 3 days or in the freezer for up to 6 months.

TO MAKE THE LIME YOGURT DIPPING SAUCE

In a small bowl, combine all the ingredients. Mix well with a spoon. Store any unoffered dipping sauce in the refrigerator for up to 3 days.

TIP: If you don't have sweet potatoes, you can replace them with finely grated carrots.

Oat-Dusted Avocado Cubes

MAKES 2 SERVINGS

¼ cup steel-cut oats
(gluten free if desired)

¼ teaspoon
onion powder

½ avocado, peeled,
pitted, and cut into
¼-inch cubes

If you're short on time, this is a quick, easy finger food to prepare for your little one. Avocados are an excellent source of healthy fats and potassium, while the oats provide plenty of fiber.

1. In a blender or food processor, pulse the oats and onion powder 10 times. Transfer to a small bowl.
2. Toss the avocado cubes in the oat powder. Shake off any excess powder. Store any unoffered cubes in the refrigerator for up to 3 days.

TIP: If you don't have oats on hand, you can replace the oat powder with wheat germ or almond meal.

Chop-Chop Salad

MAKES 4 SERVINGS

½ cucumber, cut
into ¼-inch dice

2 tablespoons chopped
black olives

2 tablespoons crumbled
feta cheese

¼ cup frozen
peas, thawed

¼ teaspoon minced
fresh mint

¼ teaspoon
dried oregano

1 teaspoon olive oil

Simply dice some soft veggies, toss them with some fresh herbs, crumbled cheese, and olive oil, and you've got a salad your baby will love. This one contains bits of olives, which are a great source of healthy fats, antioxidants, and lots of flavor.

In a small bowl, combine all the ingredients and toss to mix. Store any unoffered salad in the refrigerator for up to 3 days.

Pea Cakes

DF | GF option | NF | V

MAKES 4 SERVINGS

2 tablespoons flaxseed

1 cup frozen
peas, thawed

1 egg, beaten

1 teaspoon whole wheat
flour or oat flour

1 teaspoon minced
fresh basil

Starchy peas are an excellent source of protein to help your baby grow, and babies love their slightly sweet flavor. Using thawed frozen peas makes it easy to mash them quickly without having to par-cook them.

1. Preheat the broiler. Line a baking sheet with parchment.
2. In a food processor or blender, pulse the flaxseed about 10 times, until they form a powder.
3. In a small bowl, mash the peas with a fork. Add the flaxseed, egg, flour, and basil. Mix well with a spoon.
4. Form the mixture into ½-inch balls. Place the balls in a single layer on the prepared baking sheet and gently flatten into patties with the back of a spoon.
5. Broil until golden brown, 8 to 10 minutes. Flip and broil until brown on the other side, 2 to 3 minutes more. Store any unoffered cakes in the refrigerator for up to 3 days or in the freezer for up to 6 months.

TIP: You can replace the peas with any drained canned legumes, such as lentils or pinto beans.

Almond-Crusted Chicken Tenders

MAKES 4 SERVINGS

1 egg

1 cup almond flour
plus 1 tablespoon
coconut flour or 1 cup
whole wheat flour

¼ teaspoon garlic powder

¼ teaspoon
onion powder

Pinch paprika

8 ounces chicken
tenders, cut into
¼-inch-thick pieces

Using almond flour in place of wheat flour adds fiber and vitamin E to this recipe and makes these chicken tenders gluten free. If you don't have almond flour, you can make your own by pulsing blanched, slivered almonds in the food processor until powdery.

1. Preheat the oven to 475°F. Line a baking sheet with parchment.
2. Beat the egg in a small bowl. In another small bowl, combine the almond flour, coconut flour, garlic powder, onion powder, and paprika and mix well with a spoon.
3. Dip each chicken piece into the beaten egg and then coat with the almond flour mixture. Place the coated chicken pieces in a single layer on the prepared baking sheet.
4. Bake until the chicken tenders are cooked through and the crust is golden, about 20 minutes. Store any unoffered chicken tenders in the refrigerator for up to 3 days or in the freezer for up to 6 months.

TIP: Turkey cutlets make a great substitution for the chicken in this recipe.

Zucchini Pizza Bites

MAKES 4 SERVINGS

1 tablespoon olive oil

½ small zucchini, cut into ¼-inch-thick rounds

½ cup canned crushed tomatoes

¼ teaspoon garlic powder

¼ teaspoon dried oregano

½ cup finely grated mozzarella cheese

Thin zucchini rounds with marinara sauce and mozzarella cheese make a tasty vegetarian "pizza" that is the perfect size for little fingers. You can make the tomato sauce ahead of time and freeze it in single-serving portions for later use.

1. Preheat the broiler. Line a baking sheet with parchment.
2. In a large sauté pan, heat the olive oil over medium-high heat until it shimmers.
3. Add the zucchini rounds and cook until softened, about 5 minutes. Place the zucchini rounds in a single layer on the prepared baking sheet.
4. In a small bowl, combine the tomatoes, garlic powder, and oregano. Mix well with a spoon. Spoon an equal portion of the tomato sauce on each zucchini round and top with an equal portion of the grated cheese.
5. Broil until the cheese melts, about 5 minutes. Store any unoffered pizza bites in the refrigerator for up to 3 days or in the freezer for up to 6 months.

Grated Root Vegetable Salad

DF GF NF Vegan

MAKES 4 SERVINGS

1 carrot, peeled
and grated

2 beets, peeled
and grated

1 parsnip, peeled
and grated

½ teaspoon chopped
fresh tarragon

1 squeeze of juice
from a fresh orange

Grating root vegetables makes them easy for babies to grasp and eat. This salad is also colorful and filled with antioxidants to support your baby's immune system. Use the large holes on a box grater or the grating blade of your food processor to prepare the vegetables.

In a small bowl, combine all the ingredients and toss to mix. Store any unoffered salad in the refrigerator for up to 3 days or in the freezer for up to 6 months.

TIP: Add some fresh or thawed frozen green peas to the salad for a pop of color, a bit of protein, and extra flavor.

Ground Beef and Sweet Potato Mini Meatballs

MAKES 4 SERVINGS

8 ounces ground beef

¼ onion, grated

1 egg, beaten

½ cup grated
sweet potato

¼ teaspoon dried thyme

¼ teaspoon
mustard powder

¼ teaspoon garlic powder

These soft, tasty meatballs are the perfect protein source for your baby, and their small size makes them fun for tiny hands to grasp. You can offer marinara (from the Zucchini Pizza Bites recipe on page 166) as a dipping sauce, if you like.

1. Preheat the oven to 350°F. Line a baking sheet with parchment.
2. In a small bowl, combine all the ingredients and mix until well combined. Form the mixture into ½-inch balls and place them in a single layer on the prepared baking sheet.
3. Bake until cooked through, about 20 minutes. Store any unoffered meatballs in the refrigerator for up to 3 days or in the freezer for up to 6 months.

TIP: Adding up to ¼ cup grated vegetables in addition to the sweet potato is a great way to give your baby more veggies and to lighten the texture of the meatballs. Also, grated root vegetables like carrots work here in place of the sweet potato, as does grated zucchini.

Turkey and Squash Meatballs with Cranberry Sauce

DF option **GF** **NF**

MAKES 4 SERVINGS

FOR THE MEATBALLS

8 ounces ground turkey

¼ cup dried cranberries, finely chopped

¼ onion, grated

½ cup grated winter squash (such as acorn or butternut squash)

½ teaspoon dried sage

FOR THE CRANBERRY DIPPING SAUCE

2 (1-ounce) freezer tray cubes cranberry puree (page 62), thawed

¼ cup plain full-fat yogurt (nondairy if desired)

Pinch dried sage

Sage and cranberries give these meatballs a tasty fall flavor. Turkey is a great source of protein for your baby, and the winter squash is loaded with vitamin A, which supports your baby's developing eyesight.

TO MAKE THE MEATBALLS

1. Preheat the oven to 350°F. Line a baking sheet with parchment.
2. In a small bowl, combine all the ingredients and mix until well combined. Form the mixture into ½-inch balls and place them in a single layer on the prepared baking sheet.
3. Bake until cooked through, about 20 minutes. Store any unoffered meatballs in the refrigerator for up to 3 days or in the freezer for up to 6 months.

TO MAKE THE CRANBERRY DIPPING SAUCE

Combine all the ingredients in a small bowl and mix well with a spoon. Store any unoffered dipping sauce in the refrigerator for up to 3 days.

TIP: You can use grated pumpkin in place of the winter squash here. To grate the pumpkin, cut fresh pumpkin from the rind and remove the seeds and pulp. Then, grate it on a box grater.

Roasted Veggie Sticks

DF GF NF Vegan

MAKES 4 SERVINGS

½ zucchini, peeled and cut into ¼-inch-thick matchsticks

1 beet, peeled and cut into ¼-inch-thick matchsticks

¼ butternut squash, rind and pulp removed, cut into ¼-inch-thick matchsticks

1 tablespoon olive oil

¼ teaspoon ground cinnamon

¼ teaspoon ground allspice

Veggie sticks are super simple to prepare. This is also a versatile recipe since you can use any type of vegetable you have on hand in place of those called for in the recipe. The light spices add a sweet surprise.

1. Preheat the oven to 450°F. Line a baking sheet with parchment.
2. In a small bowl, combine all the ingredients and toss to mix.
3. Place the sticks in a single layer on the prepared baking sheet. Bake, stirring once or twice, until browned, 20 to 25 minutes. Store any unoffered sticks in the refrigerator for up to 3 days or in the freezer for up to 6 months.

TIP: Does your child love to dip everything? If so, you can quickly whip up an orange dipping sauce that will sweetly complement the savory fries. Just whisk together ¼ cup plain full-fat yogurt, 2 tablespoons orange juice, and a pinch of ground cinnamon.

TIP: Other veggies to try in this recipe include chayote, pattypan squash, and parsnips. You can also use hard fruits, such as apples or pears, to make the sticks.

Cod and Zucchini Cakes with Lemon Dill Sauce

GF option

MAKES 4 SERVINGS

FOR THE COD AND ZUCCHINI CAKES

8 ounces cod, cut into ½-inch cubes

½ small zucchini, grated

½ teaspoon chopped fresh dill

¼ teaspoon lemon zest

¼ teaspoon garlic powder

¼ cup almond flour or whole wheat flour

1 teaspoon coconut flour (use only if using the almond flour)

1 egg, beaten

¼ onion, grated

FOR THE LEMON DILL SAUCE

¼ cup plain full-fat yogurt

Juice of ½ lemon

¼ teaspoon chopped fresh dill

These are great snacks for your little one, and they're absolutely one of Julian's favorites. I must admit that our whole family loves them, so you might want to consider making a larger batch by doubling or tripling the recipe. Steaming the cod ahead of time makes it soft enough to work with and allows these fish cakes to cook quickly.

TO MAKE THE COD AND ZUCCHINI CAKES

1. Preheat the oven to 350°F. Line a baking sheet with parchment.
2. In a small saucepan with a steamer insert, bring 1 inch of water to a boil. Add the cod. Cover and steam until the cod is opaque, 5 to 10 minutes.
3. Chop the cod into small pieces (or flake it with a fork) and put it in a small bowl. Gently fold in the remaining ingredients.
4. Form the mixture into ½-inch balls and place on the prepared baking sheet. Gently flatten the balls with the back of a spoon.
5. Bake until the cakes are golden brown, about 20 minutes. Store any unoffered cakes in the refrigerator for up to 3 days or in the freezer for up to 6 months.

TO MAKE THE LEMON DILL SAUCE

In a small bowl, whisk together all the ingredients. Store any unoffered sauce in the refrigerator for up to 3 days.

TIP: You can substitute any type of white fish for the cod in this recipe. If you want to use salmon instead, change the flavor profile a bit by replacing the dill in the cakes and the sauce with an equal amount of chopped fresh tarragon, and replace the lemon juice in the sauce with the juice of ½ orange.

Very Berry Salad

DF GF NF Vegan

MAKES 4 (½ CUP) SERVINGS

1 cup chopped strawberries

½ cup blueberries

½ cup raspberries

1 (1-ounce) freezer tray cube blackberry puree (page 56), thawed

¼ teaspoon ground allspice

Your baby will love the sweetness of the berries in this tasty salad. It's loaded with antioxidants and vitamin C to support a healthy immune system. You can substitute an equal amount of other chopped fruits, such as 1 peach or nectarine or ½ cup chopped melon, or unsweetened shredded coconut.

In a small bowl, mix all the ingredients until well combined. Store any unoffered salad in the refrigerator for up to 3 days.

TIP: This is a great ice pop base as well. Puree the mixture in the blender, omitting the thawed puree cube and adding a little apple juice, coconut milk, or orange juice to adjust the consistency. Then freeze in ice pop molds.

Chicken and Apple Meatballs with Pear Sauce

MAKES 4 SERVINGS

FOR THE MEATBALLS

8 ounces ground chicken

½ apple, peeled, cored, and grated

¼ onion, grated

1 teaspoon chopped fresh tarragon

Pinch ground nutmeg

1 egg, beaten

FOR THE PEAR SAUCE

2 (1-ounce) cubes pear puree (page 45), thawed

¼ cup plain full-fat yogurt (nondairy if desired)

½ teaspoon chopped fresh tarragon

With apple in the meatballs and pear in the sauce, this recipe gives your baby a fruity infusion along with protein to support her growing body. Tarragon has a tasty licorice-type flavor that works well with these fruits.

TO MAKE THE MEATBALLS

1. Preheat the oven to 350°F. Line a baking sheet with parchment.
2. In a small bowl, combine all the ingredients and mix until well combined. Form the mixture into ½-inch balls and place them in a single layer on the prepared baking sheet.
3. Bake until cooked through, about 20 minutes. Store any unoffered meatballs in the refrigerator for up to 3 days or in the freezer for up to 6 months.

TO MAKE THE PEAR SAUCE

In a small bowl, whisk together all the ingredients. Store any unoffered sauce in the refrigerator for up to 3 days.

TIP: Add a little extra chewiness to the meatballs by mixing 2 tablespoons finely chopped dried apples or apricots into the meat mixture.

Mini Banana Pancakes with Almond Butter Sauce

 DF option **GF** **V**

MAKES 4 SERVINGS

FOR THE PANCAKES

1 banana, peeled

2 eggs, beaten

¼ teaspoon
ground nutmeg

Olive oil cooking spray

**FOR THE ALMOND
BUTTER SAUCE**

1 tablespoon
almond butter

1 (1-ounce) freezer tray
cube apricot puree
(page 58), thawed

¼ cup plain full-fat yogurt
(nondairy if desired)

Pinch ground nutmeg

Just three ingredients and a little oil are all you need to prepare these super easy and tasty banana pancakes. They're also a great source of protein and potassium, and your baby will love how the almond butter sauce complements the flavor of the bananas.

TO MAKE THE PANCAKES

1. In a small bowl, mash the banana. Add the eggs and nutmeg and mix well with a spoon.

2. Preheat a griddle or nonstick skillet over medium-high heat. Spritz with olive oil.

3. Working in 1- to 2-tablespoon portions, drop the batter onto the griddle or skillet. Cook until bubbles form on the top of the pancakes, about 2 minutes. Flip the pancakes and cook on the other side for an additional 2 minutes. Store any unoffered pancakes in the refrigerator for up to 3 days or in the freezer for up to 6 months.

TO MAKE THE ALMOND BUTTER SAUCE

In a small bowl, whisk together all the ingredients. Store any unoffered sauce in the refrigerator for up to 3 days.

TIP: You can dress up these pancakes by adding 2 tablespoons blueberries or chopped dried fruit to the batter.

8

12 TO 18 MONTHS
TODDLER MEALS

Congratulations! You've made it to the 1-year mark. Your baby is officially a toddler now, and you both have probably learned a lot about eating in the first year of her life. She's made the transition to solid foods now and no longer needs purees (though that doesn't mean she won't stop enjoying them—many 3- and 4-year-olds still love to eat pureed fruits and vegetables). While the meals in this chapter are specifically designed with your toddler in mind, you can also make larger batches to feed to older siblings or even the entire family. The meals contain nutritious whole foods, such as meats, whole grains, herbs, spices, vegetables, fruits, and legumes. There are many protein- and iron-rich vegetarian options, as well, if you are raising a vegetarian or vegan baby.

DEVELOPMENTALLY SPEAKING

All children are different, but your toddler will show signs of readiness that she can eat toddler meals and forego purees.

* She doesn't gag or choke when she eats chunky purees and other solid foods.
* She eats finger foods by herself without needing to be fed.
* She feeds herself (albeit messily) with a spoon.
* She shows interest in more grown-up versions of food, such as your meals.
* She enjoys foods in a variety of flavors and textures.
* Your toddler may show picky eater tendencies at this stage. Continue to offer a variety of foods.

PORTION GUIDELINES

Appetites vary greatly at this stage, so the guidelines below are very general.

* If your child is still breastfeeding, offer breast milk as a supplement to whole foods.
* Feed your toddler ¼ to ½ cup of solid foods four to six times per day.

FAQ

Q: My baby's 1 year old! Does she still need breast milk or formula?

A: While your baby may not need breast milk or formula for nutritional value as much as she did during the first year, I recommend continuing to breastfeed if you're up for it, while you can discontinue to formula feed. The breastfeeding provides not just nutrition but comfort. That said, even if you are breastfeeding, now is the time to offer your toddler dairy milk or, if you want to avoid dairy, introduce nondairy options as your little one moves away from the bottle.

Q: My toddler seems extremely picky. How can I combat this?

A: At this age, it's very common for toddlers to become selective about what they'll eat. But picky eating is not simply saying no to new foods. Kids (and adults) can have opinions of what they like or dislike, and that's not necessarily picky. Nutritionists consider children to be picky when they start to reject foods they used to enjoy, reducing the number of foods they will eat to a small number. When this happens, try not to give in by offering just the one or two things she will eat—though it'll be hard! Continue to offer a variety of foods, even foods your child rejects, but don't force anything. Bring little ones on food shopping trips and into the kitchen (in the high chair, initially) to watch you prepare food, to pique interest. Also, role modeling is just as important when it comes to food as it is to manners. Eat the foods you want your little one to eat. And keep in mind that toddlers often eat voraciously one day and hardly at all the next. This is totally normal. Think about their food consumption more on a week-to-week basis than on a day-to-day basis.

Oatmeal with Plums and Coconut

DF option GF option NF V Vegan option

MAKES 3 (3-OUNCE) SERVINGS

1 cup water

1 cup dairy or nondairy milk

½ cup steel-cut oats (gluten free if desired)

¼ cup chopped plum

1 tablespoon unsweetened shredded coconut flakes

When it comes to oatmeal, I like to make a big batch in advance so it's ready when we want it (see the tip about doing this with a slow cooker). One of the things I love about oatmeal is that it's a blank canvas to which you can add a variety of tastes and textures. If I don't have fresh plum or another stone fruit, I'll just thaw any frozen organic fruit that's in my freezer and pour some of the juices that pooled during thawing over the oatmeal for natural, nutrient-packed sweetness. We love the flavor and crunch of coconut flakes, but chia seeds or ground flaxseed are great options, too.

1. In a small saucepan, bring the water and milk to a rolling boil over medium-high heat.
2. Stir in the oats and plum.
3. Reduce the heat to low. Cover and simmer until the oats are soft, about 15 minutes.
4. Cool slightly before serving, or cool by adding a little more milk. Top with the coconut flakes.
5. Store any unoffered oatmeal in the refrigerator for up to 3 days or in the freezer for up to 6 months.

TIP: To make this recipe in the slow cooker, you'll need to make a larger batch. Double or triple the recipe as desired, and place the oats and fruit in the slow cooker. Cover and cook on low for 8 hours or on high for 4 hours. Top with the coconut flakes before serving.

Fruity Breakfast Quinoa

MAKES 4 (4-OUNCE) SERVINGS

½ cup quinoa

1 cup dairy or nondairy milk

⅛ teaspoon ground cinnamon

Pinch ground allspice

½ apple, peeled, cored, and cut into ¼-inch dice

½ pear, peeled, cored, and cut into ¼-inch dice

Quinoa has a great texture for breakfast because it closely resembles other hot cereals, while apples and pears add subtle sweetness. This is another terrific, protein-rich breakfast for the whole family.

1. Using a fine-mesh sieve, run the quinoa under cold water to rinse. Drain.
2. In a medium saucepan, combine the quinoa, milk, cinnamon, allspice, apple, and pear. Bring to a boil over medium-high heat, stirring frequently. Reduce the heat to medium-low.
3. Cover and simmer, stirring occasionally, until the liquid is absorbed, about 15 minutes. Store any unoffered breakfast quinoa in the refrigerator for up to 3 days or in the freezer for up to 6 months.

Chia Breakfast Pudding

MAKES 2 (3-OUNCE) SERVINGS

1 cup dairy or nondairy milk

2 tablespoons chia seeds

⅛ teaspoon ground cinnamon

¼ teaspoon vanilla extract

½ cup chopped fresh strawberries

Chia seeds are high in fiber and rich in omega-3 fatty acids. They are also a great source of nutrients that promote development of healthy bones. When you soak them, they make a thick, gel-like substance that is similar in texture to tapioca, and they have a neutral flavor that works with a variety of tasty ingredients.

1. Measure the milk into a 2-cup measuring cup, and then add the chia seeds, cinnamon, and vanilla. Mix well with a spoon. Refrigerate for 30 minutes.
2. Stir the strawberries into the measuring cup, and then pour the mixture into a small saucepan. Bring the mixture to a boil over medium-high heat, stirring frequently. Reduce the heat to medium-low.
3. Cover and simmer, stirring occasionally, until the liquid is absorbed, about 15 minutes. Store any unoffered breakfast pudding in the refrigerator for up to 3 days.

Scrambled Eggs with Sweet Potato and Bell Pepper

MAKES 4 SERVINGS

2 tablespoons olive oil

½ onion, finely chopped

½ sweet potato, peeled and cut into ¼-inch dice

½ red bell pepper, seeded and finely chopped

4 eggs, beaten

½ teaspoon dried thyme

¼ teaspoon sea salt

Because the bell pepper is integrated into the egg, this recipe makes a healthy one-dish meal. The pepper adds subtle sweetness, a tiny bit of crunch, and plenty of vitamins, while the eggs are an excellent source of protein.

1. In a large sauté pan, heat the olive oil over medium-high heat until it shimmers. Add the onion, sweet potato, and bell pepper. Cook, stirring occasionally, until the vegetables are browned, 7 to 10 minutes. Reduce the heat to medium-low.

2. In a small bowl, whisk together the eggs, thyme, and salt.

3. Add the eggs to the pan. Cook, stirring occasionally, until the eggs are set, about 3 minutes. Store any unoffered scrambled eggs in the refrigerator for up to 3 days or in the freezer for up to 6 months.

TIP: For extra calcium, add ¼ cup of grated cheese after the eggs have cooked.

Tofu Scramble with Zucchini and Carrots

MAKES 4 SERVINGS

2 tablespoons olive oil

1 zucchini, cut into ¼-inch dice

1 carrot, peeled and cut into ¼-inch dice

½ red onion, finely chopped

8 ounces silken tofu, cut into ¼-inch pieces

½ teaspoon dried oregano

¼ teaspoon sea salt

This is a great high-protein dish, especially for vegetarians or kids with an egg allergy. The neutral base of the tofu elevates the flavors of the sautéed vegetables. I often make this for a quickie "breakfast for dinner" option.

1. In a large sauté pan, heat the olive oil over medium-high until it shimmers. Add the zucchini, carrot, and onion and cook, stirring occasionally, until the vegetables begin to brown, 5 to 7 minutes.

2. Add the tofu, oregano, and salt. Cook, stirring occasionally, until warm, another 5 minutes. Store any unoffered tofu scramble in the refrigerator for up to 3 days or in the freezer for up to 6 months.

French Toast Fingers with Berry Sauce

GF option NF V

MAKES 4 SERVINGS

2 eggs, beaten

2 cups dairy or nondairy milk

½ teaspoon vanilla extract

½ teaspoon grated orange zest

⅛ teaspoon ground nutmeg

4 slices whole wheat or gluten-free bread, crusts removed, each cut lengthwise into four strips

1 tablespoon unsalted butter

4 (1-ounce) freezer tray cubes berry puree (page 56), thawed

Leftover fruit purees make a tasty and nutritious dipping sauce for French toast. You can choose whole wheat or gluten-free bread, depending on your preference and your baby's dietary requirements.

1. In a large bowl, whisk together the eggs, milk, vanilla, orange zest, and nutmeg.
2. Soak the bread strips in the mixture until saturated, 3 to 4 minutes.
3. Preheat a nonstick skillet over medium-high heat. Add the butter.
4. When the butter has melted, place the soaked bread in the skillet. Cook until the custard sets, about 5 minutes. Flip and cook for an additional 3 minutes. Store any unoffered French toast in the refrigerator for up to 3 days or in the freezer for up to 6 months.
5. Serve with the thawed berry puree for dipping. Store any unoffered dipping sauce in the refrigerator for up to 3 days.

TIP: Almond butter and other nut butters also make a good dipping sauce for these French toast sticks, and they add additional protein. Warm 2 tablespoons on the stove top and stir in a teaspoon or two of milk to adjust the consistency.

Pumpkin Oat Pancakes with Apple Butter

GF option NF V

MAKES 4 SERVINGS

FOR THE
APPLE BUTTER

2 pounds apples (6 to
8 apples), peeled, cored,
and chopped

¼ cup apple cider vinegar

1 teaspoon ground
cinnamon

½ teaspoon
ground ginger

FOR THE PANCAKES

1 cup oat flour
(gluten-free if desired)

½ teaspoon baking soda

¼ teaspoon ground
cinnamon

¼ teaspoon
ground ginger

Pinch ground nutmeg

Pinch sea salt

2 eggs

1 cup canned
pumpkin puree

¼ cup dairy or
nondairy milk

2 tablespoons unsalted
butter, melted, plus extra
for the skillet

1 teaspoon
vanilla extract

These pancakes make a delicious breakfast or snack that the whole family will love. To save time, you can make the apple butter in advance and freeze it. Then when you serve these pancakes, just thaw the portion you need, and enjoy.

TO MAKE THE APPLE BUTTER

In a large pot, combine all the ingredients. Simmer for 30 minutes, stirring occasionally. Transfer the apples to a blender or food processor and puree until smooth. Store unoffered apple butter in the refrigerator for up to 3 days or in the freezer for up to 6 months.

TO MAKE THE PANCAKES

1. In a medium bowl, whisk together the oat flour, baking soda, cinnamon, ginger, nutmeg, and salt.
2. In another medium bowl, beat the eggs, and then whisk in the pumpkin puree, milk, butter, and vanilla.
3. Add the wet ingredients to the dry ingredients, folding in with a rubber spatula until just combined. Do not overmix.
4. Heat a nonstick skillet over medium-high heat. Grease with butter. Working in scant ¼-cup portions, pour the batter into the skillet. Cook until bubbles form, 3 to 5 minutes. Flip and cook until the pancakes are cooked through, another 3 to 5 minutes. Store unoffered pancakes in the refrigerator for up to 3 days or in the freezer for up to 6 months.

TIP: If you can't find oat flour, you can make your own by pulsing steel-cut or rolled oats in the blender or food processor until they are finely ground and have a flour-like consistency.

Yogurt and Dried Cranberry Oatmeal

GF option NF V

MAKES 4 SERVINGS

1 cup water

1 cup orange juice

1 cup dairy or
nondairy milk

1 cup steel-cut oats
(gluten free if desired)

½ cup dried cranberries

½ teaspoon grated
orange zest

½ teaspoon
ground ginger

1 cup plain full-fat yogurt

This oatmeal serves up the sweet-tart flavor of cranberries along with a hint of spice and the gentle sweetness of orange. While the recipe doesn't call for any sweeteners, you may add a teaspoon of honey or pure maple syrup if you wish.

1. In a large saucepan, bring the water, orange juice, and milk to a boil. Stir in the oats, cranberries, orange zest, and ginger. Reduce the heat to low.
2. Cover and simmer until the oats reach the desired consistency, 15 to 20 minutes.
3. Stir in the yogurt before serving. Store unoffered yogurt and oatmeal in the refrigerator for up to 3 days or freeze the oatmeal without the yogurt for up to 6 months.

Avocado Toast

DF GF option NF Vegan

MAKES 4 SERVINGS

2 slices whole wheat
or gluten-free bread

½ avocado, peeled
and pitted

1 teaspoon lemon juice

Pinch sea salt

Pinch paprika

Something as simple as avocado and toast shouldn't need a recipe, but it's here to remind you that a rich, delicious, and nutritious meal doesn't need to be complicated. I offer a basic preparation, but consider adding thinly sliced radishes or cucumbers, a little curry powder, or mixing goat cheese with the avocado.

1. In a toaster, toast the bread to the desired darkness.
2. In a small bowl, mash together the avocado, lemon juice, salt, and paprika with a fork. Spread the avocado mash on the toast. Cut the toast into quarters. Store the avocado mash in the refrigerator for up to 3 days, with plastic wrap directly touching the surface of the avocado so it doesn't come in contact with the air.

Cottage Cheese with Flaxseed and Stone Fruit

MAKES 1 SERVING

½ cup cottage cheese

5 cherries, pitted and chopped

1 plum, pitted and chopped

1 tablespoon flaxseed

This makes a quick and healthy breakfast for your toddler, and it doesn't involve any cooking. It's also packed with protein to support your toddler's growing body, and plenty of calcium and other minerals for growing bones.

In a small bowl, combine all the ingredients. Mix well with a spoon to combine. Store any unoffered cottage cheese mixture in the refrigerator for up to 3 days.

TIP: You can swap out the cherries for any chopped fruit in this recipe. If you have any leftover fruit or veggie puree cubes, you can also thaw one or two of those and stir it in with the cottage cheese and fruit.

Almond Butter Sandwich with Raspberry Mash

MAKES 2 SERVINGS

2 slices whole wheat or gluten-free bread

2 tablespoons almond butter

8 to 12 raspberries, mashed with a fork

This simple sandwich is easy to prepare and tasty, and it's loaded with healthy nutrients. The raspberry mash takes the place of jelly or jam, which can be loaded with added sugar. If you prefer, toast the bread before spreading the other ingredients on.

1. Spread one piece of bread with the almond butter. Top it with the mashed raspberries and the other piece of bread.
2. Cut the sandwich into quarters. Store any unoffered sandwich quarters in the refrigerator for up to 3 days.

TIP: You can also use fruit-only raspberry preserves or spread (no sugar added) or a fruit puree in this sandwich.

Avocado Egg Salad Sandwich

DF option · GF option · NF · V

MAKES 4 SERVINGS

½ avocado, peeled and pitted

1 teaspoon fresh lemon juice

Pinch sea salt

½ teaspoon Dijon mustard

1 tablespoon plain full-fat yogurt (nondairy if desired)

1 tablespoon chopped fresh chives

2 hard-boiled eggs, peeled and chopped

4 slices whole wheat bread or gluten-free bread

If you hard-boil and chop your eggs ahead of time, you can make this sandwich quickly. Store any leftover egg salad in the refrigerator without the bread, and make the sandwiches as needed.

1. In a small bowl, mash the avocado, lemon juice, salt, mustard, yogurt, and chives with a fork, mixing well.
2. Gently stir in the chopped eggs.
3. Spread the egg mixture on two pieces of bread, topping each with a second piece of bread. Cut in quarters to serve. Store the egg salad in the refrigerator, separate from the bread, for up to 3 days.

TIP: To hard-boil eggs, put them in a single layer in a large saucepan covered by about an inch of water. Bring the water to a boil. Cover the pot, turn off the heat, and allow the eggs to sit for 14 minutes. Plunge the eggs into cold water to stop the cooking.

Tuna Salad Sandwich

MAKES 4 SERVINGS

¼ cup plain full-fat yogurt (nondairy if desired)

1 tablespoon lemon juice

1 teaspoon Dijon mustard

½ teaspoon dried tarragon

Pinch sea salt

1 (4-ounce) can water-packed tuna, drained

¼ cup fresh green peas

4 slices whole wheat bread or gluten-free bread

Using yogurt in place of mayonnaise here provides nutritious protein and calcium. Fresh peas add a pop of green color and a slight crunch to the sandwich. When served with your toddler's favorite fruit, this makes a nutritious, balanced meal.

1. In a small bowl, whisk together the yogurt, lemon juice, mustard, tarragon, and salt.
2. In a large bowl, combine the tuna and peas. Stir in the yogurt mixture.
3. Spread the mixture on two pieces of bread. Top each with a second piece of bread. Cut in quarters to serve. Store the tuna salad in the refrigerator, separate from the bread, for up to 3 days.

TIP: If fresh peas aren't available, add one or two thawed freezer tray cubes of pea puree or another green veggie puree, such as kale or spinach.

Grilled Cheese Sandwich

MAKES 1 SERVING

1 slice whole wheat or gluten-free bread

1 teaspoon Dijon mustard

¼ cup baby spinach, finely chopped

2 tablespoons grated Cheddar cheese

3 teaspoons unsalted butter, melted

Kids love a grilled cheese, with its gooey melty center and buttery, crisp, golden exterior. These grilled cheese fingers offer calcium, magnesium, and other bone-healthy ingredients. Plus they're really easy to make in small or large amounts.

1. Cut the bread in half. Spread the bread with the mustard. Top one half with the spinach and the grated cheese. Top that with the second half of bread.
2. Brush the melted butter on the outside of both sides of the sandwich.
3. Preheat a nonstick skillet over medium-high heat. Place the sandwich in the skillet.
4. Cook until the bread is golden and the cheese is melted, 3 to 5 minutes per side. Cut the sandwich into two pieces. These don't keep or reheat well.

Pea Soup with Ham

DF option | **GF** | **NF**

MAKES 4 SERVINGS

2 tablespoons olive oil

1 onion, chopped

4 cups chicken broth

4 cups fresh or
frozen peas

½ teaspoon sea salt

⅓ cup fresh basil leaves

½ cup dairy or
nondairy milk

4 ounces ham,
finely chopped

Rich and savory, this is comfort food that doesn't compromise on vegetables. Peas are a great source of protein, and with their healthy dose of folate, they support your baby's brain development. You can use fresh or frozen peas for this soup.

1. In a large pot, heat the olive oil over medium-high heat until it shimmers. Add the onion and cook, stirring frequently, until it is soft, about 5 minutes.

2. Add the broth, peas, and salt. Simmer until the peas are tender, about 5 minutes.

3. Transfer the soup to a blender, along with the basil and milk. Puree until smooth. Return the soup to the pot.

4. Add the ham. Simmer until the ham is warm, 3 to 4 minutes more. Store the soup in the refrigerator for up to 3 days or in the freezer for up to 6 months.

TIP: When pureeing hot liquids, first remove the center of the blender lid to allow steam to escape. Then put the lid on the blender, fold a towel over the hole in the lid to protect your hand and absorb the steam, and hold the lid in place as you puree. Pause every 10 seconds or so to allow more steam to escape.

Black Beans and Rice with Tropical Salsa

MAKES 8 SERVINGS

FOR THE BEANS AND RICE

2 tablespoons olive oil

¾ red onion, finely chopped

2 garlic cloves, minced

1 (14-ounce) can black beans, drained

½ cup vegetable broth

1 teaspoon ground cumin

¼ teaspoon chili powder

½ teaspoon sea salt

2 cups cooked brown rice

FOR THE SALSA

¼ red onion, finely chopped

1 mango, peeled, pitted, and cut into ¼-inch dice

Juice of 1 lime

2 tablespoons chopped fresh cilantro

This dish is a great source of plant-based protein, and your toddler will love the sweet flavor of the juicy salsa with the black beans. Other family members will enjoy it, too, so this is a great dish for family mealtime, with enough to go around.

TO MAKE THE BEANS AND RICE

1. In a large pot, heat the olive oil over medium-high heat until it shimmers. Add the red onion. Cook, stirring occasionally, until the onion is soft, about 5 minutes.

2. Add the garlic and cook, stirring constantly, until fragrant, about 30 seconds.

3. Add the beans, vegetable broth, cumin, chili powder, and salt. Cook for 5 minutes, stirring occasionally.

4. Stir in the rice. Cook, stirring frequently, until the rice is warm, about 3 minutes more. Store any unoffered portions in the refrigerator for up to 3 days or in the freezer for up to 6 months.

TO MAKE THE SALSA

In a small bowl, mix together all the ingredients. Spoon equal portions over the beans and rice. Store the salsa in the refrigerator for up to 3 days.

TIP: You can substitute your favorite jarred salsa for the fresh salsa to save time.

Barley with Lentils and Kale

MAKES 8 SERVINGS

2½ cups vegetable broth

1 cup barley

1 (14-ounce) can lentils, drained

1 (14-ounce) can crushed tomatoes

1 teaspoon onion powder

½ teaspoon garlic powder

½ teaspoon sea salt

2 cups stemmed and chopped kale

Barley and lentils come together to give your little one a toothsome meal that's packed with filling, nutritional goodness. Don't worry that this grain + legume + green combo might be too healthy to taste good. The broth and onion and garlic powders flavor everything nicely. If you freeze single servings of this tasty treat, you've got a healthy meatless meal ready to go without a lot of fuss.

1. In a large saucepan, bring the vegetable broth to a boil over medium-high heat. Add the barley. Reduce the heat to medium-low. Cover and cook, stirring occasionally, until the barley is tender, 40 to 50 minutes.

2. Turn the heat to medium. Stir in the lentils, tomatoes, onion powder, garlic powder, salt, and kale. Simmer, stirring occasionally, until the kale is tender, 5 to 10 minutes. Store the soup in the refrigerator for up to 3 days or in the freezer for up to 6 months.

TIP: To make homemade vegetable stock, save your vegetable trimmings such as onion and garlic skins, carrot peels, celery tops, and mushroom stems in a zip-top bag in the freezer. When you have a bunch saved up, dump them into a large pot of water and simmer for about 4 hours. Strain out the solids. The stock will keep in the freezer for up to 6 months.

Ground Beef Stir-Fry

MAKES 8 SERVINGS

2 tablespoons olive oil

1 pound ground beef

1 red pepper, seeded
and chopped

1 cup sliced mushrooms

½ onion, chopped

3 cups baby spinach

2 garlic cloves, minced

2 tablespoons
low-sodium soy sauce

Juice of ½ orange

¼ cup chicken broth

½ teaspoon
mustard powder

½ teaspoon
ground ginger

This is a classic, quick, and easy go-to dish for any season that you can improvise using any vegetables you happen to have on hand. This is another dish your whole family will enjoy, so it's a good thing that this recipe makes enough to go around the dinner table.

1. In a large sauté pan or wok, heat the olive oil over medium-high heat until it shimmers. Add the ground beef and cook, stirring frequently, until brown, about 6 minutes.

2. Add the red pepper, mushrooms, and onion. Cook, stirring frequently, until the vegetables are soft, about 5 minutes.

3. Add the spinach and cook just until it wilts, 1 minute more. Add the garlic and cook, stirring constantly, until fragrant, about 30 seconds.

4. In a small bowl, whisk together the soy sauce, orange juice, chicken broth, mustard powder, and ground ginger until smooth. Add it to the stir-fry.

5. Cook, stirring constantly, until the sauce thickens, 1 to 2 minutes more. Store the stir-fry in the refrigerator for up to 3 days or in the freezer for up to 6 months.

TIP: Serve this stir-fry over cooked brown rice, quinoa, or barley, if desired.

Macaroni with Spinach Pesto

NF option **V**

MAKES 8 SERVINGS

8 ounces whole wheat elbow macaroni

2 cups baby spinach

¼ cup fresh basil leaves

1 garlic clove, peeled

¼ cup olive oil

1 teaspoon grated lemon zest

¼ cup grated Parmesan cheese

2 tablespoons flaxseed

¼ cup chopped walnuts

¼ teaspoon sea salt

You can use any type of pasta you think your baby might enjoy, so don't feel limited to elbow macaroni. For those just getting used to using a fork, penne is another great option, as it's easy to slide the fork through. The spinach pesto is loaded with healthy antioxidants, iron, and vitamin C and also serves as a good source of vegetarian protein and calcium.

1. Cook the pasta according to the package directions. Drain and set aside.
2. In a food processor or blender, combine the spinach, basil, garlic, olive oil, lemon zest, cheese, flaxseed, walnuts, and salt. Process until smooth.
3. Toss the pesto with the warm pasta. Store unoffered portions in the refrigerator for up to 3 days or in the freezer for up to 6 months.

TIP: To make this recipe nut-free, you can replace the walnuts in this recipe with an equal amount of pumpkin seeds or sunflower seeds.

White Bean and Butternut Squash Stew

MAKES 4 SERVINGS

2 tablespoons olive oil

½ onion, finely chopped

½ butternut squash, peeled, seeded, and cut into ¼-inch dice

2 garlic cloves, minced

1 (14-ounce) can white beans, drained

1 cup canned crushed tomatoes

½ teaspoon dried rosemary

¼ teaspoon sea salt

Hearty and comforting, this is a family-friendly stew to warm everyone up on a cool winter night. To save some prep time, buy frozen organic butternut squash chunks and thaw 2 cups overnight in the refrigerator.

1. In a large sauté pan, heat the olive oil over medium-high heat until it shimmers. Add the onion and butternut squash. Cook, stirring occasionally, until the vegetables are soft, 5 to 7 minutes.

2. Add the garlic and cook, stirring constantly, until fragrant, about 30 seconds.

3. Add the beans, tomatoes, rosemary, and salt. Bring to a boil. Reduce the heat to low and simmer for 5 minutes, stirring occasionally. Store unoffered portions in the refrigerator for up to 3 days or in the freezer for up to 6 months.

TIP: White beans may also be called navy beans or cannellini beans.

Edamame and Brown Rice Stir-Fry

DF NF Vegan

MAKES 4 SERVINGS

2 tablespoons olive oil

1 leek, finely chopped

2 cups finely chopped
Swiss chard

1 carrot, peeled and
finely chopped

2 cups shelled edamame

½ teaspoon grated
fresh ginger

1 garlic clove, minced

1 cup cooked brown rice

Juice of 1 lime

¼ cup vegetable broth

1 tablespoon low-sodium
soy sauce

2 tablespoons chopped
fresh cilantro

You can find organic edamame in the freezer section of your grocery store. If you purchase edamame in the shells, remove the pods before cooking. It's a complete source of protein with a pleasant, neutral flavor.

1. In a large sauté pan, heat the olive oil over medium-high heat until it shimmers. Add the leek, Swiss chard, carrot, and edamame. Cook, stirring frequently, until the vegetables are soft, 5 to 7 minutes.

2. Add the ginger and garlic and cook, stirring constantly, until fragrant, about 30 seconds. Stir in the brown rice.

3. In a small bowl, whisk together the lime juice, vegetable broth, and soy sauce. Add to the pan. Bring to a simmer, stirring constantly. Simmer until the sauce thickens, about 2 minutes.

4. Stir in the cilantro and serve warm. Store unoffered portions in the refrigerator for up to 3 days or in the freezer for up to 6 months.

TIP: If you don't have edamame, use 2 cups diced tofu instead.

Lemon Cod with Pea Puree

MAKES 4 SERVINGS

FOR THE COD

2 (4-ounce) skinless cod fillets

Juice of ½ lemon

¼ teaspoon sea salt

¼ teaspoon chopped fresh dill

FOR THE PEA PUREE

2 cups fresh or frozen peas

1 tablespoon unsalted butter, melted

¼ teaspoon chopped fresh dill

¼ teaspoon sea salt

While this recipe calls for cod, you can use any type of white fish that's available and affordable. The lemon and dill flavors complement both the cod and the pea puree. You can puree fresh peas, as recommended in this recipe, or use thawed freezer tray cubes of pea puree.

TO MAKE THE COD

1. Preheat the broiler. Place a rack on a baking sheet.
2. Place the cod on the rack. Squeeze the lemon juice on the cod. Sprinkle it with the salt and the dill. Broil the cod until it is opaque, about 5 minutes.

TO MAKE THE PEA PUREE

1. In a medium saucepan with a steamer insert, bring 1 inch of water to a boil. Add the peas. Cover and steam for 5 minutes.
2. In a blender or food processor, process the peas, butter, dill, and salt until smooth. Store unoffered portions in the refrigerator for up to 3 days.

TIP: If you'd prefer, you can steam the peas, season them with a little dill and salt, and serve them to your toddler whole as a side dish.

Zucchini Noodles with Ground Turkey and Carrot-Tomato Sauce

MAKES 8 SERVINGS

2 tablespoons olive oil

1 pound ground turkey

½ onion, finely chopped

2 garlic cloves, minced

1 (14-ounce) can crushed tomatoes

1 carrot, peeled and grated

¼ teaspoon sea salt

1 zucchini, cut into ¼-inch-thick noodles

2 tablespoons chopped fresh basil

Zucchini noodles are a great alternative to wheat pasta. Making the "zoodles" doesn't require a spiralizer—although that can make the noodles longer and a lot more enticing to look at. You can use a julienne peeler or even a knife to cut the zucchini into spaghetti-like strands.

1. In a large sauté pan, heat the olive oil over medium-high heat until it shimmers. Add the ground turkey and onion. Cook, crumbling the turkey with a spoon, until brown, about 6 minutes.

2. Add the garlic and cook, stirring constantly, until fragrant, about 30 seconds.

3. Add the tomatoes, carrot, and salt. Bring the mixture to a boil. Reduce the heat to medium-low. Simmer for 5 minutes.

4. Stir in the zucchini noodles. Cook for 5 minutes more, stirring occasionally. Remove from the heat and stir in the basil. Store unoffered portions in the refrigerator for up to 3 days or in the freezer for up to 6 months.

TIP: Other veggies also make great "noodles." Try half a winter squash or jicama, 1 sweet potato, or 3 carrots.

White Beans with Barley and Kale

MAKES 4 SERVINGS

2 tablespoons olive oil

½ onion, finely chopped

2 cups chopped kale

1 (14-ounce) can white beans, drained

¼ cup vegetable broth

½ teaspoon grated orange zest

Juice of 1 orange

1 teaspoon dried tarragon

¼ teaspoon sea salt

2 cups cooked barley

This dish has a lovely citrus and tarragon flavor profile that your toddler is likely to respond well to, but it's tasty enough to share with the whole family. This recipe calls for cooked barley, so you can save time by preparing it in advance (see the tip).

1. In a large sauté pan, heat the olive oil over medium-high heat until it shimmers. Add the onion and kale. Cook, stirring occasionally, until the vegetables are soft, about 5 minutes.

2. Add the beans, broth, orange zest and juice, tarragon, salt, and barley. Simmer for 5 minutes. Store unoffered portions in the refrigerator for up to 3 days or in the freezer for up to 6 months.

TIP: To cook barley, bring 2½ cups of water or broth and 1 cup of barley to a boil. Reduce the heat to a simmer. Cover and cook until tender, 40 to 50 minutes.

Pizza Mac

MAKES 4 SERVINGS

2 cups whole wheat
elbow macaroni

1 tablespoon olive oil

8 ounces bulk
Italian sausage

½ onion, chopped

1 cup chopped spinach

1 garlic clove, minced

1 (14-ounce) can crushed
tomatoes

1 teaspoon dried
Italian seasoning

¼ cup grated
Parmesan cheese

Give your toddler all the flavors of pizza minus the crust with this delicious pizza macaroni.

1. Cook the pasta according to the package directions. Drain and set aside.
2. In a large sauté pan, heat the olive oil over medium-high heat until it shimmers. Add the sausage and onion. Cook, crumbling the sausage with a spoon, until brown, about 6 minutes. Add the spinach and cook for 1 minute more.
3. Add the garlic and cook, stirring constantly, for 30 seconds. Add the tomatoes and Italian seasoning. Simmer, stirring occasionally, for 5 minutes.
4. Add the cooked macaroni. Toss to coat it with the sauce. Stir in the Parmesan cheese. Store unoffered portions in the refrigerator for up to 3 days or in the freezer for up to 6 months.

TIP: It's easy to incorporate more vegetables into this recipe. Add 4 (1-ounce) freezer tray cubes of thawed veggie puree to the sauce, or stir in chopped vegetables when you cook the onions and sausage. Good options are red or orange bell peppers or peas.

Artichoke and Lemon Pesto on Whole Wheat Pasta

MAKES 4 SERVINGS

12 ounces whole wheat pasta (any type)

½ (14-ounce) can artichoke hearts, drained

¼ cup loosely packed fresh basil leaves

1 garlic clove, peeled

1 teaspoon grated lemon zest

Juice of 1 lemon

2 tablespoons olive oil

2 tablespoons grated Parmesan cheese

¼ cup chopped walnuts, pumpkin seeds, or sunflower seeds

¼ teaspoon sea salt

This nutritious pesto tastes great on pasta. You can even use it as a dip or sauce for veggies, meat, or finger foods. This recipe calls for artichoke hearts in a can, which are already cooked. When purchasing, select artichoke hearts packed in water, not oil or marinade.

1. Cook the pasta according to the package directions. Drain and set aside.
2. In a blender or food processor, combine the artichoke hearts, basil, garlic, lemon zest and juice, olive oil, Parmesan cheese, nuts or seeds, and salt. Pulse 10 to 15 times, until finely chopped.
3. Toss the pesto with the warm pasta. Store unoffered portions in the refrigerator for up to 3 days or in the freezer for up to 6 months.

TIP: You can use any green veggie puree in this recipe, such as asparagus, spinach, or kale. Use 5 (1-ounce) thawed cubes and eliminate the olive oil.

Beefaroni

MAKES 8 SERVINGS

12 ounces whole wheat elbow macaroni

2 tablespoons olive oil

1 pound ground beef

1 onion, finely chopped

2 garlic cloves, minced

1 (14-ounce) can crushed tomatoes

1 teaspoon dried oregano

¼ teaspoon sea salt

Beefaroni has always been a big hit with the little ones. This recipe makes a generous amount, and it freezes well. Store it in ½-cup servings and warm it up for a quick, no-fuss meal. It's a nutritious alternative to opening a can.

1. Cook the pasta according to the package directions. Drain and set aside.

2. In a large sauté pan, heat the olive oil over medium-high heat until it shimmers. Add the ground beef and onion. Cook, crumbling the beef with a spoon, until brown, about 6 minutes.

3. Add the garlic and cook, stirring constantly, until fragrant, about 30 seconds.

4. Stir in the tomatoes, oregano, and salt. Simmer until the sauce thickens, stirring frequently, about 5 minutes more.

5. Stir in the pasta and cook to warm it, about 2 minutes. Store unoffered portions in the refrigerator for up to 3 days or in the freezer for up to 6 months.

TIP: If you'd like, add ½ to 1 cup chopped vegetables, such as spinach or carrots, to the pan when you cook the ground beef.

Black Beans with Lime and Cilantro

MAKES 4 SERVINGS

2 tablespoons olive oil

½ onion, minced

1 carrot, peeled
and minced

1 red bell pepper, seeded
and minced

2 garlic cloves, minced

2 (14-ounce) cans black
beans, undrained

½ teaspoon grated
lime zest

Juice of 1 lime

½ teaspoon dried cumin

¼ teaspoon sea salt

¼ cup chopped fresh
cilantro

These tasty black beans have a little bit of Latin American flair, and they are a great source of protein. To enhance the protein, you can stir in a little cooked brown rice to create a complete source of protein with all essential amino acids.

1. In a large sauté pan, heat the olive oil over medium-high heat until it shimmers. Add the onion, carrot, and bell pepper and cook, stirring occasionally, until the vegetables are soft, 5 to 7 minutes. Add the garlic and cook, stirring constantly, for 30 seconds.
2. Add the black beans, lime zest and juice, cumin, and salt. Bring to a simmer. Cook, stirring occasionally, for 5 minutes.
3. Stir in the cilantro. Store unoffered portions in the refrigerator for up to 3 days or in the freezer for up to 6 months.

TIP: To add antioxidants, stir in a few tablespoons of finely chopped tomato to each portion before serving. You can also serve the beans with grated cheese on top.

Lentils with Sweet Potato and Orange

MAKES 4 SERVINGS

1 tablespoon olive oil

½ onion, minced

2 garlic cloves, minced

1 (14-ounce) can lentils, drained

½ teaspoon grated orange zest

Juice of 1 orange

5 (1-ounce) freezer tray cubes sweet potato puree (page 43), thawed

1 teaspoon dried thyme

¼ teaspoon sea salt

This recipe uses sweet potato puree cubes you've already made and frozen, although you can also make the sweet potato puree fresh if you'd like to make a larger batch and freeze it. With a hint of orange and thyme, this recipe will tickle your toddler's taste buds.

1. In a large saucepan, heat the olive oil over medium-high heat until it shimmers. Add the onion and cook, stirring occasionally, until soft, about 5 minutes.

2. Add the garlic and cook, stirring constantly, for 30 seconds.

3. Add the lentils, orange zest and juice, sweet potato puree, thyme, and salt. Bring to a simmer and cook, stirring occasionally, for 5 minutes. Store unoffered portions in the refrigerator for up to 3 days.

TIP: Other purees of orange veggies work well here, too, such as butternut or acorn squash or carrots.

Broccoli, Beef, and Barley

1 tablespoon olive oil

½ onion, finely chopped

8 ounces ground beef

1 cup small
broccoli florets

¼ cup beef broth

½ teaspoon garlic powder

½ teaspoon dried thyme

¼ teaspoon sea salt

1 cup cooked barley

This recipe is healing and great for the immune system. Filled with iron, zinc, and vitamins B12 and C, it's the perfect meal to make when you or your little one needs a health boost.

1. In a large sauté pan, heat the olive oil over medium-high heat until it shimmers. Add the onion and ground beef and cook, crumbling the beef with a spoon, until brown, about 6 minutes.

2. Add the broccoli. Cook, stirring occasionally, until it is soft, about 5 minutes more.

3. Add the beef broth, garlic powder, thyme, salt, and barley. Simmer for 4 minutes. Store unoffered portions in the refrigerator for up to 3 days or in the freezer for up to 6 months.

TIP: Stir in any frozen vegetable purees you have available (about three 1-ounce cubes, thawed) when you add the broth to boost the nutrition in this meal.

Turkey and Zucchini Meatballs with Sweet Potato Puree

MAKES 4 SERVINGS

FOR THE MEATBALLS

8 ounces ground turkey

½ onion, grated

1 cup grated zucchini

1 cup finely
chopped spinach

½ teaspoon dried thyme

½ teaspoon garlic powder

1 tablespoon
Dijon mustard

¼ teaspoon sea salt

1 egg, beaten

**FOR THE SWEET
POTATO PUREE**

1 sweet potato, peeled
and cut into 1-inch pieces

2 tablespoons
unsalted butter

¼ cup dairy or
nondairy milk

¼ teaspoon sea salt

Using zucchini instead of bread crumbs makes these meatballs lighter than usual, and adding herbs and spices gives them plenty of flavor. While this recipe calls for fresh sweet potato puree, you can also thaw freezer tray cubes of sweet potato puree; just don't refreeze the leftovers.

TO MAKE THE MEATBALLS

1. Preheat the oven to 350°F. Line a baking sheet with parchment.
2. In a medium bowl, combine all the ingredients and mix well. Roll the mixture into ½-inch meatballs and place them in a single layer on the prepared baking sheet.
3. Bake until the meatballs are cooked through, 20 to 30 minutes.

TO MAKE THE SWEET POTATO PUREE

4. In a medium saucepan with a steamer insert, bring 1 inch of water to a boil. Add the sweet potato. Cover and steam until tender, 5 to 10 minutes.
5. In a blender or food processor, process the sweet potato, butter, milk, and salt until smooth. Transfer the puree to a medium bowl and toss the meatballs with it. Store unoffered portions in the refrigerator for up to 3 days or in the freezer for up to 6 months.

Fish Fingers with Yogurt Tartar Sauce

DF option **GF**

MAKES 4 SERVINGS

**FOR THE
FISH FINGERS**

2 eggs, beaten

1 cup almond flour

½ teaspoon dried thyme

½ teaspoon
onion powder

¼ teaspoon garlic powder

¼ teaspoon sea salt

1 pound snapper, cut
into ½-inch-thick strips

**FOR THE YOGURT
TARTAR SAUCE**

½ cup plain full-fat yogurt
(nondairy if desired)

1 tablespoon
chopped pickles

1 teaspoon onion,
finely minced

½ teaspoon lemon juice

These baked fish fingers are made with snapper, but you can use any white fish in its place, such as cod or halibut. The almond crust makes this gluten free and adds vitamin E, and the tartar sauce made from yogurt adds calcium.

TO MAKE THE FISH FINGERS

1. Preheat the oven to 350°F. Line a baking sheet with parchment.
2. In a small bowl, beat the eggs. In another small bowl, whisk together the almond flour, thyme, onion powder, garlic powder, and salt.
3. Dip each fish finger in the egg, and then in the almond mixture to coat. Place the fish fingers in a single layer on the prepared baking sheet.
4. Bake until the fish is cooked through and the coating is golden, 20 to 25 minutes. Store unoffered portions in the refrigerator for up to 3 days or in the freezer for up to 6 months.

TO MAKE THE YOGURT TARTAR SAUCE

Mix all the ingredients in a small bowl until combined. Serve alongside the fish fingers. Store unoffered portions in the refrigerator for up to 3 days.

TIP: If gluten isn't a concern, you can replace the almond flour in this recipe with an equal amount of whole wheat bread crumbs or wheat germ.

Turkey with Cranberry Applesauce

MAKES 4 SERVINGS

FOR THE CRANBERRY APPLESAUCE

2 sweet-tart apples (such as Braeburn or Honeycrisp), peeled, cored, and cut into ½-inch dice

Juice of 1 orange

½ cup cranberries

¼ teaspoon ground cloves

FOR THE TURKEY

6 ounces boneless, skinless turkey breast, pounded to ⅛-inch thickness

¼ teaspoon sea salt

2 tablespoons olive oil

This is a great fall meal when fresh cranberries are available and apples are at the peak of their ripeness. Using turkey cutlets and pounding them thin makes them cook quickly and offers plenty of lean protein for your growing toddler.

TO MAKE THE CRANBERRY APPLESAUCE

1. In a small pot, combine all the ingredients and set over medium-high heat.
2. Cook, stirring frequently, until the apples are tender and the cranberries have popped, 5 to 10 minutes.
3. If desired, puree the fruit in a food processor or blender to achieve the desired consistency, or serve as is. Store unoffered applesauce in the refrigerator for up to 3 days or in the freezer for up to 6 months.

TO MAKE THE TURKEY

1. Season the turkey with the salt.
2. In a large sauté pan, heat the olive oil over medium-high heat until it shimmers.
3. Cook the turkey until cooked through, 3 to 5 minutes per side.
4. Cut into bite-size pieces and serve with the warm cranberry applesauce. Store unoffered turkey in the refrigerator for up to 3 days or in the freezer for up to 6 months.

TIP: To pound the turkey breasts, place them between two pieces of plastic wrap or parchment and pound evenly with a mallet.

Ground Beef with Lemon Pea Puree

MAKES 4 SERVINGS

1 tablespoon olive oil

½ onion, minced

8 ounces ground beef

1 garlic clove, minced

6 (1-ounce) cubes pea puree (page 54), thawed

Juice of 1 lemon

¼ teaspoon sea salt

1 tablespoon chopped fresh mint

Lemon and peas make a tasty combination, and the hint of mint adds freshness and flavor. This recipe contains vitamin C, plenty of protein, and lots of folate, so it supports your toddler's growth, development, and immunity.

1. In a large sauté pan, heat the olive oil over medium-high heat until it shimmers. Add the onion and ground beef and cook, crumbling the beef with a spoon, until brown, about 6 minutes.

2. Add the garlic and cook, stirring constantly, for 30 seconds.

3. Add the thawed pea puree, lemon juice, and salt. Bring to a simmer, stirring constantly. Stir in the mint and serve. Store unoffered portions in the refrigerator for up to 3 days.

TIP: Lemon and peas also taste wonderful with lamb; you can substitute ground lamb for the ground beef, if you'd like.

Turkey with Steamed Pear and Broccoli

MAKES 4 SERVINGS

½ cup small broccoli florets

1 pear, peeled, cored, and cut into ¼-inch dice

8 ounces turkey breast cutlet, pounded to ⅛-inch thickness

¼ teaspoon sea salt

1 tablespoon olive oil

This simple meal comes together quickly and offers your toddler plenty of protein with a healthy side of fruits and veggies. If you'd like to add a grain, mix in cooked rice or barley.

1. In a saucepan with a steamer insert, bring about 1 inch of water to a simmer. Add the broccoli and pear. Cover and simmer until tender, about 5 minutes.

2. Season the turkey with the salt. Heat the olive oil in a large sauté pan over medium-high heat until it shimmers.

3. Add the turkey and cook until it is cooked through, about 3 minutes per side. Store unoffered portions in the refrigerator for up to 3 days or in the freezer for up to 6 months; freeze the turkey and veggies separately.

Rice with Peas, Apple, and Chicken

MAKES 4 SERVINGS

2 tablespoons olive oil

8 ounces ground chicken

½ onion, minced

2 garlic cloves, minced

1 apple, peeled, cored, and cut into ¼-inch dice

1 cup fresh or frozen peas

1 cup cooked brown rice

½ cup apple juice

¼ teaspoon ground ginger

¼ teaspoon sea salt

While the method is similar to making fried rice, this is a different take on the dish without any Asian flavors. The recipe calls for cooked brown rice, which means you can put this nutritious meal together in less than 15 minutes. This is a good one to double, because it freezes well and gives you extra meals on the go.

1. In a large sauté pan, heat the olive oil over medium-high heat until it shimmers. Add the chicken, onion, garlic, apple, and peas and cook, crumbling the chicken with a spoon, until brown, about 6 minutes.

2. Add the rice, apple juice, ginger, and salt. Cook, stirring constantly, for 3 minutes more. Store unoffered portions in the refrigerator for up to 3 days or in the freezer for up to 6 months.

TIP: Pears make a good substitute for the apples here; you can also use pear juice or just stick with the apple juice.

Cauliflower Fried Rice

DF NF V Vegan option

MAKES 4 SERVINGS

½ head cauliflower, broken into florets

2 tablespoons olive oil

½ onion, minced

2 carrots, peeled and minced

¼ cup small broccoli florets

½ red bell pepper, seeded and minced

¼ cup chopped mushrooms

2 garlic cloves, minced

½ teaspoon ground ginger

3 eggs, beaten (optional)

1 tablespoon low-sodium soy sauce

Juice of 1 lime

1 tablespoon chopped fresh cilantro

When you process cauliflower to the texture of rice, it makes a great base for all types of flavor profiles; it's also high in fiber and nutrients. While this is a vegetarian version, you can mix it with any type of cooked meat you'd like for extra protein. Chopped tofu is a good option, too.

1. In a food processor or blender, pulse the cauliflower a few times until it resembles rice. Set aside.

2. In a large sauté pan, heat the olive oil over medium-high heat until it shimmers. Add the onion, carrots, broccoli, bell pepper, and mushrooms and cook, stirring frequently, until the vegetables begin to brown, 5 to 7 minutes.

3. Add the cauliflower and cook until it softens, stirring occasionally, about 4 minutes. Add the garlic and ginger and cook, stirring constantly, for 30 seconds.

4. Add the eggs and cook, stirring, until they are set, 1 to 2 minutes more. Add the soy sauce and lime juice. Cook, stirring, for 1 minute more. Stir in the cilantro. Store unoffered portions in the refrigerator for up to 3 days or in the freezer for up to 6 months.

Pinto Beans with Quinoa and Greens

MAKES 4 SERVINGS

2 tablespoons olive oil

½ onion, minced

2 cups stemmed and chopped kale

2 garlic cloves, minced

1 (14-ounce) can pinto beans, drained

½ cup orange juice

1 ½ cups cooked quinoa

1 teaspoon dried thyme

¼ teaspoon sea salt

This flavorful bean stew is a tasty source of protein to support your toddler's growth and development, while the dark leafy greens are loaded with iron and healthy antioxidants to support blood formation and immunity.

1. In a large saucepan, heat the olive oil over medium-high heat until it shimmers. Add the onion and kale and cook, stirring occasionally, until soft, about 5 minutes.

2. Add the garlic and cook, stirring constantly, for 30 seconds.

3. Add the pinto beans, orange juice, quinoa, thyme, and salt. Cook, stirring occasionally, for 4 minutes. Store unoffered portions in the refrigerator for up to 3 days or in the freezer for up to 6 months.

TIP: Other grains work well here, including rice or barley, both of which combine with the beans to make a complete source of protein. If using barley, remember it is not gluten free.

Turkey Meatballs with Artichoke, Spinach, and Lemon Sauce

MAKES 4 SERVINGS

FOR THE MEATBALLS

8 ounces ground turkey

½ onion, grated

1 cup finely chopped mushrooms

1 egg, beaten

1 teaspoon Dijon mustard

1 teaspoon dried thyme

¼ teaspoon sea salt

FOR THE SAUCE

2 (1-ounce) cubes spinach puree (page 47), thawed

2 (1-ounce) cubes artichoke puree (page 67), thawed

Juice of 1 lemon

¼ teaspoon sea salt

Spoon this savory and nutritious sauce over the turkey meatballs, or offer it on the side as a dip. If you'd like to add a starch, serve the meatballs on a bed of sweet potato puree (see page 43) with the sauce spooned over the top of both.

TO MAKE THE MEATBALLS

1. Preheat the oven to 350°F. Line a baking sheet with parchment.
2. In a large bowl, combine all the ingredients and mix well. Roll the mixture into ½-inch balls and place on the prepared baking sheet.
3. Bake until the meatballs are cooked through, 20 to 25 minutes. Store the meatballs in the refrigerator for up to 3 days or in the freezer for up to 6 months.

TO MAKE THE SAUCE

In a small bowl, combine all the ingredients. Mix well with a spoon. Store in the refrigerator for up to 3 days.

TIP: The best way to combine meat mixtures for meatballs, meatloaf, or burgers is by using your hands. It allows you to make sure all the ingredients are evenly incorporated.

9

12 MONTHS AND UP
FAMILY DINNER

Meals the whole family can (and will!) eat together is the holy grail. I'm not saying there are any guarantees, but these recipes are intended to help you get there. They make family-size portions (if you have a big family, you can double the recipe), and they offer nutritious ingredients that support good health. In some cases, you may want to limit herbs or spices in your toddler's portion before adding them for the rest of the family. If that's the case, the recipe indicates that you should do so. Otherwise, have at it, allowing your toddler to partake of the family meal, or at the very least sniff at it. This may be an especially good option for toddlers who are starting to show picky-eating tendencies, as they may be more likely to try a new food they see the entire family eating and enjoying.

DEVELOPMENTALLY SPEAKING

Chances are that between the ages of 12 and 24 months, your toddler has started to develop a "food identity" in which she has preferences for certain foods and dislikes of others. However, these preferences don't have to be set in stone. Offering a variety of "grown-up" foods with mild herbs and spices can help your toddler's palate continue to develop. The most important thing is that you're offering your toddler an array of nutritious choices. She can then selectively eat from the foods you offer to satisfy her personal appetites.

PORTION GUIDELINES

As mentioned in the previous chapter, your toddler will likely eat between ¼ and ½ cup of food three to four times per day. To avoid wasting food, offer small amounts and give your toddler more as needed.

FAQ

Q: I'm concerned that my toddler's preference for "white" foods such as pasta and rice means he's not getting enough protein. How can I possibly get him to eat the right amount of protein?

A: This is probably the most common question I get from clients and friends. It's actually pretty easy for kids to meet their protein needs. For toddlers, protein intake should be in the range of 13 to 16 grams per day. Odds are good that your child is getting enough protein. Keep this in mind:

FOOD	PROTEIN
1 egg	6 grams
1 cup yogurt	8 grams
¼ cup beans	3 grams
1 oz chicken	7 grams
1 tablespoon peanut butter	4 grams
½ cup cooked quinoa	4 grams
½ avocado	2 grams
½ cup cooked broccoli	2 grams

White Fish with Mango Black Bean Salsa

MAKES 6 SERVINGS

6 (4- to 6-ounce) white fish fillets (such as snapper, cod, or halibut)

1 teaspoon ground cumin

¼ teaspoon sea salt, plus a pinch

Pinch black pepper

2 mangos, peeled, pitted, and cut into ¼-inch dice

½ red onion, very finely minced

2 cups canned black beans, drained

Juice of ½ lime

¼ cup chopped fresh cilantro

The mild mango salsa pumps up the flavor of the fish in this recipe and offers plenty of nutrition. This is a simple meal that comes together quickly. Serve it with steamed brown rice on the side or a sweet potato mash.

1. Preheat the oven to 400°F. Line a baking sheet with parchment.
2. Season the fish with the cumin and a pinch each of salt and pepper. Place the fish on the prepared baking sheet and bake until flaky, about 15 minutes.
3. In a small bowl, combine the mangos, onion, black beans, lime juice, cilantro, and ¼ teaspoon of salt. Spoon the mixture over the white fish fillets. Store unoffered portions in the refrigerator for up to 3 days.

TIP: If you have family members who like the salsa a bit spicier, remove your toddler's portion first, and then add a minced jalapeño and a pinch of cayenne to the salsa.

Spaghetti Squash with Ground Turkey Tomato Sauce

DF option **GF** **NF**

MAKES 4 SERVINGS

1 spaghetti squash, halved lengthwise and seeded

4 tablespoons olive oil, divided

1 pound ground turkey

1 onion, finely chopped

4 garlic cloves, finely minced

1 (14-ounce) can tomato sauce

1 (14-ounce) can chopped tomatoes, drained

1 tablespoon dried Italian seasoning

½ teaspoon sea salt

4 ounces grated Parmesan cheese (optional)

Spaghetti squash makes a nutritious stand-in for pasta in this healthy family meal. When you run a fork along the cooked spaghetti squash, it creates long "noodles" that pair beautifully with antioxidant-rich tomato sauce and protein-filled ground turkey. You can prepare the sauce while the squash bakes, so the entire meal is easy to assemble.

1. Preheat the oven to 375°F. Line a baking sheet with parchment.

2. Brush the cut sides of the spaghetti squash with 2 tablespoons of olive oil. Place the squash, cut-side down, on the prepared baking sheet and bake for 40 minutes. When the squash is cooked, run a fork along the cut side to remove the squash in spaghetti-style strands.

3. In a large sauté pan, heat the remaining 2 tablespoons of olive oil over medium-high heat until it shimmers. Add the turkey and cook, crumbling it with a spoon, until brown, about 6 minutes.

4. Add the onion and cook, stirring occasionally, until soft, 3 to 5 minutes. Add the garlic and cook, stirring constantly, until fragrant, about 30 seconds.

5. Add the tomato sauce, chopped tomatoes, Italian seasoning, and salt. Bring to a simmer. Simmer, stirring occasionally, for 5 minutes to allow the flavors to meld.

6. Serve the sauce on top of the squash, sprinkled with the Parmesan cheese, if using. Store unoffered portions of the squash and sauce separately in the refrigerator for up to 3 days or in the freezer for up to 6 months.

TIP: There are all kinds of substitutions you can make here depending on your family's preferences. For example, you can replace the turkey with ground beef, mild Italian sausage, or a vegetarian protein option like cooked lentils.

Ground Turkey and Broccoli Stir-Fry with Brown Rice

MAKES 6 SERVINGS

2 tablespoons olive oil, plus more as needed

1 pound ground turkey

3 cups small broccoli florets

1 cup sliced shiitake mushrooms

½ onion, finely chopped

2 garlic cloves, minced

1 teaspoon grated fresh ginger

¼ cup low-sodium soy sauce

¼ cup orange juice

1 tablespoon honey

3 cups cooked brown rice

Ground turkey is flavorful and really easy for your toddler to eat, and the broccoli adds texture and nutrition. You can also substitute broccolini in this recipe, which has a slightly milder flavor and a more tender bite than broccoli.

1. In a large pot or wok, heat the olive oil over medium-high heat until it shimmers. Add the ground turkey and cook, crumbling it with a spoon, until brown, about 6 minutes.

2. Using a slotted spoon, remove the turkey from the oil and set it aside in a bowl. If needed, add a bit more oil to the pot.

3. Add the broccoli, mushrooms, and onion. Cook, stirring occasionally, until the vegetables soften, about 5 minutes. Add the garlic and ginger and cook, stirring constantly, until fragrant, about 30 seconds.

4. Return the turkey to the pot. Add the soy sauce, orange juice, and honey. Cook, stirring frequently, until the liquid reduces slightly and coats the meat and vegetables, about 5 minutes more.

5. Spoon the meat and veggies over the brown rice to serve. Store unoffered portions of the stir-fry and rice separately in the refrigerator for up to 3 days or in the freezer for up to 6 months.

TIP: Cutting the vegetables small makes them easier for your toddler to eat, and it speeds up cooking time.

Pork Tenderloin with Sweet Potato Mash and Applesauce

MAKES 4 SERVINGS

FOR THE TENDERLOIN

1 (1- to 2-pound) pork tenderloin

1 bunch fresh basil

1 bunch fresh chives

1 bunch fresh thyme, stems removed

3 garlic cloves, peeled

2 tablespoons Dijon mustard

2 tablespoons olive oil

½ teaspoon sea salt

¼ teaspoon black pepper

FOR THE SWEET POTATO MASH

4 sweet potatoes, peeled and cut into ½-inch cubes

½ cup milk

¼ cup butter, melted

½ teaspoon sea salt

¼ teaspoon black pepper

FOR THE APPLESAUCE

4 sweet-tart apples (such as Honeycrisp), peeled, cored, and chopped

¼ cup water

½ teaspoon ground ginger

¼ cup pure maple syrup

Crusting your pork tenderloin with a mustard and herb sauce adds lots of flavor. If your toddler isn't a fan of the crust, you can easily scrape it away before serving it to her. The rest of your family will enjoy the sweet flavors with the pork along with the traditional applesauce and sweet potato mash sides. To save a bit of time (and compromise a bit of flavor), buy organic, unsweetened applesauce.

TO MAKE THE TENDERLOIN

1. Preheat the oven to 350°F. Line a baking sheet with parchment and place the pork on top.
2. In a food processor or blender, combine the basil, chives, thyme, garlic, mustard, olive oil, salt, and pepper. Pulse until it forms a paste. Spread the paste all over the pork.
3. Bake until the pork reaches an internal temperature of 145°F, about 60 minutes.

TO MAKE THE SWEET POTATO MASH

1. Put the sweet potatoes in a large pot, cover with an inch of water, and bring to a boil over medium-high heat. Cook, uncovered, until the potatoes are soft, about 10 minutes. Drain.
2. Transfer the potatoes to a large bowl and add the milk, butter, salt, and pepper. Use an electric mixer to whip the potatoes.

TO MAKE THE APPLESAUCE

In a large pot, bring the apples and water to a simmer over medium-high heat. Cook, uncovered, stirring frequently, until the apples are a saucy consistency, about 10 minutes. Stir in the ginger and maple syrup.

STORAGE: Leftovers of the tenderloin, sweet potato mash, and applesauce can all be stored separately in the refrigerator for up to 3 days, or in the freezer for up to 6 months.

Sweet Potato and Leek Soup

DF **GF** **NF** **Vegan**

MAKES 4 SERVINGS

2 tablespoons olive oil

1 onion, chopped

3 leeks, chopped

3 garlic cloves, minced

6 cups vegetable broth

4 sweet potatoes, peeled and chopped

1 teaspoon ground ginger

Pinch ground nutmeg

½ teaspoon sea salt

¼ teaspoon black pepper

1 cup canned coconut milk

Leeks have a very clean and earthy taste. They bring out the natural sweetness of the sweet potato as well as the flavors of ginger and nutmeg. This soup is rich in antioxidants, vitamin A, and anti-inflammatory superstars.

1. In a large pot, heat the olive oil over medium-high heat until it shimmers. Add the onion and leeks and cook, stirring occasionally, until soft, about 7 minutes. Add the garlic and cook, stirring constantly, until fragrant, about 30 seconds.

2. Add the vegetable broth, sweet potatoes, ginger, nutmeg, salt, and pepper. Bring to a simmer. Reduce the heat to medium-low. Simmer, stirring occasionally, until the sweet potatoes are soft, about 10 minutes.

3. Transfer the soup to a blender or food processor. Add the coconut milk. Process until smooth. Store unoffered portions in the refrigerator for up to 3 days or in the freezer for up to 6 months.

TIP: To clean leeks, cut them into pieces and put them in a bowl full of water. Agitate the water and allow the dirt to settle at the bottom of the bowl. Scoop out the leeks and drain the water, then rinse out the bowl. Do this several times, until no dirt settles in the bottom of the bowl.

Orange-Tarragon Orzo with Turkey and Spinach

DF **NF**

MAKES 4 SERVINGS

2 tablespoons olive oil, plus more as needed

1 pound ground turkey

1 onion, chopped

3 cups baby spinach

2 cups whole wheat orzo (uncooked)

Juice of 2 oranges

Zest of ½ orange

6 cups chicken broth

2 teaspoons dried tarragon

½ teaspoon sea salt

¼ teaspoon black pepper

Orzo looks a little bit like rice, but it's made from the same flour as pasta. This is a simple one-pot meal that minimizes cleanup time, giving you more time to spend with your family after the meal.

1. In a large pot, heat the olive oil over medium-high heat until it shimmers. Add the turkey and cook, crumbling it with a spoon, until brown, about 6 minutes. Using a slotted spoon, remove the turkey from the oil and set it aside in a bowl. If needed, add a bit more oil to the pot.

2. Add the onion and spinach and cook, stirring occasionally, until the onion is soft, about 5 minutes. Add the orzo and cook, stirring constantly, for 1 minute more.

3. Add the orange juice and use the side of a spoon to scrape up any browned bits from the bottom of the pan. Add the orange zest, chicken broth, tarragon, salt, and pepper. Cook, stirring frequently, until the liquid is absorbed, 15 to 20 minutes.

4. Stir in the ground turkey. Cook, stirring, for 3 minutes more. Store unoffered portions in the refrigerator for up to 3 days or in the freezer for up to 6 months.

TIP: To make a lemon thyme orzo instead, replace the orange juice and zest with lemon juice and the tarragon with thyme. Then add ½ teaspoon of garlic powder along with the salt and pepper.

Black Bean Chili

DF GF NF

MAKES 4 SERVINGS

2 tablespoons olive oil, plus more as needed

1 pound ground beef

1 onion, chopped

3 garlic cloves, minced

1 (2-ounce) can mild green chiles, drained

2 (14-ounce) cans black beans, drained

1 (14-ounce) can tomato sauce

1 (14-ounce) can crushed tomatoes

1 tablespoon chili powder

1 teaspoon smoked paprika

1 teaspoon ground cumin

1 teaspoon sea salt

This is a mild chili, which is perfect for tender palates. After you've scooped out your toddler's portion, feel free to pump up the seasoning by adding a pinch of cayenne (or however much the rest of your family enjoys) and simmering for another 5 minutes.

1. In a large pot, heat the olive oil over medium-high heat until it shimmers. Add the ground beef and cook, crumbling it with a spoon, until brown, about 6 minutes. Using a slotted spoon, remove the beef from the oil and set it aside in a bowl. If needed, add a bit more oil to the pot.

2. Add the onion and cook, stirring occasionally, until soft, about 5 minutes. Add the garlic and cook, stirring constantly, until fragrant, about 30 seconds.

3. Return the ground beef to the pot, along with the chiles, black beans, tomato sauce, crushed tomatoes, chili powder, smoked paprika, cumin, and salt. Bring to a boil. Reduce the heat to medium-low. Simmer, stirring occasionally, for 10 minutes. Store unoffered portions in the refrigerator for up to 3 days or in the freezer for up to 6 months.

TIP: This is a great slow-cooker meal as well. Simply brown the ground beef beforehand and add it to the slow cooker with all the other ingredients. Cover and cook on low for 8 hours.

Minestrone Soup

MAKES 4 SERVINGS

2 tablespoons olive oil

1 onion, chopped

1 red bell pepper, seeded and chopped

1 carrot, peeled and chopped

2 celery stalks, peeled and chopped

4 garlic cloves, minced

1 cup green bean pieces (½-inch pieces)

1 (14-ounce) can crushed tomatoes

1 (14-ounce) can kidney beans, drained

6 cups vegetable broth

1 teaspoon dried Italian seasoning

½ teaspoon sea salt

¼ teaspoon black pepper

Soup is great family food. It takes only one pot, and it's easy to load with nutritious vegetables and lots of flavor. While minestrone is classically a vegetable soup, you can add browned ground meat to add more protein, or for more vegetarian protein, add a cup of shelled edamame.

1. In a large pot, heat the olive oil over medium-high heat until it shimmers. Add the onion, bell pepper, carrot, and celery. Cook, stirring occasionally, until the vegetables soften, about 5 minutes. Add the garlic and cook, stirring constantly, until fragrant, about 30 seconds.

2. Add the green beans, crushed tomatoes, kidney beans, vegetable broth, Italian seasoning, salt, and pepper. Simmer, stirring occasionally, until the vegetables are tender, 5 to 10 minutes. Store unoffered portions in the refrigerator for up to 3 days or in the freezer for up to 6 months.

TIP: Some people like to add pasta or rice to minestrone. If you'd like to, stir in 2 cups cooked elbow macaroni, barley, or brown rice just before serving, allowing the soup to heat up the grains.

White Bean, Kale, and Potato Soup

DF GF NF Vegan

MAKES 4 SERVINGS

3 tablespoons olive oil

1 onion, chopped

1 red bell pepper, seeded and chopped

1 pound kale, stemmed and chopped

4 garlic cloves, minced

8 cups vegetable broth

2 large potatoes, peeled and cut into cubes

2 large carrots, peeled and cut into coins

1 (14-ounce) can white beans, drained

1 teaspoon dried thyme

½ teaspoon sea salt

¼ teaspoon black pepper

Pinch red pepper flakes

This nourishing and warming soup is perfect for chilly fall or winter evenings. The potatoes and white beans make the soup hearty, and the herbs and spices offer plenty of flavor. Kale adds valuable fiber and antioxidants to keep the whole family healthy.

1. In a large pot, heat the olive oil over medium-high heat until it shimmers. Add the onion, bell pepper, and kale. Cook, stirring occasionally, until the vegetables soften, about 5 minutes. Add the garlic and cook, stirring constantly, until fragrant, about 30 seconds.

2. Add the vegetable broth, potatoes, carrots, white beans, thyme, salt, black pepper, and red pepper flakes. Bring to a simmer. Reduce the heat to medium-low. Cook, stirring occasionally, until the potatoes and carrots soften, about 10 minutes. Store unoffered portions in the refrigerator for up to 3 days or in the freezer for up to 6 months.

TIP: In the spring, you might be able to find garlic scapes at your farmers' market. They have a delicious, mild garlic flavor that works well in this soup. If you want to add scapes to this soup, cut them into ¼-inch pieces and add them along with the potatoes and carrots.

Shepherd's Pie

`NF`

Shepherd's pie is a traditional Irish dish made from lamb mince, peas, and carrots topped with whipped potatoes. This version sticks pretty close to the original. It's a tasty, hearty, warming meal your entire family will love.

FOR THE POTATOES

4 large potatoes, peeled and cut into cubes

½ cup milk

¼ cup unsalted butter, melted

½ teaspoon sea salt

¼ teaspoon black pepper

FOR THE MINCE

2 tablespoons olive oil

1 pound ground lamb

1 onion, chopped

2 carrots, peeled and diced

2 cups fresh or frozen peas

1 garlic clove, minced

2 tablespoons flour

1 tablespoon Worcestershire sauce

1 cup chicken broth

1 teaspoon dried thyme

½ teaspoon dried rosemary

½ teaspoon sea salt

¼ teaspoon black pepper

TO MAKE THE POTATOES

1. Put the potatoes in a large pot and cover with an inch of water. Bring to a boil over medium-high heat. Cook until the potatoes are soft, about 10 minutes. Drain.
2. Transfer the potatoes to a large bowl and add the milk, butter, salt, and pepper. Use a mixer or potato masher to mash the potatoes.

TO MAKE THE MINCE

1. In a large sauté pan, heat the olive oil over medium-high heat until it shimmers. Add the ground lamb, onion, carrots, and peas and cook, crumbling the lamb with a spoon, until brown, about 6 minutes.
2. Add the garlic and cook, stirring constantly, for 30 seconds. Add the flour and cook, stirring constantly, for 1 minute more.
3. Add the Worcestershire sauce, chicken broth, thyme, rosemary, salt, and pepper. Cook, stirring constantly, until the liquid thickens, 1 to 2 minutes.

TO ASSEMBLE

1. Preheat the oven to 400°F.
2. Spread the mince mixture in a large casserole dish. Top with the potatoes, spreading to cover the mince. Bake for 25 minutes. Store unoffered portions in the refrigerator for up to 3 days.

TIP: This dish is also delicious with a sweet potato topping. Use an equal amount of sweet potatoes in place of the white potatoes.

Shrimp and Grits

GF **NF**

MAKES 4 SERVINGS

FOR THE GRITS

4 cups chicken broth

½ teaspoon sea salt

¼ teaspoon black pepper

1 cup grits

2 tablespoons
unsalted butter

2 cups grated
Cheddar cheese

FOR THE SHRIMP

3 bacon slices,
cut into pieces

1 pound shrimp, peeled
and deveined

Juice of 1 lemon

1 garlic clove, minced

2 tablespoons chopped
fresh parsley

This cheesy, tasty dish is a Southern favorite that your family is sure to love. The grits are warming and filling, while the shrimp is flavorful and provides tasty protein. The recipe also gets smoky flavors from bacon. Serve with a simple salad for a delicious meal.

TO MAKE THE GRITS

In a large saucepan, bring the broth, salt, and pepper to a boil over medium-high heat. Add the grits and cook, stirring frequently, until the liquid is absorbed, about 20 minutes. Remove from the heat and stir in the butter and cheese.

TO MAKE THE SHRIMP

1. In a large sauté pan, cook the bacon over medium-high heat, stirring occasionally, until brown, about 5 minutes. Remove the bacon from the fat with a slotted spoon and set aside.
2. Add the shrimp and cook, stirring occasionally, until pink, 3 to 5 minutes. Add the garlic and cook, stirring constantly, for 30 seconds.
3. Add the lemon juice and return the reserved bacon to the pan. Cook for 1 minute.
4. Remove from the heat and stir in the parsley. Serve the grits topped with the shrimp. Store unoffered portions in the refrigerator for up to 3 days.

TIP: If the rest of the family would like slightly spicier shrimp, remove your toddler's portion and add a pinch of cayenne when you add the lemon juice.

Fish Tacos with Jicama Slaw

DF GF NF

MAKES 4 SERVINGS

FOR THE FISH

Juice of 2 limes

¼ cup olive oil

1 teaspoon ground cumin

1 teaspoon chili powder

½ teaspoon onion powder

¼ teaspoon sea salt

1 pound white fish (such as cod or snapper)

FOR THE SLAW

1 jicama, peeled and julienned

2 cups shredded cabbage

3 scallions, thinly sliced

Juice of 2 limes

¼ cup olive oil

2 garlic cloves, minced

¼ teaspoon ground cumin

¼ teaspoon sea salt

Pinch cayenne

2 tablespoons chopped fresh cilantro

FOR THE ASSEMBLY

8 soft corn tortillas, warmed

Taco night is popular with many families, and this fish taco recipe allows you to create a nourishing meal for your entire crew. Using soft corn tortillas makes it gluten free if anyone has sensitivity in your house, although you can also use soft wheat tortillas if you choose. A spoonful of salsa finishes off these tacos with a traditional flair—Turkey Burgers with Summer Salsa (page 247) includes a good salsa recipe.

TO MAKE THE FISH

1. In a small bowl, whisk together the lime juice, olive oil, cumin, chili powder, onion powder, and salt.
2. In a zip-top bag, combine the fish with the marinade. Marinate in the refrigerator for 30 minutes.
3. Preheat the oven to 425°F. Place a rack on a baking sheet.
4. Remove the fish from the marinade and place it on the rack. Bake until the fish is flaky, 15 to 20 minutes. Cut the fish into pieces.

TO MAKE THE SLAW

1. In a large bowl, combine the jicama, cabbage, and scallions.
2. In a small bowl, whisk together the lime juice, olive oil, garlic, cumin, salt, cayenne, and cilantro. Toss with the slaw.

TO ASSEMBLE

Load up warmed tortillas with the fish and top with the slaw. Store the fish and slaw separately in the refrigerator for up to 3 days.

TIP: One of the best ways to warm soft tortillas is to wrap them in a damp towel and microwave them for 30 seconds to 1 minute. The towel keeps them moist and soft as they heat.

Ratatouille with Whole Wheat Pasta

MAKES 4 SERVINGS

12 ounces whole wheat rotini pasta

2 tablespoons olive oil

1 onion, chopped

1 eggplant, peeled and cut into ½-inch cubes

1 red bell pepper, seeded and chopped

1 medium zucchini, cut into ½-inch cubes

4 garlic cloves, minced

1 (14-ounce) can crushed tomatoes

1 teaspoon dried Italian seasoning

½ teaspoon sea salt

1 tablespoon chopped fresh parsley

1 tablespoon chopped fresh basil

Now that it's the name of an animated movie, it's easy to forget that ratatouille is also a tasty and nourishing stewed vegetable dish. This one is loaded with tomatoes, veggies, herbs, and spices that will make everyone's taste buds sing.

1. Cook the pasta according to the package directions. Drain and set aside.
2. In a large pot, heat the olive oil over medium-high heat until it shimmers. Add the onion, eggplant, bell pepper, and zucchini and cook, stirring occasionally, until the vegetables begin to brown, 7 to 10 minutes.
3. Add the garlic and cook, stirring constantly, for 30 seconds. Add the tomatoes, Italian seasoning, and salt. Cook, stirring occasionally, for 5 minutes more.
4. Stir in the parsley and basil. Toss with the noodles. Store unoffered portions in the refrigerator for up to 3 days or in the freezer for up to 6 months.

TIP: If you'd like your ratatouille a bit spicier, remove your toddler's portion and then add a pinch of red pepper flakes. Cook for 3 to 4 minutes more.

Spinach and Pepper Frittata

MAKES 4 SERVINGS

8 eggs

¼ cup milk

½ teaspoon sea salt

¼ teaspoon black pepper

Pinch nutmeg

2 tablespoons olive oil

½ onion, chopped

½ red bell pepper, seeded and chopped

2 cups baby spinach

3 garlic cloves, minced

¼ cup grated Parmesan cheese

This simple frittata makes for a delicious family meal, and it's colorful, with vibrant red peppers and green spinach. It's also a great vegetarian meal and takes less than 15 minutes to cook, so it's a perfect weeknight meal for busy families.

1. Preheat the broiler.
2. In a medium bowl, whisk together the eggs, milk, salt, pepper, and nutmeg. Set aside.
3. In a large, ovenproof sauté pan, heat the olive oil over medium-high heat until it shimmers. Add the onion and bell pepper. Cook, stirring occasionally, until the vegetables soften, about 5 minutes.
4. Add the spinach and cook, stirring constantly, until it wilts, about 1 minute. Add the garlic and cook, stirring constantly, for 30 seconds more.
5. Carefully pour the egg mixture from step 2 over the vegetables. Cook over medium heat until the eggs start to set around the sides. Using a rubber spatula, carefully pull the edges of the eggs away from the sides of the pan, tilt the pan, and allow any runny eggs to run into the sides. Cook until the sides start to set again.
6. Sprinkle the frittata with the Parmesan. Transfer to the broiler. Broil until the frittata puffs and the cheese browns, 3 to 4 minutes. Store unoffered portions in the refrigerator for up to 3 days.

Italian Wedding Soup

NF

MAKES 4 SERVINGS

FOR THE MEATBALLS

8 ounces ground beef

8 ounces ground pork

1 onion, grated

4 garlic cloves, minced

1 egg, beaten

½ cup whole wheat bread crumbs

½ cup grated Parmesan cheese

1 tablespoon dried Italian seasoning

¼ teaspoon sea salt

⅛ teaspoon black pepper

FOR THE SOUP

10 cups chicken broth

1 pound kale, chopped

½ teaspoon sea salt

¼ teaspoon black pepper

2 eggs, beaten (optional)

Wedding soup doesn't actually have anything to do with weddings. The Italian name for the soup is *minestra maritata*, which means married soup, which is descriptive of how the meat and vegetables work well together to create the rich flavor.

TO MAKE THE MEATBALLS

In a large bowl, combine all the ingredients and mix well. Form the mixture into ½-inch balls.

TO MAKE THE SOUP

1. In a large pot, combine the chicken broth, kale, salt, pepper, and meatballs. Bring to a simmer over medium-high heat. Reduce the heat and simmer until the meatballs are cooked through, about 10 minutes.

2. Using a fork, drizzle strands of the beaten eggs, if using, into the hot soup to form "noodles." Store unoffered portions in the refrigerator for up to 3 days or in the freezer for up to 6 months.

TIP: If you'd like, you can add 2 cups cooked brown rice to this soup.

Lentil, Barley, and Mushroom "Risotto"

GF option | NF | V

MAKES 4 SERVINGS

2 tablespoons olive oil

1 onion, finely chopped

2 carrots, peeled and chopped

8 ounces mushrooms, sliced

4 garlic cloves, minced

1 (14-ounce) can lentils, drained

4 cups cooked barley

2 cups vegetable broth

1 teaspoon dried thyme

½ teaspoon sea salt

⅛ teaspoon black pepper

½ cup cream cheese

¼ cup grated Parmesan cheese

While this isn't a true risotto, it has a creaminess that is reminiscent of the rice dish. It's a lot higher in fiber than risotto, which is made from white Arborio rice. The mushrooms, lentils, and barley combine for a nice savory flavor, and spinach adds nutritious vitamins and minerals.

1. In a large pot, heat the olive oil over medium-high heat until it shimmers. Add the onion, carrots, and mushrooms and cook, stirring occasionally, until the vegetables start to brown, 6 to 8 minutes.

2. Add the garlic and cook, stirring constantly, for 30 seconds. Add the lentils, barley, vegetable broth, thyme, salt, and pepper. Bring to a simmer. Cook, stirring frequently, for 5 minutes.

3. Stir in the cream cheese and Parmesan cheese. Cook, stirring constantly, until the cheese melts and is incorporated, 2 to 3 minutes more. Store unoffered portions in the refrigerator for up to 3 days or in the freezer for up to 6 months.

TIP: To make this gluten free, you can substitute an equal amount of quinoa or brown rice for the barley.

Maple-Glazed Salmon with Roasted Green Beans

MAKES 4 SERVINGS

This recipe uses pure maple syrup on salmon to add a sweet smoky flavor to the sweet flesh of the salmon. The roasted green beans are soft and flavorful with a slightly caramelized flavor profile your family will love.

**FOR THE
GREEN BEANS**

1 pound green beans, cut into 1-inch pieces

2 tablespoons olive oil

¼ teaspoon sea salt

⅛ teaspoon black pepper

FOR THE SALMON

¼ cup pure maple syrup

¼ cup low-sodium soy sauce

Juice of ½ lemon

4 (4-ounce) salmon fillets, skin removed

TO MAKE THE GREEN BEANS

1. Preheat the oven to 400°F. Line a baking sheet with parchment.
2. In a large bowl, toss the green beans with the olive oil, salt, and pepper. Place the beans in a single layer on the prepared baking sheet. Bake for 20 minutes.

TO MAKE THE SALMON

1. Preheat the broiler.
2. In a small bowl, whisk together the maple syrup, soy sauce, and lemon juice. Marinate the salmon in the refrigerator for 10 minutes.
3. Remove the salmon from the marinade and place on a broiler pan. Broil the salmon until opaque, 3 to 5 minutes. Store unoffered portions in the refrigerator for up to 3 days.

TIP: Add some zip to the salmon marinade by adding 1 teaspoon grated fresh ginger.

Butternut Squash Soup

MAKES 4 SERVINGS

2 tablespoons olive oil

1 onion, finely chopped

2 garlic cloves, minced

6 cups vegetable broth

1 butternut squash, peeled, seeded, and cut into cubes

1 teaspoon dried thyme

½ teaspoon sea salt

¼ teaspoon black pepper

1½ cups canned coconut milk

This soup has a sweet flavor and is loaded with vitamins and minerals everyone in your family needs for good health, including vitamins C and A, along with a healthy portion of fiber, magnesium, and calcium. Plus, it tastes great and freezes well, so you can make a double batch to have freezer meals ready for busy evenings.

1. In a large pot, heat the olive oil over medium-high heat until it shimmers. Add the onion and cook, stirring occasionally, until soft, about 5 minutes. Add the garlic and cook, stirring constantly, for 30 seconds.

2. Add the broth, squash, thyme, salt, and pepper. Bring to a boil and reduce the heat to medium-low. Simmer until the squash is tender, about 20 minutes.

3. In a food processor or blender, puree the soup with the coconut milk. Store unoffered portions in the refrigerator for up to 3 days or in the freezer for up to 6 months.

TIP: This version of squash soup uses savory herbs for flavor; however, you can also use sweeter spices. Try replacing the dried thyme with ½ teaspoon each ground ginger and allspice.

Cauliflower Mac 'n' Cheese

MAKES 4 SERVINGS

1 head cauliflower,
cut into florets

4 ounces cream cheese,
cut into pieces

1 cup milk

2 tablespoons
unsalted butter

1 tablespoon
Dijon mustard

½ teaspoon
onion powder

¼ teaspoon garlic powder

2 cups grated
Cheddar cheese

½ teaspoon sea salt

¼ teaspoon black pepper

Mac 'n' cheese is a family favorite, and this version pumps up the nutrition by replacing the macaroni with nutritious cauliflower. While the flavors and textures are similar, cauliflower adds beneficial fiber and a heaping portion of vitamin C. This dish is also rich in calcium, magnesium, and protein for growing bones and bodies.

1. Bring a large pot of water to a boil over medium-high heat. Add the cauliflower and cook for 5 minutes. Drain.

2. Preheat the oven to 375°F. Grease a 9-by-13-inch baking dish.

3. In a small saucepan, combine the cream cheese, milk, butter, mustard, onion powder, and garlic powder over medium-low heat. Cook, whisking constantly, until the cream cheese and butter are melted, about 5 minutes.

4. Whisk in the Cheddar cheese, salt, and pepper, stirring constantly, until the Cheddar melts, another 3 to 4 minutes.

5. Spread out the cauliflower in the prepared baking pan. Pour the cheese sauce over the top. Bake until bubbly, about 15 minutes. Store unoffered portions in the refrigerator for up to 3 days or in the freezer for up to 6 months.

TIP: If gluten is not a concern, top the casserole with ½ cup whole wheat bread crumbs mixed with another ½ cup grated Cheddar cheese. While you can use any Cheddar here, a combination of half sharp and half medium yields the best flavor.

Cheese Quesadillas with Guacamole

MAKES 4 SERVINGS

FOR THE QUESADILLAS

1 (14-ounce) can vegetarian refried beans

12 soft corn tortillas

2 cups grated Monterey Jack cheese

2 tablespoons olive oil

FOR THE GUACAMOLE

2 avocados, peeled, pitted, and cut into cubes

¼ red onion, minced

1 garlic clove, minced

Juice of 1 lime

¼ teaspoon sea salt

1 tablespoon chopped fresh cilantro

You already know that quesadillas are dead simple to make. By adding beans, you up the nutritional content without sacrificing the easy promise of a quesadilla dinner. You can have this meal on the table in about 20 minutes, so it's perfect for busy weeknights or when everyone is on the go.

TO MAKE THE QUESADILLAS

1. Preheat the oven to 200°F.

2. Spread the refried beans on 6 of the tortillas and top with the cheese. Top that with the remaining tortillas. Brush the outsides of the tortillas with the olive oil.

3. Heat a large sauté pan over medium-high heat. Working with one quesadilla at a time, cook until browned and the cheese melts, 3 to 5 minutes per side. Transfer to a baking sheet and keep warm in the preheated oven while the remaining quesadillas cook. Cut into wedges. Store unoffered portions in the refrigerator for up to 3 days.

TO MAKE THE GUACAMOLE

In a small bowl, combine all the ingredients, mashing with a fork to mix. Store unoffered portions in the refrigerator for up to 3 days.

Mini Meatloaves with Cauliflower Mash

NF

MAKES 4 SERVINGS

Mini muffin tins allow you to make bite-size meatloaves that are fun to eat. These meatloaves are topped with a sweet-and-sour tomato glaze that adds plenty of flavor. While the traditional accompaniment to meatloaf is mashed potatoes, this one opts for veggies, with a cauliflower mash that is similar in texture.

FOR THE MEATLOAVES

8 ounces ground pork

8 ounces ground beef

1 onion, grated

1 egg, beaten

½ cup milk

1 cup whole wheat bread crumbs

1 tablespoon Dijon mustard

1 tablespoon Worcestershire sauce

1 teaspoon dried thyme

½ teaspoon sea salt

¼ teaspoon black pepper

¼ cup sugar-free ketchup

2 tablespoons blackstrap molasses

2 tablespoons apple cider vinegar

FOR THE CAULIFLOWER MASH

1 head cauliflower, broken into florets

4 tablespoons unsalted butter, melted

¼ cup milk

½ teaspoon sea salt

¼ teaspoon black pepper

TO MAKE THE MEATLOAVES

1. Preheat the oven to 375°F. Line a mini muffin tin with paper liners.
2. In a large bowl, combine the ground pork, ground beef, onion, egg, milk, bread crumbs, mustard, Worcestershire, thyme, salt, and pepper and mix well.
3. Roll the mixture into 12 balls and pat them into the muffin tin cups.
4. In a small bowl, whisk together the ketchup, molasses, and vinegar. Spread the mixture over each mini meatloaf.
5. Bake until the loaves are cooked through, about 30 minutes. Store unoffered meatloaves in the refrigerator for up to 3 days or in the freezer for up to 6 months.

TO MAKE THE CAULIFLOWER MASH

1. Fill a large pot with water and bring it to a boil. Add the cauliflower. Cook until the cauliflower is soft, about 15 minutes. Drain.
2. Transfer the cauliflower to a large bowl and add the butter, milk, salt, and pepper. Use an electric mixer or potato masher to mix or mash until smooth. Store unoffered portions in the refrigerator for up to 3 days or in the freezer for up to 6 months.

TIP: You can also make these meatloaves without the ground pork by using an additional 8 ounces of ground beef instead.

Zucchini Pasta Bolognese

MAKES 4 SERVINGS

4 tablespoons
olive oil, divided

1 pound ground beef

1 onion, finely chopped

4 ounces
mushrooms, sliced

1 celery stalk,
thinly sliced

1 carrot, peeled and
finely chopped

4 garlic cloves, minced

2 tablespoons
tomato paste

1 (14-ounce) can
tomato sauce

1 teaspoon dried oregano

1 teaspoon dried
Italian seasoning

¼ teaspoon
ground nutmeg

½ teaspoon sea salt

¼ teaspoon black pepper

Pinch red pepper flakes

4 medium zucchini, cut
into ¼-inch-thick noodles

Zucchini makes a great substitute for noodles in this pasta dish. To cut the zucchini into noodles, use a vegetable peeler to make long, thin, ribbons of the zucchini. Leave the peel on—it gives the "zoodles" a lovely green outline that adds color to the dish.

1. In a large pot, heat 2 tablespoons of olive oil over medium-high heat until it shimmers. Add the ground beef, onion, mushrooms, celery, and carrot. Cook, crumbling the beef with a spoon, until brown, about 6 minutes.

2. Add the garlic and cook, stirring constantly, for 30 seconds. Add the tomato paste and cook, stirring constantly, for 1 minute more.

3. Add the tomato sauce, oregano, Italian seasoning, nutmeg, salt, black pepper, and red pepper flakes. Bring to a simmer. Reduce the heat and cook, stirring occasionally, for 10 minutes.

4. In a large sauté pan, heat the remaining 2 tablespoons of olive oil over medium-high heat until it shimmers. Add the zucchini ribbons and cook, stirring occasionally, until they are crisp-tender, 3 to 5 minutes.

5. Toss the zucchini with the sauce. Store unoffered portions in the refrigerator for up to 3 days or in the freezer for up to 6 months.

TIP: This sauce works well with traditional pasta, too. Try it with cooked whole wheat spaghetti or fettuccine.

Honey-Glazed Salmon with Sautéed Spinach

MAKES 4 SERVINGS

¼ cup honey

2 tablespoons
low-sodium soy sauce

Juice of 1 orange, divided

Pinch cayenne

4 (4-ounce) pieces
of salmon

2 tablespoons olive oil

4 cups baby spinach

¼ teaspoon sea salt

⅛ teaspoon black pepper

This one-pan meal comes together quickly, so it's great for busy weeknights. It's also full of nutrients, including healthy omega-3 fatty acids, iron, vitamin C, and a healthy dose of B vitamins. The slightly sweet honey glaze flavors the salmon and adds a little sweetness to the spinach.

1. In a medium bowl, whisk together the honey, soy sauce, half of the orange juice, and the cayenne. Marinate the salmon in the refrigerator for 10 minutes.

2. In a large sauté pan, heat the olive oil over medium-high heat until it shimmers. Remove the salmon from the marinade and add it to the pan, skin-side up. Cook for 4 minutes. Flip the salmon and cook for an additional 3 minutes, or until the salmon is cooked through. Set aside the salmon on a platter, tented with foil.

3. Add the spinach to the pan with the salt, pepper, and remaining orange juice. Cook, stirring frequently, until the spinach wilts, 2 to 3 minutes more. Store unoffered portions in the refrigerator for up to 3 days.

TIP: Be sure to debone the salmon before you cook it. Use a small, clean pair of pliers to remove any small pin bones from the fish.

Tuna Patties with Lemony Swiss Chard

MAKES 4 SERVINGS

FOR THE TUNA PATTIES

3 (6-ounce) cans water-packed tuna, drained

¾ cup whole wheat bread crumbs

½ onion, finely diced

1 egg, beaten

2 tablespoons mayonnaise

1 tablespoon Dijon mustard

1 teaspoon grated lemon zest

1 tablespoon lemon juice

1 teaspoon dried dill

½ teaspoon sea salt

¼ teaspoon black pepper

2 tablespoons olive oil

FOR THE SWISS CHARD

2 tablespoons olive oil

4 cups stemmed and chopped Swiss chard

1 teaspoon grated lemon zest

Juice of 1 lemon

¼ teaspoon sea salt

⅛ teaspoon black pepper

These tuna patties are incredibly flavorful. Here, they are paired with sautéed Swiss chard that has a hint of garlic and lemon, which perfectly complements the flavors in the tuna. Consider using the patties as burgers when you want to make a heartier meal.

TO MAKE THE TUNA PATTIES

1. In a large bowl, combine the tuna, bread crumbs, and onion.
2. In a small bowl, whisk together the egg, mayonnaise, mustard, lemon zest and juice, dill, salt, and pepper. Fold the mayonnaise mixture into the tuna mixture. Shape the mixture into four patties.
3. In a large nonstick sauté pan, heat the olive oil over medium-high heat until it shimmers. Add the tuna patties. Cook until browned, about 5 minutes per side. Store unoffered portions in the refrigerator for up to 3 days or in the freezer for up to 6 months.

TO MAKE THE SWISS CHARD

1. In a large sauté pan, heat the olive oil over medium-high heat until it shimmers. Add the Swiss chard, lemon zest and juice, salt, and pepper.
2. Cook, stirring occasionally, until the chard is wilted, about 5 minutes. Store unoffered portions in the refrigerator for up to 3 days or in the freezer for up to 6 months.

TIP: You can use any type of greens, such as kale, spinach, or collard greens, in this recipe.

Whole Wheat Orzo with Peas and Butternut Squash Sauce

DF NF Vegan

MAKES 4 SERVINGS

12 ounces whole
wheat orzo

2 tablespoons olive oil

1 onion, finely chopped

1 butternut squash,
peeled, seeded, and
cut into cubes

4 garlic cloves,
finely minced

2 cups vegetable broth

Pinch nutmeg

½ teaspoon sea salt

¼ teaspoon black pepper

2 cups fresh or
frozen peas

Peas and whole wheat orzo combine to make a complete plant-based protein. The butternut squash sauce adds valuable nutrients like vitamin A and vitamin C, and it also has a nice, gentle garlic flavor that goes well with the pasta.

1. Cook the orzo according to the package instructions. Drain and set aside.
2. In a large sauté pan, heat the olive oil over medium-high heat until it shimmers. Add the onion and cook, stirring occasionally, until soft, about 5 minutes. Add the butternut squash and cook, stirring occasionally, for 5 minutes more. Add the garlic and cook, stirring constantly, for 30 seconds.
3. Add the vegetable broth, nutmeg, salt, and pepper. Cook, stirring occasionally, until the butternut squash is soft, 5 to 10 minutes more. Transfer the sauce to a food processor or blender and puree until smooth.
4. Return the sauce to the pot. Add the cooked orzo and the peas. Cook over medium-high heat, stirring occasionally, until the peas are warmed through, 3 to 5 minutes more. Store unoffered portions in the refrigerator for up to 3 days or in the freezer for up to 6 months.

TIP: Stir in 2 tablespoons chopped fresh basil just before serving to add a bright herbal note to this dish.

Black Bean Burritos

NF V

MAKES 4 SERVINGS

2 (14-ounce) cans black beans, drained

2 cups prepared mild salsa

Juice of 1 lime

1 teaspoon ground cumin

1 teaspoon onion powder

½ teaspoon chili powder

½ teaspoon ground coriander

¼ teaspoon garlic powder

¼ teaspoon sea salt

½ cup grated Monterey Jack cheese

4 large whole wheat tortillas

1 tomato, finely chopped

These easy vegetarian burritos are sure to be a hit with your whole family. The black beans are highly seasoned to create a savory filling for the tortillas.

1. Preheat the oven to 350°F. Line a baking sheet with parchment.
2. In a large saucepan, combine the black beans, salsa, lime juice, cumin, onion power, chili powder, coriander, garlic powder, and salt. Cook, stirring occasionally, until the beans are warm, about 5 minutes.
3. Use a potato masher to mash the beans, mixing well as you do.
4. Spoon the beans onto the tortillas and top with the cheese. Fold them into burritos. Place the burritos on the prepared baking sheet.
5. Bake until the cheese is bubbly, about 20 minutes. Top with the chopped tomato. Store unoffered portions in the refrigerator for up to 3 days or in the freezer (without the tomatoes) for up to 6 months.

TIP: Instead of the chopped tomatoes, you can make a fresh pico de gallo to top these burritos. Mix 1 finely chopped tomato, ¼ cup of finely chopped red onion, the juice of 1 lime, 2 tablespoons of chopped fresh cilantro, and a pinch of sea salt.

Lamb Kofta with Minted Peas

MAKES 4 SERVINGS

FOR THE LAMB KOFTA

1 pound ground lamb

4 garlic cloves, minced

1 tablespoon ground coriander

1 teaspoon ground cumin

¾ teaspoon sea salt

½ teaspoon ground cinnamon

½ teaspoon ground allspice

¼ teaspoon ground ginger

¼ teaspoon black pepper

FOR THE MINTED PEAS

2 cups fresh or frozen peas

¼ teaspoon sea salt

2 tablespoons chopped fresh mint

Typically, you make lamb kofta on kebabs on the grill, which you can do here if you wish. However, this recipe calls for baking them in mini muffin tins so the kofta is almost like a meatball. Your family will love the savory flavors of this kofta along with the bright mint in the peas.

TO MAKE THE LAMB KOFTA

1. Preheat the oven to 350°F. Line a mini muffin tin with paper liners.
2. In a large bowl, combine all the ingredients and mix well. Form the mixture into 12 balls and place one in each cup of the muffin tin.
3. Bake until the lamb is cooked through, 20 to 30 minutes. Store unoffered portions in the refrigerator for up to 3 days or in the freezer for up to 6 months.

TO MAKE THE MINTED PEAS

1. In a medium saucepan with a steamer insert, bring about 1 inch of water to a simmer. Add the peas. Cover and steam until tender, about 5 minutes.
2. Stir in the salt and mint. Store unoffered portions in the refrigerator for up to 3 days or in the freezer for up to 6 months.

TIP: You can also make the minted peas into a dipping sauce for the kofta. To do so, puree the steamed peas, mint, and salt, thinning with water, lemon juice, or milk to achieve the desired consistency.

Chicken Satay with Almond Butter Sauce

MAKES 4 SERVINGS

**FOR THE
CHICKEN SATAY**

Juice of 1 lime

2 tablespoons
low-sodium soy sauce

1 tablespoon olive oil

1 teaspoon fish sauce or
additional soy sauce

2 garlic cloves, minced

1 teaspoon grated
fresh ginger

½ teaspoon ground
coriander

1 pound chicken tenders,
cut into strips

**FOR THE ALMOND
BUTTER SAUCE**

¾ cup almond butter

½ cup canned
coconut milk

1 tablespoon honey

1 teaspoon toasted
sesame oil

1 teaspoon lime juice

1 teaspoon fish sauce or
low-sodium soy sauce

2 scallions, chopped

1 garlic clove, peeled

2 tablespoons chopped
fresh cilantro

Chicken satay is a flavorful dish that goes really well with nut butter sauces. This version calls for the dipping sauce to be based on almond butter, which is a great source of vitamin E. Serve with steamed brown rice and a fruit salad for a nutritious meal.

TO MAKE THE CHICKEN SATAY

1. In a large bowl, whisk together the lime juice, soy sauce, olive oil, fish sauce, garlic, ginger, and coriander. Marinate the chicken in the refrigerator for 30 minutes.
2. Preheat the oven to 350°F. Line a baking sheet with parchment.
3. Remove the chicken from the marinade. Place the chicken on the prepared baking sheet and bake until cooked through, 25 to 35 minutes. Store unoffered portions in the refrigerator for up to 3 days or in the freezer for up to 6 months.

TO MAKE THE ALMOND BUTTER SAUCE

In a blender, combine all the ingredients and blend until smooth. Store unoffered portions in the refrigerator for up to 3 days or in the freezer for up to 6 months.

TIP: If you have an indoor grill, you can grill the marinated chicken for about 5 minutes per side.

Turkey Burgers with Summer Salsa

DF NF

MAKES 4 SERVINGS

FOR THE BURGERS

1 pound ground turkey

1 teaspoon garlic powder

1 teaspoon onion powder

1 teaspoon ground cumin

½ teaspoon ground coriander

½ teaspoon sea salt

¼ teaspoon black pepper

2 tablespoons olive oil

4 whole wheat burger buns, toasted

FOR THE SALSA

1 avocado, peeled, pitted, and cut into cubes

1 cup fresh corn

2 tomatoes, chopped

1 cup canned black beans, drained

½ red onion, finely chopped

¼ cup chopped fresh cilantro

½ teaspoon sea salt

Juice of 1 lime

These tasty turkey burgers are perfect for summer, when fresh corn and tomatoes are widely available at your local farmers' market. Make the burgers as indicated here, or create mini sliders for small hands. Serve with seasonal fruit on the side.

TO MAKE THE BURGERS

1. In a large bowl, mix the ground turkey, garlic powder, onion powder, cumin, coriander, salt, and pepper until well combined. Form the mixture into four patties.

2. In a large sauté pan, heat the olive oil over medium-high heat until it shimmers. Add the turkey burgers. Cook until browned and cooked through, about 5 minutes per side.

3. Serve the burgers on the buns, topped with the salsa. Store unoffered burgers (without buns) in the refrigerator for up to 3 days or in the freezer for up to 6 months.

TO MAKE THE SALSA

In a medium bowl, combine all the ingredients. Mix well to combine. The salsa does not store well, so make it fresh if you are serving thawed burgers made previously.

TIP: These burgers are great for outdoor grilling. Grill on direct heat for 5 to 7 minutes per side.

Black Bean Burgers with Red Pepper Mayo

MAKES 4 SERVINGS

FOR THE BURGERS

1 (14-ounce) can black beans, drained

½ red bell pepper, seeded and chopped

½ red onion, seeded and chopped

3 garlic cloves, minced

1 teaspoon ground cumin

½ teaspoon ground coriander

½ teaspoon sea salt

¼ teaspoon black pepper

½ cup whole wheat bread crumbs

1 egg, beaten

2 tablespoons olive oil

4 whole wheat burger buns, toasted

FOR THE RED PEPPER MAYONNAISE

1 (7-ounce) jar roasted red peppers, drained

¼ cup mayonnaise

½ teaspoon sea salt

Black bean burgers are a great alternative to burgers made with ground meat. Topped with a red pepper mayonnaise, these tasty burgers will be a delicious treat for the whole family. You can use any type of canned beans or legumes (such as lentils, chickpeas, or kidney beans) in place of the black beans; they'll taste just as great.

TO MAKE THE BURGERS

1. In a food processor, combine the beans, red pepper, red onion, garlic, cumin, coriander, salt, and pepper, and pulse about 10 times, until well mixed but still chunky. Transfer to a large bowl.

2. Add the bread crumbs and egg and mix until well combined. Form the mixture into four patties.

3. In a large nonstick sauté pan, heat the olive oil over medium-high heat until it shimmers. Cook the patties until browned, about 4 minutes per side. Serve on the buns, spread with the red pepper mayonnaise. Store unoffered burgers (without buns or sauce) in the refrigerator for up to 3 days or in the freezer for up to 6 months.

TO MAKE THE RED PEPPER MAYONNAISE

In a blender or food processor, blend the red peppers, mayonnaise, and salt until smooth. Store unoffered sauce in the refrigerator for up to 3 days.

Salmon with Blackberry Sauce and Spinach

MAKES 4 SERVINGS

The sweet, juicy flavor of blackberries enhances the salmon here. You can often find blackberries growing wild in mid- to late summer, so this is a great summer recipe.

FOR THE SALMON

4 (4-ounce) salmon fillets

½ teaspoon sea salt

¼ teaspoon black pepper

1 teaspoon dried tarragon

2 tablespoons olive oil

1 shallot, minced

2 garlic cloves, minced

3 cups blackberries

1 cup chicken broth

FOR THE SPINACH

2 tablespoons olive oil

4 cups baby spinach

½ teaspoon grated lemon zest

Juice of 1 lemon

1 teaspoon dried thyme

¼ teaspoon sea salt

⅛ teaspoon black pepper

TO MAKE THE SALMON

1. Preheat the broiler. Place a rack on a baking sheet.
2. Season the salmon with the salt, pepper, and tarragon. Place the fish on the rack and broil until cooked through, about 5 minutes.
3. In a large saucepan, heat the olive oil over medium-high heat until it shimmers. Add the shallot and cook, stirring occasionally, until soft, 3 to 4 minutes. Add the garlic and cook, stirring constantly, for 30 seconds.
4. Add the blackberries. Bring the mixture to a simmer. Cook, stirring occasionally and mashing the berries with a spoon, until the blackberries are saucy, about 4 minutes.
5. Add the chicken broth to the blackberries. Simmer, stirring constantly, until the sauce thickens, 2 to 3 minutes more. Spoon the sauce over the cooked salmon. Store unoffered portions in the refrigerator for up to 3 days or in the freezer for up to 6 months.

TO MAKE THE SPINACH

1. In a large sauté pan, heat the olive oil over medium-high heat until it shimmers. Add the spinach and cook, stirring occasionally, until it wilts, about 3 minutes.
2. Add the lemon zest and juice, thyme, salt, and pepper. Cook, stirring constantly, for 2 minutes more. Store unoffered portions in the refrigerator for up to 3 days or in the freezer for up to 6 months.

TIP: Halibut is another fish that works really well with blackberry sauce. Replace the salmon with four (4-ounce) halibut fillets and follow the recipe as written.

Peanut Butter Noodles with Broccoli

MAKES 4 SERVINGS

12 ounces whole wheat spaghetti

2 cups broccoli florets

1 cup peanut butter

1 cup canned coconut milk

2 tablespoons low-sodium soy sauce

1 tablespoon honey

1 tablespoon lime juice

½ teaspoon fish sauce or additional soy sauce

2 garlic cloves, peeled

3 scallions, chopped

1 teaspoon grated fresh ginger

¼ cup chopped fresh cilantro

Kids love these peanut butter noodles hot or cold. They make a tasty, protein-filled vegetarian meal that comes together easily. The only cooking required is boiling the noodles and steaming the broccoli, so it's a fast, easy meal anytime.

1. Cook the spaghetti according to the package instructions. Drain and set aside.

2. In a medium saucepan with a steamer insert, bring about 1 inch of water to a boil. Add the broccoli. Cover and steam until tender, 5 to 10 minutes.

3. In a food processor or blender, combine the peanut butter, coconut milk, soy sauce, honey, lime juice, fish sauce, garlic, scallions, ginger, and cilantro. Blend until smooth.

4. Toss the sauce with the hot noodles and broccoli. Store unoffered portions in the refrigerator for up to 3 days or in the freezer for up to 6 months.

TIP: If you're not vegetarian, Chicken Satay (page 246) is a great addition to this tasty family meal, offering extra protein and flavor.

Baked Egg and Red Pepper Mini Muffins

8 eggs

½ cup milk

1 tablespoon Dijon mustard

1 teaspoon onion powder

½ teaspoon sea salt

⅛ teaspoon black pepper

1 (7-ounce) jar roasted red peppers, drained and chopped

1 cup grated Parmesan cheese

There's good reason why "breakfast for dinner" is a thing. Not only is it fun to switch up mealtime expectations, breakfasts tend to be more indulgent meals. Round out these egg muffins with a side of baked sweet potato fries and even a simple green salad.

1. Preheat the oven to 350°F. Line a mini muffin tin with paper liners.
2. In a large bowl, whisk together the eggs, milk, mustard, onion powder, salt, and pepper. Fold in the red peppers and cheese. Pour the mixture into the muffin tin cups.
3. Bake until the eggs are set, 20 to 30 minutes. Store unoffered portions in the refrigerator for up to 3 days or in the freezer for up to 6 months.

TIP: If you'd like to add animal protein to this dish, you can stir in 4 ounces flaked smoked salmon or chopped ham when you add the red peppers.

Lentils and Brown Rice with Tomato Sauce

MAKES 4 SERVINGS

2 tablespoons olive oil

1 onion, finely chopped

1 carrot, peeled
and chopped

1 celery stalk, chopped

3 garlic cloves, minced

2 (14-ounce) cans
lentils, drained

1 (14-ounce) can crushed
tomatoes

1 teaspoon dried oregano

1 teaspoon dried thyme

½ teaspoon sea salt

¼ teaspoon black pepper

2 cups cooked brown rice

Here's a great vegan family meal you can make in one pot. It comes together more quickly if you have precooked rice on hand. This dish is a great source of protein, and it's really flavorful, so your whole family will love it.

1. In a large pot, heat the olive oil over medium-high heat until it shimmers. Add the onion, carrot, and celery. Cook, stirring occasionally, until the veggies soften, 5 to 7 minutes. Add the garlic and cook, stirring constantly, for 30 seconds.

2. Add the lentils, tomatoes, oregano, thyme, salt, and pepper. Bring to a simmer and cook, stirring frequently, for 5 minutes.

3. Stir in the rice. Simmer until the rice is warmed through. Store unoffered portions in the refrigerator for up to 3 days or in the freezer for up to 6 months.

TIP: This lentil mixture, minus the rice, also makes a delicious pasta sauce. Spoon it over cooked whole wheat pasta, such as spaghetti.

Roast Chicken with Brussels Sprout and Bacon Hash

MAKES 4 SERVINGS

FOR THE CHICKEN

1 (3-pound)
whole chicken

1 teaspoon sea salt

¼ teaspoon black pepper

1 rosemary sprig

1 thyme sprig

½ onion

FOR THE HASH

4 bacon slices,
cut into pieces

½ onion, chopped

1 pound Brussels sprouts,
julienned

2 tablespoons apple
cider vinegar

2 tablespoons pure
maple syrup

½ teaspoon sea salt

¼ teaspoon black pepper

Pinch cayenne (optional)

Roast chicken is an ideal main course for a Sunday family dinner. The chicken takes about an hour in the oven, but the prep time is minimal. While the chicken cooks, make the sweet, slightly spicy and smoky Brussels sprout and bacon hash as a tasty and nutritious side dish.

TO MAKE THE CHICKEN

1. Preheat the oven to 350°F. Place a rack in a large roasting pan.
2. Season the chicken all over with the salt and pepper. Stuff the cavity with the rosemary, thyme, and onion. Put the chicken, breast side up, on the roasting rack.
3. Bake until the breast reaches an internal temperature of 165°F, about 1 hour and 15 minutes.
4. Allow the chicken to rest for 20 minutes before carving. Store unoffered portions in the refrigerator for up to 3 days or in the freezer for up to 6 months.

TO MAKE THE HASH

1. In a large sauté pan, cook the bacon over medium-high heat, stirring occasionally, until browned, about 5 minutes. Using a slotted spoon, remove the bacon from the pan and set aside.
2. Add the onion and Brussels sprouts to the pan. Cook, stirring occasionally, until the vegetables soften and begin to brown, 7 to 10 minutes.
3. Add the vinegar, maple syrup, salt, black pepper, and cayenne. Cook, stirring frequently, until the liquid is partially evaporated, 5 minutes more. Return the bacon to the pan. Cook for 1 minute more. Store unoffered portions in the refrigerator for up to 3 days or in the freezer for up to 6 months.

TIP: In place of the Brussels sprouts, you can use a head of shredded cabbage for the hash.

Whole Wheat Pasta with Kale-Walnut Pesto

MAKES 4 SERVINGS

12 ounces whole
wheat rotini

2 cups stemmed and
chopped kale

3 garlic cloves, peeled

½ cup chopped walnuts

½ cup grated
Parmesan cheese

1 teaspoon grated
orange zest

¼ cup olive oil

½ teaspoon sea salt

¼ teaspoon black pepper

Pesto is a super-easy sauce to make. Once prepared, all that's left is to cook the pasta, so this recipe comes together in minutes. This is a perfect meal when you're short on time or in the summer when it's just too hot to spend much time in the kitchen. Walnuts add protein and flavor, but you can replace them with any type of tree nuts you enjoy, such as almonds or pine nuts.

1. Cook the pasta according to the package instructions. Drain and set aside.

2. In a blender or food processor, process the kale, garlic, walnuts, cheese, orange zest, olive oil, salt, and pepper until the mixture forms a paste. Toss the pesto with the hot pasta. Store unoffered portions in the refrigerator for up to 3 days or in the freezer for up to 6 months.

TIP: Pulse the blender several times, pausing between pulses to stir the pesto and scrape down the sides with a rubber spatula for consistency.

Veggie Lasagna

MAKES 4 SERVINGS

2 (14-ounce) cans
crushed tomatoes

2 garlic cloves, peeled

¼ cup chopped
fresh basil

½ teaspoon sea salt

3 large zucchini, cut
into ¼-inch-thick noodles

8 ounces part-skim
ricotta cheese

2 cups thawed
frozen spinach, liquid
squeezed out

8 ounces grated
Swiss cheese

Zucchini ribbons take the place of pasta noodles in this recipe, making it gluten free and full of nourishing vitamins and minerals. Simply use a vegetable peeler to make long, thin ribbons of the zucchini.

1. Preheat the oven to 350°F.
2. In a blender or food processor, puree the crushed tomatoes, garlic, basil, and salt until smooth.
3. Spread a layer of the tomato mixture over the bottom of a 9-inch square pan. Add a layer of zucchini noodles. Follow with a layer of ricotta cheese and spread evenly. Follow with a layer of spinach, then a layer of Swiss cheese. Add another layer of zucchini noodles and more sauce. Continue layering in this manner until you've filled the pan. Top with the remaining cheese.
4. Bake the lasagna until the cheese is bubbly, about 1 hour. Store unoffered portions in the refrigerator for up to 3 days or in the freezer for up to 6 months.

TIP: Lasagna is notorious for bubbling over in the oven. To keep your oven clean, place the lasagna on a baking sheet when you put it in the oven, to catch any drips.

Chicken and Spinach Roll-Ups

MAKES 4 SERVINGS

4 (4-ounce) boneless, skinless chicken breast halves

½ teaspoon sea salt

¼ teaspoon black pepper

4 thin prosciutto slices

2 cups thawed frozen spinach, liquid squeezed out

4 ounces grated Swiss cheese

A fun way to serve spinach to your family is to roll it up inside thinly pounded chicken. This recipe calls for frozen spinach, which helps these tasty roll-ups come together quickly. Serve with a side of your favorite grain, such as brown rice, barley, or quinoa.

1. Preheat the oven to 350°F. Line a baking sheet with parchment.
2. Using a mallet, pound each chicken breast between two layers of parchment or plastic wrap until they are ⅛ inch thick. Place the chicken on the prepared baking sheet and season with the salt and pepper.
3. Place a slice of prosciutto on each piece of chicken. Top with the spinach and grated cheese.
4. Roll the chicken around the filling and tie it with kitchen twine to hold it together.
5. Bake until the chicken is cooked through, 45 to 50 minutes. Allow to rest for 10 minutes before slicing and serving. Store unoffered portions in the refrigerator for up to 3 days or in the freezer for up to 6 months.

TIP: In place of the spinach, you can roll the chicken and prosciutto around three steamed asparagus spears before baking.

Lemon Pepper Cod and Kale

MAKES 4 SERVINGS

4 (4-ounce) cod fillets

½ teaspoon sea salt

½ teaspoon black pepper

2 tablespoons olive oil

1 lemon

5 cups stemmed and chopped kale

This simple cod dish cooks in one pot in about 20 minutes, and it's a nutritious, high-fiber, high-protein meal your family will enjoy. If you can't find cod, feel free to substitute any other white fish, such as snapper. You can also use greens other than kale, such as collard greens or escarole.

1. Season the cod with the salt and pepper.
2. In a large sauté pan, heat the olive oil over medium-high heat until it shimmers. Add the cod and cook until it is cooked through, about 4 minutes per side. Squeeze the lemon over the cod and continue to cook for 1 more minute. Remove the cod from the pan and set it aside, tented with foil to keep it warm.
3. Add the kale to the pan. Cook, stirring occasionally, until the kale is soft, about 5 minutes. Store unoffered portions in the refrigerator for up to 3 days.

TIP: Your little one may be sensitive to too much pepper, so adjust the pepper on her fillet accordingly.

Taco Soup

DF option GF NF

MAKES 6 SERVINGS

2 tablespoons olive oil

1 pound ground beef

1 onion, chopped

4 garlic cloves, minced

6 cups chicken or beef broth

1 (14-ounce) can crushed tomatoes

1 (14-ounce) can kidney beans, drained

1 (2-ounce) can chopped chiles, drained (optional)

1 cup fresh or thawed frozen corn

1 teaspoon ground cumin

1 teaspoon chili powder

½ teaspoon ground coriander

1 teaspoon sea salt

¼ teaspoon black pepper

4 ounces grated Cheddar cheese (optional)

1 avocado, peeled, pitted, and chopped (optional)

Soup is a fantastic dish to serve your family because it's quick and easy and cooks in a single pot, which minimizes cleanup. The other great thing about soup is that you can add your own flair, use up any leftovers, and easily create your own recipes. This soup is a great way to use up any leftover taco meat, if you have it, or you can make it from scratch as suggested here.

1. In a large sauté pan, heat the olive oil over medium-high heat until it shimmers. Add the ground beef and onion. Cook, crumbling the beef with a spoon, until brown, about 6 minutes.

2. Add the garlic and cook, stirring constantly, for 30 seconds. Add the broth, tomatoes, kidney beans, chiles (if using), corn, cumin, chili powder, coriander, salt, and pepper. Simmer, stirring occasionally, for 15 minutes.

3. Top individual servings with Cheddar cheese and avocado, if using. Store unoffered portions (without toppings) in the refrigerator for up to 3 days or in the freezer for up to 6 months.

TIP: To use leftover taco meat, eliminate the ground beef and the cumin, chili powder, and coriander. Cook the onion in the olive oil. Add the meat about 5 minutes before the soup is done.

At-a-Glance Cooking Chart for Purees

FOOD	AMOUNT	COOK TIME
AVOCADOS	3	n/a
APPLES	4	Steam 10 minutes
APRICOTS	5	Steam 10 minutes (whole fruit) or 5 minutes (chopped)
ARTICHOKE HEARTS	3	Steam 1 hour (whole)
ASPARAGUS	1½ pounds (trimmed)	Steam 5 to 10 minutes
BANANAS	3 peeled	n/a
CEREAL (Barley, Brown rice, Farro, Oat, Quinoa)	½ cup ground grains	Simmer 10 minutes
BEANS	1 cup dried	Soak overnight; Boil 45 minutes to 2 hours
BEETS	4 or 5	Steam 5 to 10 minutes (cubed) or 45 to 60 minutes (whole)
BELL PEPPERS	6 medium	Steam 10 minutes
BERRIES (blackberries, raspberries, strawberries)	2 cups	n/a
BLUEBERRIES	2 cups	Steam 5 minutes
BROCCOLI OR CAULIFLOWER	1 head (chopped)	Steam 10 minutes
BROWN RICE	½ ground cup	Simmer 10 minutes
BUTTERNUT OR ACORN SQUASH	1 small (cubed)	Steam 10 to 12 minutes
CARROTS OR PARSNIPS	5 (cubed)	Steam 5 to 10 minutes
CHERRIES	3 cups	Steam 5 minutes
CHICKPEAS (canned)	2 cups	Boil 5 minutes
CRANBERRIES	6 cups	Boil 5 minutes
DRIED FRUIT	2 cups	Soak 10 minutes

FOOD	AMOUNT	COOK TIME
EDAMAME	1½ pounds (shelled)	Steam 5 minutes
FISH	1½ pounds (skinned, boned, and chopped)	Steam 5 to 10 minutes
GREEN BEANS	5 cups	Steam 5 to 10 minutes
GREENS (chard, collards, kale, spinach)	1½ pounds (stemmed, chopped)	Steam 5 to 10 minutes
LENTILS	1 cup (dried)	Soak overnight; Boil 30 minutes
MANGO OR PAPAYA	2 fruit	n/a
MEAT (beef, pork)	1½ pounds (boneless, trimmed, cubed)	Steam 10 to 15 minutes
MELON	1 small	n/a
PEAS	1½ pounds	Steam 5 to 7 minutes
PEACHES OR NECTARINES	5 fruits	Steam 7 to 10 minutes
PLUMS	7 plums	Steam 7 to 10 minutes
POTATOES	3 medium (cubed)	Steam 10 minutes
POULTRY	1½ pounds (boneless, skinless, cubed)	Steam 10 to 15 minutes
PRUNES	2 cups	Soak 20 minutes
PUMPKIN	1½ pounds (cubed)	Steam 10 minutes
SWEET POTATOES OR YAMS	2 medium (cubed)	Steam 10 minutes
TOFU	12 oz.	n/a
ZUCCHINI	3 small (cubed)	Steam 10 minutes

Sample Food Introduction Schedule

Consider this 6-week food schedule to be a guide, not a mandate. It's here to help you make early food choices but don't feel you need to follow it to the letter. Perhaps you'll start with avocado puree, and then serve it every day for a week. That's great. Go at your own pace, and your baby's.

For those who want to vary it up, this schedule gives you a new option every few days. Always make sure that your child can tolerate an ingredient before adding a new one to it.

WEEK 1

DAY 1	Avocado Puree (page 42)
DAY 2	Avocado Puree (page 42)
DAY 3	Avocado Puree (page 42)
DAY 4	Sweet Potato Puree (page 43)
DAY 5	Sweet Potato Puree (page 43)
DAY 6	Sweet Potato Puree (page 43)
DAY 7	Carrot Puree (page 46)

WEEK 2

DAY 1	Carrot Puree (page 46)
DAY 2	Carrot Puree (page 46)
DAY 3	Banana Puree (page 44)
DAY 4	Banana Puree (page 44)
DAY 5	Banana Puree (page 44)
DAY 6	Avocado and Banana Puree (page 76)
DAY 7	Avocado and Banana Puree (page 76)

WEEK 3

DAY 1	Avocado and Banana Puree (page 76)
DAY 2	Sweet Potato and Spinach Puree (page 76)
DAY 3	Sweet Potato and Spinach Puree (page 76)
DAY 4	Sweet Potato and Spinach Puree (page 76)
DAY 5	Pea Puree (page 54)
DAY 6	Pea and Carrot Puree (page 82)
DAY 7	Pea and Carrot Puree (page 82)

DAY 1	Meal 1: Beet Puree (page 63)
	Meal 2: Avocado and Banana Puree (page 76)
DAY 2	Meal 1: Mix Beet Puree (page 63) and Carrot Puree (page 46)
	Meal 2: Mix Avocado Puree (page 42) and Spinach Puree (page 47)
DAY 3	Meal 1: Beet Puree (page 63) with fennel
	Meal 2: Pea Puree (page 54) with mint
DAY 4	Meal 1: Apple Puree (page 45)
	Meal 2: Mix Pea Puree (page 54) and Avocado Puree (page 42)
DAY 5	Meal 1: Mix Apple Puree (page 45) and Carrot Puree (page 46)
	Meal 2: Sweet Potato and Spinach Puree (page 76)
DAY 6	Meal 1: Oat and Banana Puree (page 87)
	Meal 2: Mix Sweet Potato Puree (page 43) and Pea Puree (page 54)
DAY 7	Meal 1: Mix Oat Cereal (page 68) and Apple Puree (page 45)
	Meal 2: Avocado Puree (page 42) with cumin

DAY 1	Meal 1: Mix Banana Puree (page 44) and yogurt
	Meal 2: Pea Puree (page 54) with mint
DAY 2	Meal 1: Mix Beet Puree (page 63) and yogurt
	Meal 2: Mix Pea Puree (page 54) and Avocado Puree (page 42)
DAY 3	Meal 1: Mix Banana Puree (page 44) and yogurt
	Meal 2: Mix Cauliflower Puree (page 52) and Sweet Potato Puree (page 43)
DAY 4	Meal 1: Avocado and Banana Puree (page 76)
	Meal 2: Cauliflower Puree (page 52) with cumin
DAY 5	Meal 1: Blueberry and Yogurt Puree (page 80)
	Meal 2: Mix Cauliflower Puree (page 52) and Carrot Puree (page 46)

DAY 6	Meal 1: Blueberry and Yogurt Puree (page 80)
	Meal 2: Mix Sweet Potato Puree (page 43) and Avocado Puree (page 42)
DAY 7	Meal 1: Green Bean Puree (page 48)
	Meal 2: Mix Beet Puree (page 63) and Apple Puree (page 45)

DAY 1	Meal 1: Green Bean Puree (page 48) and Carrot Puree (page 46)
	Meal 2: Pea and Carrot Puree (page 82)
DAY 2	Meal 1: Green Bean and Sweet Potato Puree (page 79)
	Meal 2: Mix White Bean Puree (page 69) and Avocado Puree (page 42)
DAY 3	Meal 1: Oat and Banana Puree (page 87)
	Meal 2: Mix White Bean Puree (page 69) and Spinach Puree (page 47)
DAY 4	Meal 1: Mix Green Bean Puree (page 48) and Carrot Puree (page 46)
	Meal 2: White Bean and Leek Puree (page 105) – blend until smooth
DAY 5	Meal 1: Banana and Mango Puree (page 109) – blend until smooth
	Meal 2: Sweet Potato and Spinach Puree (page 76)
DAY 6	Meal 1: Banana and Mango Puree (page 109) with yogurt – blend until smooth
	Meal 2: Butternut Squash Puree (page 89) with ground nutmeg
DAY 7	Meal 1: Blueberry and Yogurt Puree (page 80) with banana – blend until smooth
	Meal 2: Pea and Butternut Squash Puree (page 89)

The Dirty Dozen and the Clean Fifteen

The Environmental Working Group (EWG) is a nonprofit, nonpartisan organization dedicated to protecting human health and the environment. Its mission is to empower people to live healthier lives in a healthier environment. This organization publishes an annual list of the twelve kinds of produce, in sequence, that have the highest amount of pesticide residue—the Dirty Dozen—as well as a list of the fifteen kinds of produce that have the least amount of pesticide residue—the Clean Fifteen).

THE DIRTY DOZEN

The 2016 Dirty Dozen includes the following produce. These are considered among this year's most important produce to buy organically:

1. Strawberries
2. Apples
3. Nectarines
4. Peaches
5. Celery
6. Grapes
7. Cherries
8. Spinach
9. Tomatoes
10. Bell peppers
11. Cherry tomatoes
12. Cucumbers
+ Kale/collard greens*
+ Hot peppers*

*The Dirty Dozen list contains two additional items—kale/collard greens and hot peppers—because they tend to contain trace levels of highly hazardous pesticides.

THE CLEAN FIFTEEN

The least critical to buy organically are the Clean Fifteen list. The following are on the 2016 list:

1. Avocados
2. Corn
3. Pineapples
4. Cabbage
5. Sweet peas
6. Onions
7. Asparagus
8. Mangos
9. Papayas
10. Kiwi
11. Eggplant
12. Honeydew
13. Grapefruit
14. Cantaloupe
15. Cauliflower

Measurement Conversions

VOLUME EQUIVALENTS (LIQUID)

US STANDARD	US STANDARD (ounces)	METRIC (approximate)
2 tablespoons	1 fl. oz.	30 mL
¼ cup	2 fl. oz.	60 mL
½ cup	4 fl. oz.	120 mL
1 cup	8 fl. oz.	240 mL
1½ cups	12 fl. oz.	355 mL
2 cups or 1 pint	16 fl. oz.	475 mL
4 cups or 1 quart	32 fl. oz.	1 L
1 gallon	128 fl. oz.	4 L

OVEN TEMPERATURES

FAHRENHEIT (F)	CELSIUS (C) (approximate)
250°F	120°C
300°F	150°C
325°F	165°C
350°F	180°C
375°F	190°C
400°F	200°C
425°F	220°C
450°F	230°C

VOLUME EQUIVALENTS (DRY)

US STANDARD	METRIC (approximate)	US STANDARD	METRIC (approximate)
⅛ teaspoon	0.5 mL	½ cup	118 mL
¼ teaspoon	1 mL	⅔ cup	156 mL
½ teaspoon	2 mL	¾ cup	177 mL
¾ teaspoon	4 mL	1 cup	235 mL
1 teaspoon	5 mL	2 cups or 1 pint	475 mL
1 tablespoon	15 mL	3 cups	700 mL
¼ cup	59 mL	4 cups or 1 quart	1 L
⅓ cup	79 mL		

WEIGHT EQUIVALENTS

US STANDARD	METRIC (approximate)
½ ounce	15 g
1 ounce	30 g
2 ounces	60 g
4 ounces	115 g
8 ounces	225 g
12 ounces	340 g
16 ounces or 1 pound	455 g

References

Barański, Marcin, Dominika Średnicka-Tober, N. Volakakis, Chris J. Seal, Roy Sanderson, G. B. Stewart, Charles Benbrook, et al. "Higher Antioxidant and Lower Cadmium Concentrations and Lower Incidence of Pesticide Residues in Organically Grown Crops: A Systematic Literature Review and Meta-Analyses." *British Journal of Nutrition* 112, no. 5 (September 2014): 794–811. doi:10.1017/S0007114514001366.

Średnicka-Tober, Dominika, Marcin Barański, Chris J. Seal, Roy Sanderson, Charles Benbrook, Håvard Steinshamn, Joanna Gromadzka-Ostrowska, et al. "Higher PUFA and n-3 PUFA, Conjugated Linoleic Acid, α-Tocopherol and Iron, but Lower Iodine and Selenium Concentrations in Organic Milk: A Systematic Literature Review and Meta- and Redundancy Analyses." *British Journal of Nutrition* 115, no. 6 (March 2016): 1043–60. doi:10.1017/S0007114516000349.

Średnicka-Tober, Dominika, Marcin Barański, Chris J. Seal, Roy Sanderson, Charles Benbrook, Håvard Steinshamn, Joanna Gromadzka-Ostrowska, et al. "Composition Differences between Organic and Conventional Meat: A Systemic Literature Review and Meta-analysis." *British Journal of Nutrition* 115, no. 6 (March 2016): 994–1011. doi:10.1017/S0007114515005073.

Strom, Stephanie. "Paying Farmers to Go Organic, Even Before the Crops Come In." *New York Times.* July 14, 2016. www.nytimes.com/2016/07/15/business/paying-farmers-to-go-organic-even-before-the-crops-come-in.html

Index

Acknowledgments

Thank you to my husband Andrew for being my partner through this entire journey. You taught me the joy of cooking, to have fun in the kitchen, and to find my voice. To my son, Julian, you were (and still are) such a happy and willing tester. I simply cannot wait to watch you grow up. The two of you will always be my "quinoa pigs." I look forward to all the various journeys we will take.

Terry and Linda, Julian and I couldn't be luckier to have the two of you in our lives. Your caring and devotion to the both of us is nothing short of remarkable.

To my fabulous team at Middleberg Nutrition: Eliza, Sydney, Pegah, Hanna, Beth, and Ilana. You have been tremendous supporters, researchers, brilliant dietitians, and collaborators. Without all of you there would be no Middleberg Nutrition. Thank you to Nicole who helped make our own introduction to solids as easy a time as I hope our readers have.

Thank you the entire Callisto Media team. My wonderful editor, Stacy Wagner-Kinnear, you made this first-time author comfortable with what seemed like a daunting endeavor. You were a dream to collaborate with, quick to encourage my philosophy and nutritional approach, and willing to make changes, even after the last minute. Thank you to Katy Brown, the book's designer, who brought my words to life, and to Shannon Douglas, whose beautiful photography made me grin from ear to ear. And to Karen Frazier, the incredibly talented chef who helped pull my vision together.

To my dear friends, you know who you are, you keep me laughing, smiling, and centered.

And of course, to my family: Dad, Mom, Melissa. Who would have ever thought this picky eater would build a career around food? You have all supported me from Day 1 and, most importantly, let me find my own path.

CPSIA information can be obtained
at www.ICGtesting.com
Printed in the USA
LVHW01s1613201017
552610LV00001BA/1/P